Laboring in the Shadow of Empire

Inequality at Work: Perspectives on Race, Gender, Class, and Labor

Series Editors: Enobong Hannah Branch and Adia Harvey Wingfield

Inequality at Work: Perspectives on Race, Gender, Class, and Labor provides a platform for cultivating and disseminating scholarship that deepens our knowledge of the social understandings and implications of work, particularly scholarship that joins empirical investigations with social analysis, cultural critique, and historical perspectives. We are especially interested in books that center on the experiences of marginalized workers; that explore the mechanisms (e.g., state or organizational policy) that cause occupational inequality to grow and become entrenched over time; that show us how workers make sense of and articulate their constraints as well as resist them; and have particular timeliness and/or social significance. Prospective topics might include books about migrant labor, rising economic insecurity, enduring gender inequality, public and private sector divisions, glass ceilings (gender limitations at work) and concrete walls (racial limitations at work), or racial/gender identity at work in the Black Lives Matter era.

Laboring in the Shadow of Empire

Race, Gender, and Care Work
in Portugal

CELESTE VAUGHAN CURINGTON

Rutgers University Press

New Brunswick, Camden, and Newark, New Jersey

London and Oxford

Rutgers University Press is a department of Rutgers, The State University of New Jersey, one of the leading public research universities in the nation. By publishing worldwide, it furthers the University's mission of dedication to excellence in teaching, scholarship, research, and clinical care.
Library of Congress Cataloging-in-Publication Data

Names: Curington, Celeste Vaughan, 1988– author.
Title: Laboring in the shadow of empire : race, gender, and care work in Portugal / Celeste Vaughan Curington.
Description: New Brunswick : Rutgers University Press, [2024] | Series: Inequality at work: perspectives on race, gender, class, and labor | Includes bibliographical references and index.
Identifiers: LCCN 2023051599 | ISBN 9781978827950 (paperback) | ISBN 9781978827967 (hardcover) | ISBN 9781978827974 (epub) | ISBN 9781978827981 (pdf)
Subjects: LCSH: Women foreign workers—Portugal—History—21st century. | Africans—Portugal—History—21st century. | Women—Employment—Portugal. | Women caregivers—Portugal. | House cleaning—Portugal. | Portugal—Race relations.
Classification: LCC HD8598.5.B55 C87 2024 | DDC 331.4/813620425089960469—dc23/eng/20240407

LC record available at https://lccn.loc.gov/2023051599

A British Cataloging-in-Publication record for this book is available from the British Library.

rutgersuniversitypress.org

Contents

Laboring in the Shadow
of Empire

Introduction

••••••••••••••••••••••••

> The myth of a tolerant Portuguese society, one of the pillars of the national identity narrative, has prevented the explicit recognition of racism as a systemic and structural practice. It denies or normalizes racism, it accepts violence and oppression, it tolerates the intolerable.
> —Beatriz Gomes Dias, *O estado do racismo em Portugal* (translation by author)

At age twenty-four, Maria left Santiago, Cabo Verde. She had worked for more than half her life, sometimes as a field hand, sometimes as a domestic worker. Back when she was twelve, her mother had sent her to Praia, the capital of Santiago, for a domestic position in a government worker's home. It was 1993, less than twenty years since Cabo Verde achieved its independence, when Maria settled her son in a rural village under the watchful eyes of her sisters and their aging mother. Still, it was a rather daunting thing to consider the transnational journey from this West African archipelago—just ten islands, three hundred nautical miles from Senegal's coastline—to Europe. Alone, she set out for Portugal, the very country that claimed her homeland as a colony for more than five hundred years.

A short, dark-skinned Black woman with a crop of salt-and-pepper coils, Maria remembered her urgency. "The only solution was to immigrate," she began. "I left my family and came here in 1993. I wanted a better life." In her tidy, fourth-floor Lisboan apartment, decorated with family photographs and colorful fabrics she collected from visits to Cabo Verde, Maria told the story.

1

Perhaps the decision seemed easier because life in Cabo Verde had been so difficult. Maria's relationship with her partner, Carlos, had deteriorated years before. Everyone on the islands was being squeezed, inflation making it harder and harder to pay for everyday staples. She knew other Cabo Verdean women were migrating to Portugal, where higher wages allowed domestic workers to remit money to their families. And so, like them, she got a tourist visa to enter Portugal. Like them, she overstayed her visa.

Maria's voice was flat, almost indifferent, as she spoke about her first day working in the home of a *senhora* (a married Portuguese woman). About two weeks after settling in at a relative's apartment in Cova da Moura, Amadora, Maria took a taxi to the coastal community of Cais Cais, where she was greeted at gunpoint. "That's how they were in those days," she sighed. The white men with their fingers on the triggers turned out to be the *senhora*'s husband and son: "They needed to know that I wasn't some dangerous *pr-ta*.¹" The situation was absurd. Even with two decades' distance, Maria's voice bubbled with laughter as she remembered being a newly arrived Black woman, an immigrant racialized as inescapably inferior by the same white Portuguese families that sought her labor.

The job wasn't ideal, though it allowed her to send regular remittances to her family in Cabo Verde. With time, she set down roots in Portugal. She had two more children. And in 2001, Maria was granted residency status under a short-term regularization program for unauthorized migrants. She secured work in institutional cleaning services through an employment agency and eventually became a naturalized Portuguese citizen. Today, she lives with her eleven-year-old son and fourteen-year-old daughter in a public housing complex that's home to a multiracial, multigenerational community of Africans and African descendants.

Maria remains somewhat ambivalent about her life in Portugal. Though she has achieved citizenship and prefers her cleaning job to the domestic work she did in the past, Maria still bristles as she laments living paycheck to paycheck, performing emotionally and physically stressful labor, and weathering the perpetual instability of employment opportunities. And then there's the racism. There's always the racism:

Listen *fidju*,² I live day-to-day, and I have to interact and coexist with the Portuguese in transportation, in work, on the streets, in the commercial centers. A person takes notice of the racism. There has always been racism in Portugal, and racism will continue here in Portugal. Just in our transportation you see it. . . . There's a white person sitting there, a *pessoa negra* [Black person] enters and sits down, and a *pessoa branca* [white person] gets right up—right up! It's just that—racism is getting better, but nevertheless it exists a lot. It exists! Sometimes they see us on the street and say, "Oh those *pr-tos* [Blacks]." . . . They think that we are here, we *negros*, to steal and . . . do all bad things.

As if to underscore her personal, lived experience, Maria added, "I feel this way because I have gone through it all already."

Maria's struggles are shared by many Black women care workers in Portugal and Europe. Her transnational journey from Cabo Verde to Portugal mirrors the global economy's increased dependence on migrant care laborers, while her entrance into formalized care work in Lisbon reflects the racialized and gendered occupational structure of a postindustrialized nation. Like other southern European nations, Portugal has been shaped by demographic and structural changes, including rapid urbanization, the hypersegregation of racialized and immigrant populations (especially African migrants from former European colonies), an aging population, and the economic stagnation that settled over the continent after the turn-of-the-century "EU Boom."

Lisbon's racial segregation is readily apparent when I arrive to begin my fieldwork in 2015. The outer, fringe neighborhoods I visit are overwhelmingly populated by racialized minority communities, particularly Black African descendants and Romani. I take note of the characteristics familiar to any migrant enclave in any large city in the world. Locals duck into tiny, crowded shops to make long-distance calls, purchase unlocked phones, or cash checks. Northeast and Southeast Asian–managed dollar stores sit side by side with corner markets offering specialty goods (including culturally specific foods) and hair salons where the nimble-fingered owners, stylists, and braiders often look and sound just like their clients. An African migrant can buy Afro-centric hair products, African food items, urban clothing, and electronics, all without leaving her neighborhood.

The neighborhoods are not, however, African satellites. They are marked by a distinct mixture of migrant and Portuguese culture. Elderly Portuguese men sit around in public squares, nestled behind their newspapers or gathered into large, chatty groups. A typical Portuguese *pasteleria* (bakery café) marks each corner, giving people another place to meet, eat, argue over soccer games and politics, or grab a quick espresso to fuel their daily commutes into Lisbon. From the high rail, you can look down to the remnants of the informal housing constructed during African decolonization to the spray-painted bedsheets that serve as both doors and billboards: "There's no justice," one reads. Another, in lurid red paint, exclaims, "Violence!" Flyers are pasted, stapled, and taped to just about anything standing still, the walls, windows, and bus stops converted into splashy ads for upcoming concerts and parties featuring Cabo Verdean and Angolan artists like Anselmo Ralph or G-Amado.

To catch the morning commuters, Cabo Verdean women wearing traditional *pánu di téras*[3] line the tunnels leading to Center City station and sell homemade treats like *doce di coco*,[4] *pastel*,[5] and *toresma*.[6] Black people of all ages, all skin tones, all types wait for the morning train. There are Black women in aprons, carrying buckets full of cleaning supplies, and Black men tapping their heavily worn construction boots. Later in the day, they will return home covered in

FIG. 1 A woman walks past posters in a Lisbon periphery neighborhood. Photo by author.

dust and soot—the evidence of their labor. After 4 p.m., Black youth tumble from the train, making their way home from school, but not without the playful jostling and shouting of schoolkids everywhere. Out in the street, I hear the Afro house, Kizomba and Zouk beats, and African hip-hop from their tinny portable speakers and the shouted flirtations as groups of young boys and girls move down the streets: "Oi, vida boa . . . tudu dret!"[7] All around me, I hear Portuguese, Cabo Verdean *kriolu*, a diasporic dialect, or a combination of the two.

Tourists don't tend to come to these neighborhoods. They are focused on meandering through the medieval castles, cobblestone villages, and picturesque city squares plastered across tourist guides extolling Europe's "hidden gem." But they are constantly crossing paths with the other side of Portugal. Throughout Lisbon's bustling streets, commercial centers, and public spaces, there are Black, African-descendant women wearing uniforms, headed to and from their jobs or cleaning up after the deluge of tourists and city residents passes through. Because of their work in caretaking for the elderly, Black women's presence is also apparent in the "gray zones," those Lisboan neighborhoods marked by an overrepresentation of older residents. They may walk, arm in arm, with a white Portuguese elder; push wheelchairs over the difficult terrain of Lisbon's narrow, cobblestoned streets; or be spotted meeting up in the commercial center to exchange keys and discuss schedules with their peers. Persistently present but often unseen, Black women's invisibility is a paradox in this "new," contemporary, immigrant-receiving nation often lauded for its successful immigrant integration policies.[8]

The Shadow of the Empire

The scholarship on global care migration to Europe and the United States tends to prioritize migrant workers who are unauthorized and informal workers. This framing assumes that the solution to the care gap and the exploitation that migrant care workers often face is to regulate the market and regularize migrants' immigration status. Yet these pages reveal that focusing on legality and labor formality versus informality *alone* fails to improve the poor living and working conditions they face. That is because I center the continued racialized and gendered marginalization of African-descendant women (Cabo Verdeans) who are permanent residents and/or citizens of Portugal and work within its formal labor markets. If legality obviated discrimination, I'd have little to report. Instead, race and gender color access to work even in this society, where race is not supposed to matter. The resulting labor exploitation produces the subjugated class position of African-descendant women and restricts their inclusion in substantive citizenship and Portuguese society.

In conversation after conversation, throughout my research, people like Maria repeatedly referred to their contradictory social location. As care workers who labor in stigmatized care occupations, they feel simultaneously hypervisible yet invisible within the greater Portuguese society that upholds an ideology of antiracialism—that is, the sociopolitical supposition that Portugal is a multicultural society where one's racial identity allegedly does not matter. I argue that, in these documented experiences, we begin to sense what I refer to as the *shadow of the empire*—the social remnants of a colonialism that lingers and finds reinforcement in the present when a society fails to come to terms with its past or remedy its replicated harms.

Portugal was the longest-lived colonial empire in European history, lasting nearly six centuries. Like other former colonial empires, the Portuguese empire was deeply involved in the transatlantic slave trade and has a long history of enforcing colonial labor hierarchies in and outside of Portugal. It has also seen the continuous flow of migration streams bringing Cabo Verdean and other lusophone African-descendant men and women into Portugal prior to and after African decolonization in the 1970s. The expansion of industrial capitalism in the late twentieth century reinforced race and gender as central to Portugal's labor system, as these Africans and African descendants were summoned to perform low-paid, precarious, and feminized work (including caring, construction, and institutional cleaning work in the country's expanding urban centers). I weave together hundreds of hours of participant observation in greater Lisbon with data gathered in hundreds of informal interviews and nearly sixty formal interviews to trace the historical construction of labor from the imperial period and how its vestiges remain firmly ensconced in postcolonial law and migration regimes. I also demonstrate how the gendering and racialization of labor are reinforced and reproduced in localized practices today as African-descendant women care workers live and labor in the shadow of the empire.

I use the shadow metaphor, in other words, as an allegory for the contemporary fact of "coloniality" made apparent in the viewpoints of the "postcolonial" transnational care migrant in Portugal. Coloniality refers to the intricate machinery that entangles global racial/ethnic/gender/sexual hierarchies, divisions of labor, and hegemonic European epistemologies.[9] Under coloniality, contemporary Cabo Verdean women care workers in Portugal experience invisibility and hypervisibility as an effect of what Maria Lugones refers to as the "the modern/colonial gender system," rooted in colonization's implementation of racialized gender as a tool for human differentiation, social domination, and exploitation.[10] Colonialism thus created new patterns of power previously unknown to the world; supraexploitative conditions such as chattel slavery and coercive or forced labor regimes became the groundwork for the production of new (and enduring) social categories, including race, gender, *and* human belonging.

Such colonial legacies bring me back to my original animating question: *Why is it that women racialized as Black, specifically, across space, time, and national context, often carry out some of the most stigmatized professions in society, such as cleaning and caring?* As argued by feminist scholars for decades, caring labor marks a specific relationship among capital, identity, and inequality.[11] That is, while caring necessarily reproduces labor power in a capitalist system, the gendered, racial, and ethnic segmentation of people into caring work demonstrates the sector's societal devaluation, as well as the marginalization of the people that perform that work. This itself is a colonial (even feudal) holdover, associating care work with servility, in which vulnerable people must negotiate the performative or affective dimensions of caring labor. They must meet the demands of assumed servility, deference, passivity, and emotional and affective labor, all within a gendered occupation in which the entrenched racial and class hierarchies of privilege and power prevail.[12] Employment in both the "nurturant" care sector, which often involves direct relationships with individuals (work in nursing homes, home care, domestic work, babysitting, etc.), and the "nonnurturant" care sector (laundry, janitorial, restaurant services, etc.) furthers this replication by providing low wages, scant to absent labor protections, and little to no opportunities for advancement.[13] Given the overrepresentation of racial and ethnic minorities in this work, caring labor gives us a productive lens through which to examine how coloniality shapes the structure of social groups within the shadow of empire.

This fact of coloniality is apparent if we situate the contemporary migration of Cabo Verdean care migrants in the long history of its genesis—the *longue durée* of colonial and postcolonial African women's reproductive labor. In Lisbon, African women's ontology remained deeply racialized as they carried out the "dirty work," or what many of my study informants described as *trabadju sujo*, as far back as the fifteenth and sixteenth centuries. They served as city cleaners, personal domestics, washerwomen, and street vendors and carried out the arduous task of fetching water under the colloquial sobriquet *negras do pote*, or Black women of the fountain.[14] As José Ramos Tinhorão's work has shown, the colonial assignation of the hardest, most stigmatized and menial work to enslaved Africans and African freedmen has continued to shape symbolic and sociocultural conceptions of race and servility in Portuguese society[15] such that lusophone Black women with ties to the former Portuguese colonies remain overrepresented among the nation's cleaning and caring workers.[16] I specifically focus on Cabo Verdeans because they are the largest PALOP (Países Africanos de Língua Oficial Portuguesa) African-descendant community in Portugal and because their multigenerational networks of immigrant families are common to Lisbon. I particularly look to those women who work in eldercare and institutional cleaning services because they represent two major occupational niches open to regularized Black immigrant women in this region.[17]

Laboring in the Shadow of Empire thus reorients the literature on care and migration to consider not only Black women's long-standing participation in caring labor but also how colonialism is not in the past but rather relived in gendered systems of migrant mobility and the social organization of reproductive labor. My focus on a postcolonial setting enhances the important scholarship on the Global North, which, as I mentioned, tends to prioritize unauthorized care migration in compounding the marginalization experienced by migrant care workers.[18] That crucial work illustrates how the more recent liberalization and globalization of immigration policy have ensured a continuous flow of temporary, exploitable workers with few pathways to regularize their status. As globalization unfolds, Saskia Sassen's research reveals, the world's economy generates a strong demand for feminized immigrant labor; new growth sectors require vast expansions of low-wage service jobs, thus shaping the gendered survival circuits that find women supporting their families by providing paid care for others abroad.[19]

Scholarship that prioritizes the transnationalization of the care economy, however, has frequently de-emphasized the *contemporary* role of the colonial in preserving the stigmatization of care work. Nina Sahraoui explains that this extant scholarship conceals the "post-continuities and the underpinning racialisation processes through which bodies are categorised, not exclusively in articulation with the migration status."[20] Heeding Sahraoui's words, I broaden the analysis beyond the illegality-informal nexus, situating migrant care work within both global and local contexts in which racialized and gendered labor hierarchies, rooted in coloniality, find expression and reinforcement within capitalist labor markets of the twenty-first century.

This work also brings literature on care migration in the Global South into conversation with the economic and global transformations that altered the structure of caring work in the twentieth and twenty-first centuries. Here, research shows how local configurations of indigeneity and Blackness, as well as long-standing colonial hierarchies of labor, are incorporated into a capitalist mode of production and local labor market mechanisms, reproducing power distinctions among an array of citizens and noncitizens alike. For example, scholarship on the rural-to-urban migration of African women in postapartheid South Africa tracks how the intersections of colonial racial and ethnic marginalization with labor and welfare policy result in a racialized and gendered labor regime, with rural Black women performing domestic work for affluent and middle-class white urban families.[21] Crossing the Atlantic, a robust group of scholars and activists spotlight how Black and Indigenous South American women's exploitation via domestic work remains one of the most visible legacies of colonial servitude, patronage, and slavery in the modern era.[22] Similarly, I argue, the incorporation of Black women into paid caring labor in Europe is intertwined with a political economy of care that rejuvenates long-standing colonial discourses and practices of gendered racialization.[23]

Together, extant literature illustrates the likelihood of a global structure of *gendered anti-Blackness*[24] in which racialized and gendered conceptions of humanity, servility, and belonging are linked to postcolonial migratory settings, such as Portugal's. Thus, while attention to home care and institutional cleaning service work in Portugal gives us a perspective on larger economic inequities across regions or distant localities, it also reveals how, under coloniality, macroprocesses collide with enduring local systems to construct occupational hierarchies in which Black women are assigned to the bottom rungs.

Laboring in the Shadow

The assumption that *light* and *good* are linked, against *darkness* and *evil*, is a fitting allegory for the shadow, or the omnipresent persistence of gendered anti-Blackness in the present-day context. Black feminist scholars such as Katherine McKittrick and Hortense Spillers implicate the gendered afterlife of colonialism, which has violently and epistemologically denied Black women's *existence* under the haunting idea that Black womanhood is pathological or rightfully, to the colonial logic, nonexistent.[25] Sociologist Avery Gordon, in her book *Ghostly Matters*, makes artful use of the language of haunting, that which does not disappear but perpetually lingers, in exploring the durable structuring impacts of the transatlantic slave trade and the failure of Reconstruction in the United States.[26] Likewise, intersectional scholar Stefanie Boulila documents this lingering in her discussion of postracial Europe, where "race unfolds its power in the shadow of its erasure."[27] In *Laboring in the Shadow of Empire*, I use the word *shadow* in multiple ways, primarily to invoke the ways modern Portuguese society is haunted by the unresolved political, economic, emotional, and social effects—the *human* effects—of its imperial and colonial racialized violence. Left unattended, these hover over the whole of society, a naturalized spectral sorting that, when brought into the light, might fall to pieces.

I also use the shadow metaphor to capture the variegated visibility of care workers in Portuguese society. As activist-scholar-revolutionary Amílcar Cabral asserts, in Portugal and much of Europe, a colonial and neocolonial episteme occludes the reality of anti-Black violence and oppression.[28] Afro-feminists such as Akwugo Emejulu and Francesca Sobande further remind us that the intersecting structures of race, gender, class, legal status, and nation thrust African-descendant women into a social location characterized by their *invisibility* (assumed to be irrelevant and absent in Europe) and *hypervisibility* (assumed to be angry, out of place, deviant, hypersexual, and irrational).[29] In a context like Portugal, where the ideological strength of antiracialism pervades, this collides with a particular type of what Stephen Small terms "ambiguous hypervisibility": African-descendant care workers are obvious to anyone who looks around Lisbon, as is their concentration in service jobs, which is oddly amplified and naturalized by their relative absence from other professions such as in politics, academics, medicine, and other more prestigious, flexible, and well-paid occupations.[30] When scholars speak of these women's paid work, it is often under the category of "invisible labor,"[31] not because it is hidden, but because it is so frequently taken for granted. This introduces a dynamic where Black African-descendant women navigate a duality as they and their bodies are racialized as Other, out of place and invisible as they work and traverse the city, yet their bodies are also constructed as hypervisible and appropriate targets for insult, violence, and control. My aim here is not to reify workers as powerless and subservient by framing them as *shadows* but rather to highlight how the long *shadow of empire*—the enduring legacy of colonialism—intersects with contemporary hierarchical dynamics of race, class, nationality, gender, and human belonging to shape the social location and ontology of Cabo Verdean women in ostensibly "postcolonial" Portugal.

Drawing from key Black and Afro-feminist scholarship that ties the power-knowledge of outsider locations to the stimulation of resistance, I further offer the shadow as a site of clandestine work, of subversive potential.[32] Katherine McKittrick argues that the gendered anti-Blackness confronted by Black women results not only in their marginalization and erasure; Black women also draw from their marginalized subject position to initiate "everyday contestations" and "philosophical demands."[33] Likewise, as the shadow follows all those who are marginalized, it is also a sort of umbrella, shielding the development of collective spaces, consciousness, and resistance efforts from those with a vested interest in maintaining the status quo.[34] Throughout this work, as Cabo Verdean care and service workers express a collective racial and gender consciousness that destabilizes the contradictions of their daily lives, the shadow always speaks back.

The African Diaspora and Caring Labor

Though global care migration literature has infrequently centered the migration histories of African care workers in Europe, this does not mean they are either uncommon or unimportant.[35] In the case of Portugal, it is the complex and centuries-old history of colonial slavery and labor migration with its now-former colonial territories that continues to facilitate the migration and settlement of Cabo Verdean families within its borders.[36] Cabo Verdean women labor as postcolonial subjects, a reality that distinguishes their experiences as migrants to Portugal from those who, in newer waves, arrive from places such as Eastern Europe.[37]

Also, given that Cabo Verdeans may enter Portugal through formalized migration pathways, eventually accessing naturalization, their experiences often differ from those of the undocumented care migrants studied most frequently in literature at the nexus of work and global migration. While this crucial literature illustrates how migrant workers encounter restrictive conditions of membership in their host society,[38] the women I interviewed work in expanding institutional care services in the formalized market, they are not subject to what scholar Rhacel Salazar Parreñas calls "legal servitude" in that they are free to change employers, and many of them have families living with them in Portugal.[39] As long-standing African migration flows matured, many of these women sought and secured regularization and came to combine waged work with family obligations. This, as argued by Sónia Pereira, results in disparate job preferences, with African workers "tend[ing] to prefer stable, lower-paid jobs . . . that allow them to look after their family" instead of the more unstable and "live-in" domestic work often picked up by single, undocumented migrants in Portugal.[40] In this case, the "preference" is not inherent to a racial or ethnic group but tied to obligations *and* limited opportunities; nonetheless, the pattern it produces further racializes, others, and naturalizes the subjugation of a specific group of Black, African-descendant women.

This changing care labor demographic in the Portuguese context fits well with several groundbreaking studies. Evelyn Nakano Glenn's foundational work on a "racialized division of reproductive labor" argues that migrant Asian and Latina women's entrance into U.S. care work comes as Black women's exodus from that same occupational sector began.[41] Rhacel Salazar Parreñas's theory of the "international division of reproductive labor" furthers Glenn's work by identifying how the globalization of the market economy has extended the politics of reproductive labor on an international level, generating new patterns of marginalization around immigrant women's paid labor.[42] As sending and receiving states restrict access to citizenship and implement inadequate measures to support families, class-privileged women purchase the low-wage services of migrant women, prompting migrant women to simultaneously purchase the even lower-wage services of poorer women left behind.

Thus, an international division of reproductive labor reflects how citizenship protects workers, as employers are able to exert a greater level of control over undocumented migrant women and, therefore, exploitable workers.[43] However, as this book illustrates, as opposed to a one-dimensional exodus, Cabo Verdean women who are naturalized citizens or residents and some native-born Portuguese women of Cabo Verdean descent have increasingly found work within institutional service and care settings, such as home care and institutional cleaning services in public (commercial centers, transportation terminals) and semipublic settings (business offices and storefronts), while their undocumented counterparts perform paid domestic private household work and join other migrant groups such as those from Brazil, Guinea-Bissau, and Angola, as well as growing numbers from Ukraine, Moldova, Russia, Romania, and the Philippines.[44] In the Portuguese context, then, African migrant women are sorted into care work but then additionally sorted into documented and undocumented as well as formal and informal realms. Against the background of a twenty-first-century Lisboan service sector reliant on migrant and racial and ethnic minority labor, home care (or *apoio domiciliário*) and institutional cleaning work (or *limpeza*) depend on both a steady supply of regularized workers and their social networks, which draws in sisters, aunts, mothers, friends, and cousins. That dependence reveals the entanglement of feminized migration and gendered and racialized colonial labor regimes informing the Cabo Verdean community's presence in and around Lisbon.[45]

The formal organization of home care and cleaning enterprises in Portugal departs from the traditional domestic work model in which individual employers enter the marketplace to supplement the family's informal care with the paid care of a domestic worker. As numerous studies show, this traditional model of domestic work has resulted in a two-tiered division of labor, reproduced across national contexts, with predominantly white and class-privileged women hiring poor, working-class, and immigrant women of color to perform the most intimate family tasks.[46] While research finds that domestic work draws from a documented and undocumented immigrant labor force in Portugal and remains one of the sectors that has the highest level of informal employment, the home care and cleaning workers I talked to in Portugal all achieved legislative status.

Further, under the agency-based home care and institutional cleaning enterprise model I document in Portugal, a triangular relationship among manager / service worker / client or care recipient replaces the two-tiered hierarchical dyad of service interactions. For home care, families or individuals seek care through the agency, which delegates the performance of care through managers and supervisors who oversee home care workers' labor. In their nurturant caring labor, home care workers must navigate relationships with employers and with elders under their direct care. Meanwhile, in providing institutional cleaning services in public or semipublic settings through commercial enterprises, these workers again depart from the traditionally understood service interactions of domestic work; institutional cleaning workers have supervisors, managers, and colleagues, yet they also negotiate spontaneous, brief, and frequently powerful workday interactions with customers and clients who frequent their workspaces. Thus, for both occupations, as I will illustrate in the following chapters, there are multiple layers of interactions in which the importance of race, class, nation, and gender inequalities and ideologies may unfold for Cabo Verdean care workers.

The comparative perspective provided by examining eldercare and cleaning work especially shows the context-specific, structurally mediated, and interactional dimensions of Cabo Verdeans' gendered racialization in Portugal. As noted, both home care and institutional cleaning work are underpaid, challenging for working mothers who are balancing the care of their own families, and often absent of advancement opportunities. Using the work of Evelyn Nakano Glenn as a guide, I argue that both forms of reproductive labor constitute "care work" given their direct relationship to personal and social care (caring for the socially vulnerable aged population and maintaining hygienic and healthy living conditions).[47] The more direct care work, home care, is considered "nurturant" labor, involving the individualized and physical care of elders and, often, negotiation with family members. Unlike domestic cleaning work that is carried out within private homes and is more often described in the literature on care work, institutional cleaning work, on the other hand, is a sort of indirect care work encompassing "nonnurturant" tasks carried out in a mix of public-private work settings, including hauling trash, scrubbing, buffing, washing, and sanitizing.[48]

Further, as Eileen Boris and Rhacel Salazar Parreñas argue, labor organized around "dirt, bodies, and intimacy" produces and reinforces social distinctions that are as much affective and symbolic as they are material.[49] Indeed, nurturant care work for elderly people has been characterized as a *socially valuable* form of devalued "dirty work" given its intimate proximity to aged death, disease, and dying and due to its centrality to the physical cleaning of the aged, dependent body and its discharges (blood, urine, and excrement).[50] Meanwhile, nonnurturant cleaning domestic work, as Bridget Anderson argues, has been characterized as *dishonorable* "dirty work" because it is constructed as dirty, menial, and degrading;[51] cleaning work is like home care in its association with the body and its discharges, but this relationship manifests in a more distant and less intimate way. Still, the distinction between nurturant and nonnurturant caring labor that this book unpacks also reveals the pervasiveness of gendered anti-Black racism across both sectors; though it is apparent in different ways, colonial imagery remains intertwined with racialized and gendered affective rules and expectations of racialized femininity in both spheres. In short, study participants' stories reveal how the historical context of Portugal clearly matters for the experience of oppression, while the organizational context of how their work is carried out mediates the reenactment of and resistance to such oppression in unique ways.

Portuguese Antiracial Ideology

Centering and privileging the voices of African-descendant care workers in the shadow of empire is a deeply radical act in the Portuguese context. Most centrally, Portugal joins several European contexts in its state-level adherence to antiracial ideology,[52] a collective political imagination positing racism as a bygone problem and race, therefore, as a no-longer-relevant social category.[53] Antiracial ideology joins other racial ideologies across the globe as linked components of *epistemologies of ignorance*—to borrow from the work of philosopher Charles Mills[54]—where a white epistemological framework writes out the fact of white supremacy and colonial modernity. These epistemologies of ignorance signify collective manifestations of dominant groups' social positions and, in fact, are outcomes of a racialized social system—what sociologist Eduardo Bonilla-Silva defines as "societies in which economic, political, social, and ideological levels are partially structured by the placement of actors in racial categories or races."[55] As the development of racial categories in racialized social systems across the globe illustrates, racial states have long defined, redefined, or altogether rejected racial categories to service white supremacy. Antiracialism and other epistemologies of ignorance may hold several key similarities, particularly with regard to their outcomes, but the specificity of historical, social, economic, cultural, and political context matters. Indeed, as David Theo Goldberg has argued, distinct ways of expressing race and justifying racial dominance are found alongside the global historical materiality of race.[56]

Unlike color-blind or mestizaje ideologies that neutralize contemporary and historical realities of systemic racism by framing race as a *depoliticized identity* (in the case of color-blindness in the United States) or emphasizing a *shared national multiethnic and cultural identity* (in the case of several Latin American countries), in an antiracial state, the mere use of the language of race is eschewed altogether. The uniqueness of Europe as a raceless context stands at the forefront, and the problem of "race" is placed elsewhere—specifically, in places like the United States, where the age-old problem of the "color line" endures. As argued by Trica Danielle Keaton, the danger of hegemonic ideologies of racelessness lies in their "capacity to invisibilize *racial* structures that have historically advantaged and individualized whitened people while effacing their racialization of self and others, and thereby their respective accrued benefits and disadvantages."[57] In all three examples of global epistemologies of ignorance, the negation of race itself normalizes the systemic racism perpetuated by racial states.[58]

This ideological "death" of racism inherent to European antiracialism traces to disavowals of scientific racism and the formal racial categorization of the human species following the Holocaust. Yet Western elites *also* promoted antiracialism to manage anticolonial, anti-imperial political movements: depoliticizing racism allowed powerbrokers to curtail claims of redistributive politics. Slavery and colonialism's determinative roles in producing the modern European nation-state and the racialized relationships between the "West and the Rest"[59] were obscured in the global shift to Nazism as the key twentieth-century referent for racial and ethnic discrimination.[60]

The power of antiracialism is that it becomes acceptable to ignore calls for serious political directives aimed at ameliorating systemic racism—even when, as we saw at the turn of the twenty-first century, several European nations developed antidiscrimination policies.[61] For instance, when the European Union developed its first Racial Equality Directive in 2000 as a response to rising anti-immigration and radical right political parties throughout Europe, the denial of race that accompanies antiracialism stripped conversations around inequalities patterned by race (in housing, education, and policing, to name but a few) of any explicit discussion of racism at all.[62] In Portugal, the principle of antiracialism can be found embedded in the Data Protection Act of 1988, which forbids the collection of information regarding ethnic or racial origin, and in the way some academic researchers, politicians, and policymakers subsequently avoid studying or addressing race and racial oppression.[63] While Portugal has since strengthened its antidiscrimination policy, critics charge that the law continues to deny the existence of systemic racism through the individualization of racism as a matter of irrational behavior (i.e., a few bad apples). Meanwhile, the continued reluctance of the public to report racism to appropriate bodies reveals public distrust and fears of retaliation or repeated revictimization.[64] Antiracialism also permeates civil society, where individuals who detail encounters of racial oppression are often silenced, chastised, or deemed ignorant.[65] Amid data scarcity, policy dodges, and social circumscription, racism is rendered ideologically invisible, naturalizing the inequality faced by Africans and African descendants in Portugal, as well as other racialized and minoritized communities.[66]

The pervasiveness of Portuguese antiracial ideology cannot be understood without historical context. Influenced by Brazilian scholar Gilberto Freyre's work, cultural narratives of "lusotropicalism" posit that Portugal is an exemplar of "benevolent colonialism" due to a history of increased "miscegenation" and "intercultural exchanges" in the former colonies and during precolonial times in the Iberian Peninsula.[67] In short, lusotropicalist ideology suggests that Portuguese people's history of interracial and interethnic mixing—namely, with Africans, Muslims, and Jewish groups—has given the Portuguese people the ability to participate in cross-cultural exchanges and, in fact, to transcend race.[68] These cultural narratives held particular political sway in the twentieth century, when African national liberation movements took hold and Portugal's fascist dictator, António de Oliveira Salazar, sought to rebrand colonialism as a mutually beneficial cultural exchange and his own Estado Novo regime as a multiracial yet postracial state. Lusotropicalism served a political function, hiding or obscuring injustice as Salazar and his peers continued to promote white supremacy. Portuguese scholars Marta Araújo and Silvia Maeso are especially incisive in revealing the insidiousness of this intersection, charging that contemporary discourse around diversity and race in Portugal remains a rhetorical evasion of ongoing institutional racism and oppression and an instrument to depoliticize the legacies of European colonialism.[69]

Opposition and activism, however, have their own long history in Portuguese society and scholarship. Simply documenting disparities is a radical act in this climate. Researchers report, for instance, that PALOP immigrants, including Cabo Verdeans, are heavily concentrated in racially segregated neighborhoods on Lisbon's outer fringes and are overrepresented in low-wage, precarious service and care work occupations.[70] They draw attention to alarming educational disparities, in which African students are far more likely than others to be grade retained (held back to repeat a year or more of education) and referred to vocational courses, both outcomes evidencing institutionalized racism.[71] And scholars, along with Portuguese antiracist and feminist organizations such as Plataforma Negra, Djass, SOS Racismo, Plataforma Gueto, and Femafro, as well as international monitoring bodies like the European Commission against Racism and Intolerance and the European Network Against Racism, continue to denounce the racialized surveillance of and police violence directed against African and African-descendant neighborhoods in Lisbon and communities throughout Portugal.[72] Conservative politicians and pundits counter that, because race does not *matter* in an antiracial hegemony, these disparate outcomes relate not to oppression but to cultural differences and individual choices. This is reminiscent of how "postracial" and "color-blind" ideologies are documented throughout the world, including, prominently, in the United States, where claims about "not seeing race" have regularly stifled institutional initiatives aimed at reducing racial inequality.[73]

While antiracial ideology attempts to make race unspeakable, this book's privileging of Black women's experiences builds on the crucial studies of Black Europe to present an alternative narrative that reflects the social significance of race in a context in which it is, theoretically and allegedly, nonexistent.[74] To that end, *Laboring in the Shadow of Empire* takes a historically informed approach to revealing systemic intersectional oppression in Portugal, particularly attending to the ways the physically, socially, and ideologically violent colonial encounter lives on in the daily experiences of individuals racialized as Black women as well as the socially structured acceptance of white European superiority (so visible in ongoing and multifaceted inequalities). In this sense, "race" refers to the relative social positions of differentially positioned groups in the shadow of empire, shaped by ongoing and intersecting histories of empire, colonialism, anti-Blackness, heteropatriarchy, and white supremacy and subtly inflected by lingering notions of racial essentialism.[75]

How Race and Gender Matter for Care Laborers

In this work I draw from the rich tradition of Black feminist and intersectional scholarship, as it provides a much-needed analytical approach and theoretical lens through which we can understand the joint influence of race and gender, along with other salient social statuses, on African-descendant women's work in Portugal.[76] Intersectionality—first coined by legal scholar and activist Kimberlé Crenshaw in 1989[77]—recognizes that structural identities do not exist independently of each other and are rather co-constructed, often creating a complex convergence of oppression and privilege. While an antiracial epistemology of ignorance attempts to normalize the depth of systemic oppression in society through the silencing of the most marginalized, intersectionality begins with the premise that we must start from the vantage point of the marginalized in order to truly unearth the possibilities for social change. Specifically, I center analysis on the everyday gendered anti-Black racism experienced by Cabo Verdean women—what Philomena Essed describes as the manifestations of the mundane practices of intersectional racisms that are normalized by the dominant group and gain meaning in relation to one another through their repetition.[78] These cumulative instantiations both reinforce and are reinforced by the intersectional systems of domination within a society.

The intersectional approach I forward in this book is crucial to study the complex inequalities faced by African-descendant care workers in Portugal. Foremost, centering on the everyday experiences of gendered anti-Black racism allows for an exploration of how intersectional identities that are not recognized by the state (i.e., the racial and gendered identity of "Black woman") are nevertheless made salient every day through various institutional and systemic mechanisms of oppression. For example, research finds rampant gender-based occupational segmentation in this labor market[79] such that occupations such as "personal service workers," "cleaners and helpers," and "clerks" are heavily dominated by women, but occupations that require economic decision-making and leadership are far more male dominated than in the rest of the European Union.[80] Gender inequality also persists in salaries, with men outearning women across many occupational levels.[81] Sociologists have long attributed this form of occupational segregation via feminization to the maintenance of gender and class inequalities.[82] Yet few large-scale studies have focused specifically on the particular discrimination and work experiences faced by African-descendant women in the contemporary Portuguese labor force.[83]

Intersectional theorizing thus shows us that much can be learned from paying attention to the everyday experiences of people who exist at the intersection of coloniality, white supremacy, patriarchy, economic exploitation, and nationalism. As I will discuss in the next chapter, changes ushered in by decolonization, Portugal's entrance into the European Union, and the rapid urbanization of its major cities in the late twentieth century drastically altered the sociocultural and occupational landscape for women. As white Portuguese middle-class women saw their relative status in Portuguese society rise through increased access to education and expanded family work policies, they nevertheless experienced conflict between their roles as mothers and workers. Decreased fertility and Portuguese women's increased labor market participation resulted, too, in white middle-class women seeking to "buy out" of gendered constraints and family obligations, including by employing paid eldercare workers. At the same time, Cabo Verdean women were moving into the institutional cleaning market, where the growth in the service sector and the suburban middle class also increased service demand.[84] Because higher demand collided with existing racialized and gendered stereotypes—colonial mindsets—pertaining to African immigrant women as an "appropriate" population for carrying out stigmatized, or "dirty," service work, the gendered impacts of economic change were also inescapably raced.[85]

Laboring in the Shadow of Empire thus illustrates how much gendered racialization is required by a labor system regulating ethnic and racial minority women to lower-tier marginal jobs. At the site of work, omnipresent practices of everyday gendered anti-Black racism are manifest in labor hierarchy and performance, affect, and racialized expectations of femininity through which domination is both justified and actively resisted. I stress, however, that addressing this complex web of oppressions that Cabo Verdean care workers face is not simply about listing the social problems they face. It is also about showing that African and African-descendant care workers are not "duped" by systemic social forces; they are active agents, and their voices and experiences offer a unique window into how inequality is produced and perpetuated and perhaps how it may be abolished. Discussion with the women in my research reveals how they have equipped themselves with the political consciousness to challenge and resist marginalization.[86] It is to this end that several intersectional scholar-activists, such as Beatriz Dias, Carla Fernandes, Grada Kilomba, Iolanda Évora, Inocência Mata, Joacine Katar Moreira, and Cristina Roldão, among many others, have argued for the critical necessity of placing Africans' and African descendants' experiences at the center of social justice organizing in Portugal.[87] Similarly, because I firmly believe that we cannot understand and address persistent systemic inequality without taking into account the lived reality of intersectional oppression, I have centered this book on the Black women laborers disadvantaged by the vestiges of colonial discourses and their continued power within the modern Portuguese occupational landscape.

The Research

The ethnographic data in these pages primarily come from seventeen months of participant observation in the greater metropolitan region of Lisbon. I conducted this fieldwork in stages during the years 2015, 2016, and 2019. I further supplemented my study with five weeks of supplementary field visits to Cabo Verde in 2015, fifty-nine in-depth and semistructured interviews with Cabo Verdean eldercare and cleaning workers, and hundreds of informal interviews with informants and their friends and families.

Starting in January 2015, I spent nine months in the field riding along with eldercare workers as they commuted in metropolitan Lisbon, observing eldercare home visits, sleeping in my field informants' homes, and helping out with their childcare needs. During this time, I informally interviewed and observed eldercare workers and their families as they went through their daily routines. A five-week field visit to Praia, Cabo Verde, allowed me to add to these data through extended conversations with family members and friends of the participants I met in Portugal. I returned to Portugal in the summer of 2016 to conduct additional interviews with care workers and to continue my participation observation schedule, as well as in 2019, when I followed up with past informants during a four-month field visit. In the latter, I was able to interview further family members and collect a subset of interviews with institutional cleaning workers of Cabo Verdean descent (see the methodological appendix for greater detail and an exploration of the impact of author positionality in this fieldwork).

My interest in Cabo Verdean care migrants has been shaped by several intersecting dimensions of my personal history. During my childhood I had witnessed the myriad trials and tribulations of immigrant life in my own extended family as well as from within the classes in which I learned, the parks in which I played, and the neighborhoods in which I lived, made friends, and forged memories. I am a Black, mixed-race woman from an interracial and immigrant family who was raised in a working-class city in New Jersey in which well over 70 percent of the population had ties to the Caribbean, Mexico, and Central and South America. My husband is a Cabo Verdean immigrant to the United States, raised in the fishing town of New Bedford, Massachusetts, and my stepfather is a Mexican immigrant from Tehuacán, Puebla, who was undocumented during my childhood and has long worked alongside his siblings and cousins as an interior painter. My biological father, a former jazz musician with southern roots, instilled in me a profound appreciation for the power of stories, always urging me to question why things were the way they were. Over the years and over meals, several of my relatives shared our complex family histories of laboring in undervalued and precarious employment—ranging from "hauling slag," sharecropping, and "cleaning house" in small coal- and coke-mining towns in Tennessee to the more present realities of caring for the elderly or the disabled in Chattanooga. They treated our stories as testimonies of the hardship all our families have endured, as well as reminders of the fortitude our ancestors—and we—possessed.

Though several family members, friends, and neighbors back in New Jersey also worked in caring occupations during my formative years and likewise had *many* stories to tell, my interest in the racialized dimensions of Black women's caring work emerged after a conversation with my cousin that occurred during a family visit to Chattanooga when I was twelve years old. We sat on her porch during a hot summer afternoon in Chattanooga, Tennessee, surrounded by the scenic forges of the river city. With bright eyes, she shared her story of working as a home health worker as she looked up toward what my great-aunt referred to as the "rich white people's houses" that peered, ominously, through the trees atop of Lookout Mountain: "Celeste, do you know what's the worst thing that someone could ever do to you? The worst thing a racist person who really hates you could ever do?" I shrugged and waited for her to answer. "This one white woman I watch, she can't speak, but she's a racist! She doesn't want me to touch her! And she does the worst thing she could do. She spits on me! *Every day.* Looks at me with that face, and just spits, spits, spits! That's the worst thing someone could ever do to you."

My cousin's biting words stayed with me as a doctoral student at the University of Massachusetts–Amherst. While reading through assigned material on the critically important experiences of, often, Asian and Latina domestic workers in global cities around the world, I wondered about the voices and complex life histories of the contemporary Black women care workers—both native and foreign born. I appreciated the rich accounts of Black American women's historical participation in domestic labor within homes, particularly through the mid-twentieth century, but I wanted to know more about Black native and immigrant women's *current* engagement in paid work within formalized care professions in nursing homes, institutional cleaning services, and home care— something that was clearly ongoing in the southern United States and in the New York City metro area where I had grown up. Though I would eventually become exposed to the brilliant work of feminist scholars who center on the diversity of Black care workers' contemporary experiences across the globe (such as Jacqueline Andall, Enobong Hannah Branch, Kesha Fikes, Shireen Ally, Tamara Rose Brown, and Fumilayo Showers, among others), these are the questions that remained with me as a novice graduate student trying to find my way through the unfamiliar academy.

Indeed, my specific academic interest in the Cabo Verdean community fomented after I moved, for graduate school, to Massachusetts (in many outsiders' accounts, a wholly white space). I quickly became aware that it had, in fact, a vibrant Cabo Verdean community. The friendships I forged within this community sustained me as a graduate student; in our shared meals and good laughs, I found respite from the all-too-familiar sting of good old "progressive" New England racism. But the specific topic of Cabo Verdean care migration to Portugal came to me in 2012 when I was invited by the adviser and founder of the UMass–Amherst Cabo Verdean Student Alliance to serve as graduate adviser during their trip to the Cabo Verdean islands. There, and during several subsequent visits, I met several people who had women relatives abroad working in caring professions in Europe or the United States (even in Amherst, Massachusetts) or who were planning to depart Cabo Verde themselves.

For the first time, I also bore witness to the omnipresent legacies of Portuguese colonialism. On the Cabo Verdean Island of Fogo, locals explained that the old cemetery, facing the water and adjacent to dilapidated prison cells, was colloquially referred to as the cemetery for whites (or *brancos*); in Cidade Velha, the first European colonial outpost in the tropics, we walked past a slave-trading

FIG. 2 Island of Fogo. Photo by author.

post. Colonialism was not a distant or fleeting memory for many I met. It was a haunting. In conversation after conversation, people recounted histories and personal stories of Portuguese colonial oppression, coerced migrations, drought and famine, relentless resistance, and relatives lost or entangled therein. They spoke vividly of the "here" and "there" of the contemporary, postcolonial Cabo Verdean diaspora.

Long-standing migration flows connect Cabo Verde to the United States, especially in the form of migrants departing the islands of Brava and Fogo. These Cabo Verdeans who migrate to the United States historically tend to have lighter complexions, and a great deal of research on the Cabo Verdean diaspora in the United States has focused on these migrants' complex experiences of racism *and* racial fluidity and hybridity.[88] The large body of scholarship meant that I originally expected Cabo Verdean women's stories to centrally engage racial hybridity or, perhaps, ambiguity. Instead, the women who labor in institutional cleaning and home care work taught me how an ontology of gendered Blackness seems to indelibly mark their subjectivities; racial hybridity was not particularly central to how they made sense of their work and their positions in Portuguese society. Certainly, they located their Cabo Verdean identity within a racial and ethnic formation comprising the African continent, the Cabo Verdean global diaspora, and Europe, but foremost, they pointed to institutionalized gendered racism as the major force shaping their postcolonial subjectivities in Portugal. Additionally, my respondents, the majority of whom migrated not from the major "sending" locations connected to the United States but from

FIG. 3 Island of Santiago. Photo by author.

the island of Santiago, where the population tends toward darker complexions, allowed my work in this book to interrogate the multidimensional meanings of Blackness within a diasporic African community that flows to multiple receiving contexts.

Mapping the Book

Throughout this book, I illustrate how a racialized and international division of reproductive labor shapes Cabo Verdean women's evaluations of life within the shadow of empire. I argue that it is work itself that, in creating and structuring their interactions and interdependencies with other residents of Portugal, shapes migrant Cabo Verdean women's racial and gender identity in their new homes. In other words, the conditions of cleaning work distribute social recognition in ways that rejuvenate many long-standing colonial discourses of gendered racialization.

In the first chapter, I provide an overview of the migration, labor, and nationality regimes that have facilitated the spatial movement of Cabo Verdean men and women to Portugal. I argue that colonial slavery and Portugal's implementation of a forced and coerced colonial labor recruitment apparatus in the nineteenth and twentieth centuries, alongside the retrenchment of welfare states and rapid urbanization, laid the foundation for the solidification of a contemporary racialized and international division of reproductive labor in twenty-first-century Portugal. This division of labor now compels African and Afro-descendant women to pursue only a narrow set of occupations, which reinforces their social position and influences their identity formation.

Chapter 2 describes the processes of migration and chapter 3 the postmigration process of finding work in Portugal. Through both, respondents come to recognize their own sense of racial and gender identity in an allegedly antiracial society. I capture key moments of intersectional identity formation by tracing the everyday experiences of gendered anti-Black racism respondents have with labor gatekeepers and the "rank and file" whites they encounter in public spaces, including supermarkets, bus stops, public parks, and commercial centers. I also illustrate how agentic African-descendant women resist the everyday gendered anti-Black racism they face in public spaces.

Chapters 4 and 5 examine the experiences of marginalization Cabo Verdean women report on the job in the devalued service care contexts to which they are so commonly relegated. First, I explore how white women colleagues scrutinize Cabo Verdean women's home care labor performance unfairly, thereby thwarting Black women's already scarce opportunities for advancement while achieving respectful treatment for themselves within shared workplaces. Then I reveal the tensions between Black women and the elders and families they care for—interpersonal instantiations in which antiracial ideologies about the nature of the work hide the racial tensions of these gendered workplaces. In chapter 5,

I demonstrate the impacts as patrons interact with Black women as both invisible and allegedly hypervisible laborers—invisible in the sense that women are regarded as appropriate to the work of cleaning up after others and hypervisible in that they are subject to suspicion when encountered by white (and other non-Black) patrons in bathrooms and other solitary spaces in the places in which they labor. Both chapters also center on everyday acts of resistance as workers negotiate multiple forms of quotidian invisibility and hypervisibility.

Chapter 6 addresses the issue of belonging. Cabo Verdean women, who weather and contest racialized and gendered exclusion in broader Portuguese society, co-create and frequent spaces of belonging that, like the community spaces I found in Massachusetts, make room for their performances and celebrations of their own conceptualizations of Blackness. Black femininity is devalued in wider society, but in these spaces of belonging, it is forged, sustained, and reinterpreted. It can be taken up as a cherished identity or even set aside as an unneeded burden within an almost sacred space of shared experience.

Laboring in the Shadow of Empire concludes by revisiting my main arguments and offering generative ideas for implementing social change. I point to economic power and stratification as durable barriers preventing challenges to the ongoing violence of racialized and gendered colonial systems in the present day such that the flourishing of Africans and Afro-descendants in Portugal will not come without the wholesale eradication of the intersectional occupational segregation of reproductive labor. Foremost, I stress that actions toward emancipatory change must be rooted in the subjectivities of those who are rendered invisible by the antiracial ideology of the shadow of empire.

A Final Note on Terminology

Throughout this book I describe research participants as "African" (*africana*), "Cabo Verdean" (*cabo verdiana*), "African descendant" (*afrodescendente*), and "Black" (*negra*) because I have chosen to follow informants' own naming conventions. Similarly, I use the word *kriolu* regarding their language because it reflects my informants' own spelling and pronunciation of the Cabo Verdean language they speak (and that is largely associated with the island of Santiago).[89]

1

The Making of a Gendered and Racialized Care Sector in Portugal

• •

It's Freedom Day in Lisbon—as the "Dia da Liberdade" banners swaying in the breeze attest—and the streets are filled with revelers. I'm only a few months into my fieldwork on April 25, and I'm surrounded by families, children, and community groups. Children playfully scamper into the road to gather up the red carnations strewn across the cobblestones, paying tribute to the 1974 "Carnation Revolution." The countrywide celebrations represent what some refer to as the spirit of Portugal. Citizens take to the streets, praising the political freedoms, civil liberties, and mass civil resistance encapsulated in the fateful day when, the story goes, the soldiers from the Movimento das Forças Armadas (MAF), along with men and women manual workers, led the people in the peaceful overthrow of dictator Marcelo José das Neves Alves Caetano and the Estado Novo. Ushering in Portugal's democratization and decolonization efforts, the revolutionaries placed carnations in the muzzles of soldiers' rifles and pinned them to their uniforms.

The red, green, and yellow of the Portuguese flag swirl around us, and the celebrants fill the air with chants. As they march from the statue of Marquês de Pombal, the eighteenth-century Portuguese statesman who managed the colonial slave trade, down the Avenida da Liberdade toward the Praça do Comércio, a historic and popular square where slave ships once moored on the Tagus River, onlookers cheer from the sidewalks and balconies. Yet for all its exuberance, this commemoration so important to Portuguese political life is triggering a sort of dissonance. In my relatively few months in the field, I have frequented neighborhoods filled with vibrant multigenerational African and African-descendant families laying down roots, but on this day, on these streets, the faces seemed to be almost uniformly white and light-skinned.

I drop back from the crowd. It takes only a few minutes before I come upon a different scene. A large multiracial and multiethnic congregation is gathering near an intersection along "Liberty Avenue," its members laughing, chatting, unfurling banners, and passing out pamphlets. A group of drummers warms up, their beats swelling to fill the alcove between two adjoining buildings. I thrill at the sight of this crowd, predominantly Black and South Asian, and the enormous blue-and-yellow banner that reads "Immigrantes Contra a Escravatura"—"Immigrants against slavery." Just as quickly, I am filled with dismay. A handful of participants rush toward my group, informing us that some of the political groups in the main march (such as the communists, they say) are trying to block the immigrant groups from participating. Immigrant support groups, they say, have been told they have no right to march because they are "not citizens." In the end, this assemblage of Portuguese and non-Portuguese activists chooses its own symbolic action. Adorned with red carnations, the group steps in behind the main march. It shadows the official procession, like a sort of Greek chorus, with chants and signs that contrast sharply with those they trail so closely.

"We are labor"
"No one is illegal"
"We are not immigrants, we are humans!"
"We are not Criminals!"
"Everyone is an Immigrant"
"The Struggle Continues!"

Throughout my fieldwork, I often thought back to that afternoon in 2015. I remembered the juxtaposition of the signs reading "freedom" with those reading *escravatura* (slavery). I learned that the exclusion of some from full and visible participation in Freedom Day reflected the exclusion of many hailing from former Portuguese colonies from full and visible citizenship in Portugal itself. The chanting of "La Luta Continua" (the fight continues), the rallying cry of the FRELIMO (Frente de Libertação de Moçambique) movement during Mozambique's war that was taken up by other African liberation movements, reveals the intrinsic contradictions of the Dia da Liberdade. The "bloodless" and "peaceful" Carnation Revolution that took place on Lisboan soil hinged on a history of violent racial and gender subjugation, more than a decade of deadly colonial warfare, and the Portuguese state's explicit efforts to limit migrant inclusivity as decolonization unfolded. Soon it seemed to me that a great deal of violence had been—and continued to be—implicated in the social politics of modern Portugal.

Making of Gendered and Racialized Colonial Labor Hierarchies

Studies of state-sponsored migration in EU member states have traditionally forwarded a periodization of immigration that downplays race, subordination, and colonialism, yet in my ethnographic study of Cabo Verdean institutional home care and service workers in Portugal, I have found it more fruitful to consider the issue from a *longue durée*[1] perspective that highlights the long-standing and ongoing processes of colonialism.[2] Cabo Verdeans and PALOP immigrants (those from Portuguese-speaking African countries, or Países Africanos de Língua Oficial Portuguesa) are heavily concentrated in the Lisbon metropolitan area, where their integration into the labor market has been predominantly concentrated within precarious, low-wage service and care work.[3] Research also finds that Cabo Verdeans' labor market position persists even after long periods of residence.[4] The factors that have shaped their labor market position are not limited to the internationalization and gendered racialization of care and service work but also include everything from historically charged colonial and postcolonial labor regimes, shaped by state-supported methods of coercion, to Portugal's decolonization processes and annexation to the European Union. In particular, the relegation of stigmatized "dirty work" to African and African-descendant women has remained remarkably consistent despite the historical transformation of reproductive labor from a feudal and colonial model of servitude and servility to one of service work in twenty-first-century Portugal.

Work that locates the twentieth century as the major nexus of African migration to Portugal also obscures centuries of Africans' and African descendants' presence in Portuguese society. The country was the first of the modern European empires to initiate colonialism in the fifteenth century and the last to carry out decolonization in the twentieth century, and chattel slavery, settler colonialism, and coerced labor regimes have been and remain central to the history of Portugal, its African-descendant population, and its former colonies, including Cabo Verde.[5] At the same time, Portugal deemed itself to be central to a Europe that historically deemed it distant. Once the head of the colonial empire, Portugal became economically dominated by core countries (namely, England) by the end of the seventeenth century. Boaventura de Sousa Santos refers to this unique position as a "semiperipheral country in the modern capitalist world system" located in "another South inside Europe."[6] But in part, it was through its long involvement in empire via the colonialization of Africa that Portugal established itself as part of a racialized, modern Europe.

Rather than emerging in Lisbon and other population centers in the twentieth century, there has long been an African presence in Portugal. For example, elites from the kingdom of Congo came to Lisbon to study theology and astronomy well before the emergence of the Portuguese slave trade. Enslaved Africans began arriving in Portugal in the mid-fifteenth century—a flow that would continue over a span of three hundred years.[7] A. C. De C. M. Saunders's work reveals that the largest concentration of fifteenth- and sixteenth-century Blacks in Portugal, both enslaved and free, was in the city of Lisbon, where nearly 20 percent of the population was African.[8] Lisbon's Mocambo neighborhood (known today as Madragoa) was established in 1593, providing a vibrant home to significant populations of Africans and African descendants. Historical accounts demonstrate that Afro-Lisboans' degradation was built into law and everyday colonial practice, and they document how their integration into Portuguese society, by necessity, came to include linguistic incorporation as well as adherence to the conventions of Catholic religious life. Yet in neighborhoods like Mocambo (named after the Kimbundu word for "hideout"), enslaved and freed Africans and their families resisted cultural domination through the continued production of their own cultural life—the dance traditions, festivals, music, and religious customs deemed "sorcery" or immoral by the Portuguese crown and the Catholic Church.[9]

From the start, both free and enslaved Africans in Portugal worked, meaning their labor market participation and social positions within cities began taking shape well before the current era. In *general*, regardless of race, enslaved people were associated with feudal ideologies of servility, though enslaved and free Blacks encountered specific racialized treatment in Portugal that shaped their ontology. Often, they were assigned the most stigmatized work—the kind even free servants tended to refuse. The institutionalized exploitation of Black labor had a name: *negros de ganho*, or "Blacks for profit." Under this system, masters or proprietors had a right to a portion of the meager earnings brought in by African laborers doing the "dirty" and menial work of the city. Lisboan city dwellers purchased water from Black women known as *negras do pote* who hauled water from the city fountain, counted on them for the removal of garbage and excrement to the river's edge each night, and looked to them as street vendors, or *regateiras*, by day. This assignation of the most stigmatized work to Africans racialized as Black (and, to a smaller degree, some marginalized non-Blacks) would contour the symbolic and sociocultural conceptions of race, anti-Blackness, gender, and servility in Portuguese society for centuries.[10]

Additionally, fifteenth- and sixteenth-century histories suggest that Black enslaved women had no access to legal protection against sexual violence in Portugal and the colonies. The crown's legal regulation of sexual crimes paints a distinction between white femininity and Black femininity as early as 1521, after which date a master could sue someone for assaulting or raping an enslaved woman racialized as white—no such legal stipulation "protected" enslaved women racialized as Black. In Lisbon and Evora, even religious orders made such distinctions, and the Episcopal constitutions forbade priests from owning white, but not African, slaves. Moreover, more costly Black women domestic house servants were regarded as a status symbol among the elite.[11] In this way, enslaved Black women's presence within the household also provided elite white women with the power to perform their racial dominance within a patriarchal society. Together, these historical realities point to a violent degradation of Black African femininity and dehumanization of Black women vis-à-vis white femininity.

The Age of ~~Discovery~~ Colonization of the Cabo Verdean Islands

Between 1460 and 1462, during the "age of discovery," Portuguese, Spanish, and Genoese sailors first sighted the Cabo Verdean archipelago. Though some evidence suggests otherwise, the Europeans deemed the islands unvisited and uninhabited. With the aid of land grants (*capitanias*, including one to the original "discoverer" of the archipelago, António de Noli), Portuguese settlers first colonized the island of St. Thiago (now Santiago) and founded the first colonial outpost, Ribeira Grande (modern-day Cidade Velha). In 1466, to further incentivize settlement and with the support of a Catholic civilizing mission, Portuguese king Dom Afonso V granted Santiago colonists, the majority of whom were Portuguese men, exclusive rights over the slave trade off the Guinean coast. When the crown withdrew these rights in 1472, the resulting commercial turn toward the export of locally produced goods spurred the establishment of a plantation economy.

Cabo Verde's early plantation economy was characterized by the arrival of Africans, often kidnapped from the Guinean coasts and forced to labor on sugar cane, cotton, maize, and coffee plantations while others were sold and transported to the Americas or Europe, including South America, the Caribbean, and the United States.[12] The island of Santiago, from which migration streams to Portugal historically originate, has always been the most populous. By 1582, the island of Santiago was inhabited by approximately 1,100 whites, 400 free Blacks, 10,700 enslaved adult persons, and enslaved children who are not accounted for in historical records.[13] For 150 years, Cabo Verde played a key role in the transatlantic slave trade. Its geographic location, between continental Africa and the Americas, was key to the vicious, violent, and inhumane business. White Portuguese and some mixed-race Portuguese descendants from the colonies sailed up and down the African coast, procuring human chattel by "bartering" with local African chieftains[14] and deploying armed envoys further inland. While vast numbers of enslaved Africans brought to the Cabo Verdean islands were forcefully rerouted and exported to the Americas, the remaining enslaved comprised two main groups: men and women "rural slaves," who labored on the agricultural plantation system; and "domestic slaves," who were primarily women and labored within the homes of the Portuguese elite on the islands.

With increasingly comprehensive legal support, this period of the colonial project created a globalized, racialized knowledge of the colonized, cementing a durable European association between Black Africans and taxing, stigmatized labor. Historian António Carreira describes the privileged position of the white European settler in this period. Under the Portuguese crown, they had the right

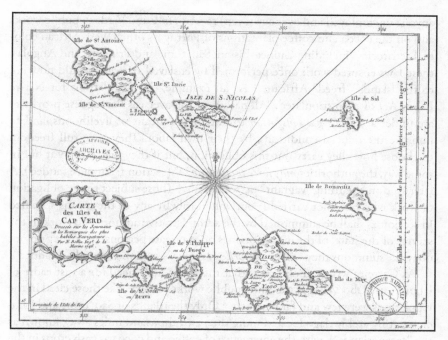

FIG. 4 Map of Cabo Verde, 1746. *Source:* Wikimedia Commons.

to own land and humans they regarded as suited to the crushing work of physical labor in the tropical climate (unlike themselves). This taxing work was, in fact, seen as appropriate for Africans. The settlers' social, racial, and economic prestige were soon enshrined in the colonial legal codes, which imported a Portuguese system of land tenure, *morgadio*, to the African colonies. The imposition disrupted systems of African land tenure not only through wholesale seizure but also by stipulating that land parcels were indivisible and transmitted intergenerationally through male family lineage. The Royal Warrant of 1472 solidified the right of settlers "to have slaves, male and female, to work for them, to enable them to live and settle better."[15] White men's powerful position, coupled with the paucity of European women on the islands, made sexual relations (including rape) between enslaved African women and white men commonplace and entirely legal.[16]

Despite its mid-nineteenth-century abolition, de facto slavery continued in Cabo Verde well into the twenty-first century in the form of a system of contracted labor and sharecropping.[17] Miguel Bandeira Jerónimo argues that these forms of compulsory labor were a central feature of the Portuguese colonial empire's *civilizing mission*, whereby colonial authorities claimed they had the moral obligation to civilize Africans by forcing them to work.[18] Ancillary laws shored up the practice, including the 1875 imposition of a colonial antivagrancy scheme. By allowing the colonial administration to force "vagrants" (defined as anyone unemployed and over age seven) to work in Cabo Verdean public works and on the cocoa and coffee plantations of Portugal's other West African colonial territories (including Guinea-Bissau, São Tomé and Príncipe, and Angola), these laws ensured work once performed by enslaved Africans would now fall to the islands' "freed" Africans.[19] As an example, the Regulations for Native Labor Act of 1899 stipulated, "All natives of the overseas Portuguese provinces are under a *moral legal obligation* to obtain the means of livelihoods, and to improve their social conditions, by their own labor. They have full freedom to choose how they carry out this obligation; but if they fail to carry it out in some way, the authorities *may force them to do so*" (section 1; emphasis added). A later section regarding "vagrant" persons reads, "Those subject to the obligation of work who have not carried it out voluntarily by any of the means specified in section 2, shall be summoned by the administrative authority to work in the service of the state, of the municipalities or of private persons. . . . If they do not obey the summons they will be *compelled to do so*" (section 31; emphasis added).

As Carreira writes, the irony is that there was little need for a vast cadre of laborers in Cabo Verde at the time; public works projects like those cited in the regulations were few and far between.[20] Only the islands of São Tomé and Príncipe (a tiny archipelago located more than two thousand miles away, known as the "cacao islands"), with the emergence of coffee and cocoa as cash crops in the second half of the nineteenth century, required substantial labor power. Instead, as Evelyn Nakano Glenn has revealed of vagrancy laws in the United States, such regulations intentionally structured the social control of subjugated racial groups (whose labor the state sought to exploit) via law enforcement and the judicial court system.[21] This social control led to one of the first waves of Cabo Verdean migration within continental Africa.

Colonialism also reinforced and transplanted racialized and gendered conceptions of belonging and nonbelonging in the metropole that normalized white masculine national identity and granted white women national belonging while denying them an independent identity from that of their husbands.[22] This normalization of feminine whiteness, however, rested on the racialization and, in fact, regulation of the bodies of women of color.[23] To extend colonialist enslavement regimes, African women in Cabo Verde were subjected to the imposition of laws like the 1856 "Law of the Free Womb," which claimed their reproductive labor in a literal sense, mandating that any children under the age of thirteen of an enslaved mother must serve their mother's masters without payment until the age of twenty.[24]

That all African women, whether enslaved or free, were generally compelled to engage in subsistence agriculture or reproductive labor through a labor peonage system additionally distanced them from the feminine status afforded to white women.[25] Black feminist scholar Hortense Spillers refers to this process as the dehumanized *ungendering* of Black women, in which historical violence (such as the reproductive economy of chattel slavery and the postemancipation labor peonage system) excludes Black women from normative kinship structures such as the nation.[26] In this case, the ungendering of Black women reflected their unique racial ontology; they and their families could not "belong" to the heter-opatriarchal colonial empire outside of their utility for exploitative commodification. In short, African women were at once *modes of production* and *modes of reproduction* as their labor would extract, shape, and circulate raw commodities for Europe and support the reproduction of human life—including the precious African human life that the empire constructed as nonhuman chattel.

Drought and Famine

As periods of relentless drought and famine threatened Cabo Verdeans' survival within the bounds of subsistence agriculture, men and women migrated from Cabo Verde to Europe, the United States, continental Africa, and Latin America.[27] Particularly during the nineteenth and twentieth centuries, this out-migration was shaped by the Portuguese colonial administration's mismanagement of relief within the islands' social infrastructure. Specifically, the colonial economic policy favored cash crops for export over subsistence production, leaving islanders particularly susceptible to famine.[28] For example, the Portuguese crown established maize as Cabo Verde's staple crop, though the island's dry soil, sparse rainfall, and frequent drought years proved enormous challenges to the grain's cultivation. Under the Portuguese colonial authority's sharecropping system—reminiscent of the post–Civil War U.S. South—poor African sharecroppers were forced to bear the cost of production and then hand over as much as 50 percent of their harvests to affluent land-owners;[29] this imported reality found its precedent in the system of *negros de ganho* institutionalized in Portugal during the sixteenth century. To historian George Brooks, Portuguese rule in Cabo Verde formed, in essence, a "gulag":

> The toll of environmental degradation mounted over the centuries. . . . Multi-year droughts precipitated famines, some to claim thousands of the archipelago's inhabitants. The archipelago's inhabitants subsisted almost entirely on agriculture, consuming little seafood. Denied use of boats, Cabo Verdeans were restricted to shore fishing along the few coves, reefs, and shoal waters. There were few possibilities to market salt-preserved or sun-dried fish, for the archipelago's destitute inhabitants had no money or commodities to barter. So impoverished were people of all social groups except Portuguese colonial administrators and plantation owners that for centuries there was practically no money in circulation, no shops, and no inter-island commerce.[30]

The cumulative effects of intense Portuguese control and intentional neglect were devastating. To wit, in just three years (1773 to 1776), nearly 50 percent of the population of Cabo Verde died from famine according to some estimates.[31] By 1900, the archipelago had lost approximately 25–35 percent of its population at least two additional times during the 1830s and 1860s.[32] The toll was some-times unevenly spread. According to estimates cited by Judy R. Aulette and Katherine Carter, from 1941 to 1943, the island of Fogo lost approximately 31 percent of its population to starvation and illness, and from 1946 to 1948, the island of Santiago (where ties were strongest to the transatlantic slave trade and migration to Portugal) lost a stunning 65 percent of its population to starvation and illness.[33]

Responses from the Portuguese state only compounded the deleterious effects of these regular famines. Corrupt local officials diverted already sub-standard relief supplies for their own profit. In 1864, ten years prior to the implementation of vagrancy laws, the governor of Cabo Verde received a royal order to export laborers from Santiago to São Tomé and Príncipe as "an effi-cient means of giving help to the inhabitants of Cabo Verde, most affected by the famine, with great utility for another Portuguese possession," later adding that the governor was commanded to "facilitate the emigration of free laborers in conditions favorable to their utilization . . . [and] employing to this end all possible means necessary."[34] In other words, if Africans were starving in Cabo Verde, they should be forcibly removed and sent into labor in other colonial outposts—a move that further damaged kinship relations, propped up colonial economies, and tidily, if technically, lowered the numbers of people starving to death on the Cabo Verdean islands. These projects consisted of the provision of money for food in exchange for men's and women's labor power and were the colonial administration's primary mode of famine relief.

As some eighty thousand Cabo Verdeans were sent to labor on the cocoa and coffee plantations of São Tomé and Príncipe over fifty-two years (taking up the work of deserted slaves, these workers joined others transported from Mozam-bique and Angola), others worked on state construction projects as late as the 1960s, using simple tools like picks, hammers, and dynamite to craft roadways and other infrastructure. Frequently, women worked alongside family in small farms, in informal sales of everyday goods (or *rabidantes*), or as domestics within the homes of the islands' Portuguese and Cabo Verdean elites.[35] Importantly, all these responses made the deleterious effects of famine and drought into reve-nue streams for Portugal: African workers were paid paltry sums, barely enough for a minimal supply of food, which facilitated the colonizers' access to a cheap labor pool even after the abolishment of slavery on the Cabo Verdean islands.[36] Thus scholars have rightly characterized the state-sponsored system of colonial labor recruitment as "forced migration," akin to slavery, under extreme coercion and control.[37] As a result, Portuguese coloniality's construction of racialized and gendered hierarchies of labor, spanning back to the fifteenth century, reinforced already existing colonial "knowledge" of some groups' inferiority and "appropri-ateness" to low-wage and stigmatized labor.[38]

Race and Color on the Islands of Cabo Verde

A long history of racial mixture has influenced the emergence of a Cabo Verdean *kriolu* identity. Inhabitants of the island have a range of skin tones from very dark to very light. As Richard Lobban's work accounts, the colonial categorization of race here was initially a basic binary system: there were *pretos* (Blacks, meaning enslaved humans) and *brancos*, or upper-class white Portuguese traveling merchants or settlers. But as mentioned previously, interracial sex (whether forced or "voluntary") was common, and the mixed-race community of Cabo Verde expanded exponentially. As Celeste Fortes and Elizabeth Challinor have noted, within these structural conditions, some enslaved women used their bodies as "a means of upward social mobility within slave society."[39] On some occasions, their "mulatto," often male, offspring could be freed by masters, then sent to the Guinean coast as the colonial administration's *lançados*, or middlemen in imperial trade. Iva Cabral's important work reveals that over time, and as a free African population emerged, skin color lost its rigid association with enslavement. Referred to as *brancos da terra*, or whites of the land, a social intermediate class consisting of mixed-race *crioulos* and Blacks arose in Cabo Verdean society.[40]

The Portuguese state manipulated the *crioulo* community by creating new racial hierarchies in which often the lighter-skinned among them became "strategic intermediaries" (like the *lançados*) throughout the colonial system. As deftly argued by Afro- and decolonial feminist Sylvia Tamale, often contradictory colonial ideologies of difference were tools to extend colonial dispossession and rule.[41] In 1930, in one of its many ploys to extend colonialism and buffer subaltern resistance to colonial rule in its southern African colonies, Portugal created a legal designation known as *assimilados* (or assimilated). This status—which implied the holder was *civilized*, as they had accepted the cultural expectations of the colonial authority by way of language, religion, and customs—was automatically granted to Cabo Verdeans. Meanwhile, the inhabitants of Portugal's other former African colonies (rebranded "provinces" by Portuguese dictator António de Oliveira Salazar in the mid-twentieth century) were dubbed *indígenas* (or Indigenous). Cabo Verdeans, often *crioulo* men from elite families, were elevated to work as colonial officers throughout the Portuguese empire[42] and encouraged to believe that they were culturally similar to the Portuguese (if still second-class citizens of the colonial state). Per Lobban, these officials "were trapped in a system in which they were simultaneously subordinated and elevated . . . both victims and victimizers in the colonial structure."[43]

An article in the newspaper *O Primero de Janeiro*, published in 1940, spotlights how pernicious Portuguese white supremacy cemented the African *assimilados* second-class status and framed *true* assimilation as an impossibility: "No matter how brilliant and effective their professional and economic activity may and should be, they [the assimilated Africans] must never fill positions of general politics; except perhaps in cases of full identification with us in terms of temperament, violation, understanding, ideas; though [such] cases are quite uncommon and improbable."[44]

In the metropole and the colonies, violent characterizations depicted African and African-descendant men and women as uncivilized, "primitive," childlike, backward, hypersexual, and often grotesque.[45] Of the *assimilados*, former governor-general of Angola Vicente Ferreira remarked in 1932, "[They] are no more than grotesque imitations of white men [keeping, in their majority,] the mentality of the primitive, concealed poorly by words, gestures and clothing, copied from the European."[46] Whiteness, let alone its privileges, could never become more than an *assimilado* pantomime, this ongoing European racial formation suggested, because the negation of Blackness was central to the construction of Portuguese racial and national identity.[47]

Twentieth-Century Migration from Cabo Verde to Portugal

At the turn of the twentieth century, Cabo Verdean migration flows were oriented primarily to intercontinental Africa and the United States. For many, as argued by Carla Indira Carvalho Semedo, contract servitude in São Tomé and Príncipe promised peril and suffering by overwork on plantations—hardly a boon when held against the possibility of death by starvation in Cabo Verde.[48] In this sense, migration to the United States seemed a viable option for sustaining life, even family. Beginning with the nineteenth-century whaling boom, Cabo Verdeans were recruited by crew members on ships stopping over for supplies during their journeys to and from places like New Bedford, Massachusetts. Desperate locals from the "forgotten island"[49] found in the northeastern United States an industrializing society with new niches for cheap laborers in the fishing and whaling industry. Their historical ties to seafaring and agriculture afforded opportunities for Cabo Verdeans, and even women and children often found work harvesting in the cranberry bogs of New Bedford; Nantucket; and nearby Providence, Rhode Island.

This migration pathway was soon jettisoned when the United States introduced racially restrictive immigration quotas under the 1924 Johnson-Reed Act. Africans were almost entirely blocked from legal entrance. As a result, Cabo Verdean migration flows redirected to Portugal. This was the era of Salazar's Estado Novo, a fascist, authoritarian government that would stretch from 1932 to 1968 and extend under Marcelo Caetano. Still, Cabo Verdeans had Portuguese passports, which eased the journey, and in Portugal they could find jobs as gardeners and street sweepers and in the other service-oriented occupations of its rapidly changing urban centers.[50] A wave of poor, rural, often dark-skinned *badia* Cabo Verdean migrants, mainly from the rural interior of the island of Santiago, entered Portugal in the 1960s, joining the often *crioulo* children of Cabo Verdean *sampajuda*[51] elites who were traveling to Portugal and other areas of Europe, taking advantage of a scholarship offered by the Casa dos Estudantes do Império (the House of Students of the Empire), a government-financed center for secondary students from the Portuguese colonies. Indeed, Portuguese university spaces would act as a training ground for African nationalists who would eventually lead the struggle against colonial rule.

The mid-twentieth-century migration to Portugal was shaped in part by an unskilled labor shortage resulting from a series of simultaneous processes. The Portuguese colonial wars of 1961–1974 drained the country of military men, while low wages and poor working conditions spurred rural Portuguese families to migrate to more affluent European nations, particularly France and the United Kingdom.[52] Further, the Estado Novo regime in Portugal began settlement programs throughout the colonies for rural peasant Portuguese families through family reunification schemes during the mid-twentieth century. By the 1960s, some two-thirds of Portuguese citizens resided overseas, in Western Europe, the Americas, and in Portuguese Africa (mainly Angola and Mozambique).[53]

Portugal's Europeanization

The 1960s were also an important moment of Portuguese economic growth, urbanization, and industrialization. The country entered the European Free Trade Association (EFTA) in 1960, paving the way for membership in the European Union in January 1986. Joining the EFTA allowed Portugal to apply for a series of infrastructure and development grants, and securing this funding created a huge need for low-skilled laborers to construct new public works. The recent exodus of broad swaths of Portugal's military families and poor rural populations left the administration looking to Cabo Verde for labor recruitment.

Thus, most Cabo Verdean migrants entering Portugal at this time were men subcontracted by the government and employed by private enterprises to construct Lisbon's underground railroads and suburban housing developments and to dig ditches for electricity and telephone cables (by the twenty-first century, Cabo Verdean men would increasingly find themselves working in the agricultural sector). These migrants were not bound to preestablished state labor contracts, so they were often able to leave their original employment situations and travel within Portugal to seek other opportunities. Further, Cabo Verdean men could petition to bring their wives and families to Portugal, easing the migration of Cabo Verdean women, though tying it to the status of the male migrant's labor recruitment.

As I have argued earlier, women from all the Cabo Verdean islands also have their own history of both interisland and international labor migration to African territories, such as São Tomé and Príncipe, Angola, and Senegal, as well as the Americas and Europe. Amid the below-market-rate pay afforded to Cabo Verdean laborers, both men and women had to work to support their families; added pressure fell to the women who stayed behind on the islands because traditional cultural ties yoked a mother's ability to earn and support her family to her ability to live up to and claim the ideals of social respectability, selfhood, and motherhood.[54] Cabo Verdean men's out-migration often left women in charge of managing households, agriculture, and food production for the home, and many of the women who migrated to Portugal during this time leveraged their reproductive labor to work as cooks, domestic workers, and informal fish-mongers (*peixeiras*) in urban areas.[55]

Cabo Verdean women also represented an important auxiliary labor force supporting Lisbon's growing construction industry of the twentieth century. Many older Cabo Verdean women who told me of migrating to Portugal in the twentieth century recounted that they or their family members had worked as day laborers in construction, working to paint, sand, and clean newly installed fixtures or haul away the rubble and toxic materials left behind at work sites. Like their male counterparts, the women's labor was central to Portugal's urbanization, and because they were engaging in heavy, often stigmatized work, it fit neatly with earlier histories of racialized, gendered work divisions in Lisbon and beyond. Past depictions have attributed Cabo Verdean women's migration to these cities to either labor seeking or family reunification, but the reality is far messier—pushes and pulls on many levels resulted in the influx of Cabo Verdeans to their colonizers' homeland, before and after independence.

Migration, Race, and Space

Sociologist Luís Batalha has traced the majority of the Cabo Verdean migrants of the mid-twentieth century first to early improvised quarters provided by white Portuguese employers, then to the informal squatter housing settlements on the outskirts of Lisbon, where what locals called *barracas* or *bairros de lata* (shacks or tin neighborhoods) would become the historical antecedents to today's migrant neighborhoods in Lisbon, including (but not limited to) Buraca, Cova da Moura, Chelas, Odivelas, and Talude.[56] Male migrant laborers, who initially slept on straw beds at construction sites or in the back rooms of white Portuguese businesses, were not, as their employers believed, "used to" living in such conditions[57] and unsurprisingly left these inadequate quarters. Priced and racially shut out of the local housing market, they settled in the cultural enclaves forming at the city's edge.[58] These communities thus emerged from marginalization and the desire to create shared community spaces to maintain Cabo Verdean culture, becoming both a response to and, ironically, evidence of migrants' "unassimilability" to mainstream white Portuguese society.[59]

The relationship between Portugal's urban landscape and its Luso-African migrant communities remains complicated. Today, Lisbon's suburban neighborhoods are home to multigenerational Africans and African descendants, standing as markers of the mid-twentieth-century Cabo Verdean labor migration streams, yet most informal housing settlements have been leveled in favor of hulking concrete-block housing. This social housing dates to 1993, when the state initiated a major public housing program called PER (Plano Especial de Realojamento). This program affected migrants regardless of nationality or legal status (Decree-Law Nos. 163/93 and 07/05) and, like similar housing policies throughout Europe, was politically purported to curb alleged migrant criminality, drug trafficking, and prostitution. In practice, as countless studies have shown, these housing programs frequently became city planning disasters. They have bred and compounded social marginalization through isolation, housing discrimination, overpolicing, and the dangers of shoddy, neglected, and mismanaged infrastructure.[60] Even so, as I will illustrate in chapter 6, my informants combined their articulations of these pressing concerns about social housing on the urban margins with characterizations of the segregated neighborhood that highlighted community, belonging, and joy.

African Decolonization and Cabo Verde's Independence

The Cabo Verdean migration must also be contextualized by exploring the relentless, African-led anticolonial resistance of the mid-twentieth century.[61] In this era, the international community increasingly rallied together to support colonial territories' bids for independence, yet António de Oliveira Salazar pushed back, working to extend formal colonialism indefinitely under the aegis of Portugal's "special relationship" to what he named its "overseas provinces."[62] As Salazar trumpeted Portugal as a multiracial nation free from racial discrimination, he found support in the Brazilian sociologist Gilberto Freyre's cultural framework of "lusotropicalism,"[63] in which the scholar presented Cabo Verde as a case study of "benevolent colonialism," as evidenced by the island's history of interracial sex.[64] Freyre further insisted that the Portuguese people's history of precolonial cross-cultural exchanges with Muslim and Jewish states imbued their society with a laudable level of "interculturality"—a particular cultural ability to participate in peaceful cross-cultural exchange. In other words, whatever anticolonial movements claimed had little to do with *Portuguese* colonial power.

Ultimately, these political and rhetorical attempts could not thwart the anticolonial struggle being led by the colonized. After six centuries of Portuguese colonial domination, a thirteen-year Portuguese colonial war, and relentless African resistance, on July 5, 1975, Cabo Verde and Guinea-Bissau united as an independent nation under the leadership of El Partido Africano da Independência da Guiné e Cabo Verde (PAIGC).[65] Decades worth of colonial dispossession and extraction, mismanagement, and neglect had taken an enormous toll throughout the African colonies. Agriculture, one of Cabo Verde's most crucial sectors, had been weakened by centuries of foreign mismanagement, absentee landlords, and unequal land distribution policies that forestalled Africans' subsistence. Some 90 percent of the nation's population was illiterate and 60–75 percent unemployed. Industrial fishing was reserved for international actors, not locals, and drought and famine plagued the country. "Benevolent colonialism" had not even yielded useful infrastructure: only 842 kilometers of the nation's roads were paved by the close of the 1960s.[66] During these initial stages of independence, the PAIGC faced huge hurdles. Its governmental policy was primarily centered on developing food sustainability, improving health and education, and shoring up the degraded natural environment.[67]

Cabo Verdean migration to Portugal increased on the eve of independence, with Africans using their Portuguese passports before new restrictions were implemented.[68] In hindsight, the move was prescient: as it undertook decolonization, the Portuguese state reversed its reliance on the principle of *jus soli* (nationality based on land ties) in favor of *jus sanguinis* (nationality based on blood ties), thereby retroactively stripping African descendants of their citizenship and ensuring they would compose an exploitable labor supply for decades. Small numbers of affluent Cabo Verdean elites with ties to the colonial administration were able, after decolonization, to regularize their status via the *retornado*[69] migration flow of colonial settlers back to the metropole; the vast majority of Cabo Verdeans could often only settle in *bairros de barracas* in Portugal.[70] In this way, an explicitly white Portuguese national identity was solidified during the democratization of the sovereign Portuguese nation-state. The fall of the Estado Novo furthered an ongoing "racial Europeanization"[71] in which nation-building and racial citizenship dovetailed at the ideological intersections of decolonization.

The restriction of citizenship did not translate to a wholesale restriction of entry, however. Decree-Law No. 97/77 of March 17 established that 90 percent of enterprises with more than five employees had to be Portuguese, for instance, but bilateral agreements excepted male Cabo Verdean migrants recruited into public industry (such as construction work). When, in 1981, Portuguese nationality law excluded immigrants' Portugal-born children from automatic citizenship, there were immediately apparent hardships for many African families. Regulation was often lax through the rest of the twentieth century, with Cabo Verdeans moving to Portugal primarily through family reunification or by overstaying visitation visas, though political commentators, Portuguese scholars, and journalists have convincingly argued that the variously enforced regime shaped the marginalization of Africans and Afro-descendants within a country in which systemic racism is made literal, built into the urban geography.[72] Over decades, the colonial distinction between "African" and "Cabo Verdean," as most clearly expressed in the *assimilated/Indigenous* dyad (see earlier), lost some social significance as postcolonial labor and citizenship mechanisms racialized African bodies.

Changing Portuguese Families

Portuguese citizens saw major political and social change with the fall of the Estado Novo regime in 1974 too. For instance, laws dating to the 1930s codified gender divisions, with men designated heads of household and women the keepers of family well-being. Salazar's regime would reinscribe this division by advocating large families, prohibiting the use of contraceptives, and prohibiting divorce. Ridding itself of social welfare obligations, the Estado Novo left religious charitable organizations and individual families to assist those in need, including the disabled or the elderly. Fertility was high, poor families received precious little help from the state, a rigidly gendered division of labor forced women to shoulder the reproductive labor, and the people were told to look only to one another for help.[73]

As a major component of democratization, the Portuguese state expanded its welfare system,[74] legalized divorce, asserted that both parents bore equal responsibility for a child's well-being, and established employment protections, including the extension of a ninety-day paid maternity leave for working mothers who contributed to social security. In compliance with European guidelines, in 1995 the state granted fathers the right to paternity leave, and in 1999 maternity leave was extended to 120 days. Preschool was established as part of the educational system, and the government expanded childcare services to support working families, particularly Portuguese mothers and women, whose social position increased alongside democratization.[75]

Notably, the fascist regime had never restricted women from paid work. Rather, it allowed a "dual-earner" model of family life based on the traditional rural system and further necessitated by the concurrent rise of industrialization and the depletion of male laborers due to colonial wars and emigration; in Lyonette, Crompton, and Wall's words, "women's employment was always accepted, if underpaid."[76] Women's high Estado Novo labor participation continues today, as Portugal has one of Europe's highest rates of working women.[77]

Coupled with the emergence of compulsory education in the early 1960s, these changes to Portuguese policy drastically altered cultural conceptions of family and parenthood. More and more white Portuguese women worked and accessed education, with labor protections raising their status as workers and mothers. Extended kinship networks steadily dispersed amid migration flows as Portuguese men fled drafts or sought opportunity elsewhere, individuals and families moved from rural to urban areas, and Portuguese fertility began a gradual decline alongside stagnating wages for both men and women (today, the single-child family dominates); given that the restructuring of the welfare state did not include support for the disabled and elderly, this erosion of tight kinship networks would still leave a great many needs unfulfilled.[78]

State Policies on Migrants and Migrant Workers

Toward the end of the twentieth century, in a push to integrate with the greater EU community, Portugal devised several waves of regularization programs to manage its undocumented population and harmonize its migration and labor policy with the growing Fortress of Europe.[79] Once a supplier of migrant labor for more affluent European countries, Portugal emerged as an important immigrant destination in southern Europe.[80] In the 1990s, like its EU counterparts, Portugal began to introduce integration and antidiscrimination laws that would, like labor protections for women, increase the available workforce. For example, and in response to the powerful collective actions of immigration and civic associations (e.g., SOS Racismo, the Cabo Verdean Association, Guinean Association for Social Solidarity, and House of Brazil), Act No. 20/98 amended the aforementioned Decree-Law No. 97/77 of March 17 so that an employer could hire any worker residing *legally* in Portugal, regardless of nationality, pursuant to the 90 percent Portuguese workers requirement on businesses. Perversely, however (and despite the fact that migrant labor laws did not bind residency to a preestablished state labor contract until the twenty-first century), the turn of the century and the global financial crisis spurred public demand for state protection against foreign job competition; throughout Europe, the social climate shifted toward anti-immigrant sentiment, and various governments criminalized the hiring of undocumented workers.[81] In this way, the opening of Portuguese labor and migration policy was actually folded into ongoing European processes of restriction and immigration control—a central feature of racial Europeanization linked to the Fortress of Europe.

Europe "abolished" borders via the Schengen Agreement in 1985, and Portugal acceded to the EU in 1986, but the Portuguese state continued to restrict access to nationality. Lusophone African immigrants, however, encountered somewhat more lax restrictions than other immigrant groups; Eastern Europeans and East and South Asians, for instance, generally had less of a cultural/historical link to Portugal and had to meet a minimum of ten years' residency versus the six required of lusophone migrants to access citizenship.[82] While it is tempting to see this as a symbol of Portugal's closeness to its lusophone African population, history suggests an alternate reading. That is, borders, as argued by Harsha Walia, entrench and retrench, often in the service of empire and capital, which force migrants and racialized communities into exploitative labor market arrangements.[83] Though Cabo Verdeans and other lusophone Africans migrated to Portugal throughout the twentieth century, their entrance was conditioned on unequal terms. Owing to their positions within the labor market and within a gendered ethnoracial hierarchy, the migrants were persistently present yet paradoxically hidden in Portugal's cities.

The twenty-first century would also bring about important changes in the state's nationality regime that would especially impact PALOP African communities that had so long taken root in Portugal. For one, the state broadened the criteria for the acquisition of nationality, allowing immediate acquisition for third-generation "immigrants" and second-generation "immigrants" whose parents had resided legally within Portugal for at least five years (Portuguese Decree-Law No. 2/2006). The word *immigrants* is, of course, misleading and reflects the systemic invisibility of African-descendant communities given that the third-generation African-descendant "immigrants" may have been born in Portugal. Still, the privilege that lusophone immigrants had in the area of residency requirements for nationality was eradicated, requiring six years of legal residence for all immigrants regardless of national status.[84] Later changes initiated in 2020 broadened the criteria for nationality, granting nationality to immigrants' children born in Portugal (Organic Law No. 2/2020).[85]

In terms of migration policy, Portugal is also considered one of Europe's most "family-friendly" countries. Temporary residents can reunite with family. Family members of legalized migrants have equal rights to work and access social benefits. And key to its reputation, the Portuguese state employs a relatively broad definition of "family," including spouses and partners, adult and minor siblings, dependent young and adult children, and parents and grandparents in its immigration laws.[86] As numerous studies have shown, however, chain migration through family reunifications frequently results in the emergence of subpopulations of working-class and working-poor immigrant families concentrated in lower-skilled labor sectors and held back because they tend to be less educated than migrants who enter through other formal avenues.[87] Cabo Verdean migrants to Portugal today fit this profile neatly: they often enter through family reunification, hold lower educational profiles than "newer" migrant populations, and are highly represented among holders of residential permits as they settle in multigenerational, metropolitan migrant communities.[88]

The Feminization of Postcolonial Migration

Beginning in the 2000s, women came to outnumber men among migrants from Cabo Verde to Portugal.[89] An eclectic body of scholarship locates this feminization of migration as a major turning point in global population circuits, though systems of mobility, as argued by Sylvia Tamale, are also racialized and gendered through colonialism and within wider fields of empire and capitalist social reproduction.[90] That is, the gendering of Cabo Verdean immigration remained a colonial reality in that economic vulnerability was upheld under "flag independence," pushing more and more women to embark on transnational migrant journeys just to care for their families and subsidize national economies through their remittance practices.

Indeed, over the last several decades, neoliberalism has become a predominant economic approach in Cabo Verde. Proponents argue that economic growth is fostered when the market is freed from state-led regulations. Thus, throughout the international political community, liberalizing the market and opening the doors to foreign investment seemed *the* cure to economic stagnation; the idea of economic self-sufficiency and socialism was increasingly regarded as untenable for this small archipelago country.[91] Under El Movimento para a Democracia (MPD), the ruling party established in 1990 and dominant in Cabo Verde for much of the twenty-first century thus far,[92] European buyers have been allowed to purchase a large majority of Cabo Verde's firms and institutions. The MPD has accrued a growing international debt burden, and the massive privatization efforts it has initiated have occurred with few regulatory restrictions in place. Where the first PAIGC government (1975–1980) once stressed the importance of social welfare for the vulnerable, such as the poor, children, women, and the ill, the MPD's political philosophy urges deregulated labor markets and the devolution of responsibility for social and care needs to the family (as seen in Portugal). The policies have resulted in lower wages, the elimination of health and safety standards, and the curtailment of social services. Most citizens feel the effects of these changes, but they are particularly damaging for precariously positioned groups, such as women laboring within and outside of the home and still falling short of subsistence.[93]

This gendered economic reality clearly cannot be divorced from conditions of coloniality. Simply put, debt is about power. As a reflection of how the long shadow of empire extends into the present day, Portugal remains the largest bilateral creditor to Cabo Verde.[94] Further, in the absence of traditional colonial administrations, many formerly colonized nations of the Global South are strong-armed by disciplinary institutions into accepting a subordinated position in the world economy. For example, the rise of neoliberalism in Cabo Verde must also be understood in the context of Europe's "underdevelopment" of Africa during colonialism as well as the continued imposition of European economic dependency after decolonization.[95] As Cabo Verde transformed from a one-party to a multiple-party country in the late 1980s and early 1990s, the stress on "democracy" from leading international lenders such as the World Bank and the International Monetary Fund (IMF) was increasingly prevalent. The donor community tied their aid to "less-developed" nations to requirements that they open their markets and deregulate foreign investment to become "equal partners" in the global economy. Among these, structural adjustment programs (SAPs)[96] are common conditions, even though they result in the privatization of government services and reductions in public spending on social services (due, in part, to debt servicing obligations).[97]

Perhaps paradoxically, Cabo Verde is often considered an African "success story"—namely, for its relative success in achieving the United Nations Development and Sustainable Development Goals (SDGs). However, development goals have long been criticized by feminists for their neoliberal framework that impedes gender justice for women on the ground.[98] In Cabo Verde, women still disproportionately shoulder the vast majority of unpaid caring responsibilities, including childcare and eldercare for an aging population.[99] Meanwhile, the opening of markets to the export of finance capital has been met with cutbacks in social services such as health and education. As a result, women's responsibility for caregiving has increased alongside the deepening of the feminization of poverty.[100] In 2015, 39 percent of female-headed households in Cabo Verde were poor (compared to 26 percent of male-headed households). In 2017, the proportion of employed women was lower than that of men (45 vs. 59 percent), and unemployment among the youth was also higher among women. Poverty is also most pronounced in rural and semiurban areas and among Cabo Verdean households with children.[101] The majority of women labor within the informal market or in agriculture, two sectors that experience minimal or lax regulation and are especially vulnerable to economic shocks. Given their overrepresentation in the agricultural workforce, rural women are also disproportionately impacted by climate change—of which colonialism and neoliberal global capitalism are historic and ongoing drivers.[102]

To be sure, there have been gains in gender equality since independence, but gender inequality persists. A half century since independence, many Cabo Verdean women find migration remains the best and most viable option to better their families' social and economic situations.[103] In this way, the feminization of both migration and poverty in Cabo Verde must be understood within a matrix of race, gender, class, and rule, together shaping the lived subjectivities of postcolonial migrant women. I next turn to how these "push" factors that compel Cabo Verdean women's migration are also amplified by the changing economic landscape of twenty-first-century Portugal.[104]

Cleaning and Caring in the Shadow of Empire

The social and political landscape white Portuguese experienced at the turn of the twenty-first century contrasted starkly with the fascism under which their parents and grandparents had lived and labored. The experiences of African and African-descendant women were, nonetheless, unique. The economic changes brought on by Portuguese democratization, urbanization, and annexation into the global economic community, mediated by EU funding, extended the existing colonial labor system and routinized the sorting of ethnic and racial minority women into low-wage, unstable, and marginal jobs.[105]

Laboring in the shadow of empire, for the African-descendant community in Lisbon, often means relegation to types of employment that are characterized by menial work, unsocial hours, and poverty wages.[106] These workers' precarity escalated with the post-2008 "fiscal adjustments" and austerity programs implemented in Portugal's recovery from the global financial crisis. Portuguese austerity measures reinforce the vulnerability of immigrants in the labor market, as their ability to secure work decreased substantially during the post-2008 economic downturn.[107] Intriguingly, the precarity itself is gendered, as care sector jobs have been differently impacted than manufacturing, construction, agriculture, and other traditional sectors for male immigrants' employment.[108] That is, while migrant women similarly weathered economic precarity, they continued to find a range of low-wage care service work throughout Lisbon and other Portuguese population centers during much of the twenty-first century.[109]

The formalized nurturant and nonnurturant care service markets attracted Cabo Verdean women at the turn of and into the twenty-first century because of several converging forces. Not only had racial discrimination foreclosed other labor sectors for these women, but the growth of Portugal's suburban middle class, in conjunction with the influx of European funding and urban expansions, raised the demand for such services.[110] Additionally, the drop in national fertility and the aging population was coupled with the withdrawal of state support for eldercare and the cultural expectation that such care falls to women.[111] In fact, within the last few years, the tendency has been for the state to outsource the provision of eldercare to charities, not-for-profit and for-profit organizations where a growing home caring staff performs the day-to-day physical and emotional nurturing of many Portuguese elders.[112] These jobs are deskilled, so the women who perform them are paid less than other health professionals such as nurses, they work long hours, and they often lack the necessary training, worker protections, and resources required to provide quality and minimally strenuous face-to-face care.[113] In this way, migrant eldercare workers subsidize the Portuguese household (and national economy) by allowing some families to outsource caring responsibilities in order to enter the labor market or even travel abroad in search of higher wages, where their higher market value offsets the cost of cheap, marginalized care workers.

Further, Portuguese urbanization has led to a bumper crop of commercial companies whose workers service the metropolitan offices, businesses and commercial centers, airports, and public transportation terminals funded by international investment. All those spaces need cleaning and maintenance, after all. The presence of high-income professionals alongside booming crowds of twenty-first-century tourists is a further boon to institutional cleaning services in the new urban economy.[114] Prior to the 1990s, as sociologist Luís Batalha writes, these cleaning and caring jobs were filled by mainly rural and poor or working-class white Portuguese women; those women's increasing access to education and other opportunities in the decades since have made retail and clerical work more viable (and desirable) options for them.[115]

To initiate family reunification as migrant flows from Cabo Verde matured, workers in home care and cleaning services fought for—and won— regularization. Today, commercial cleaning enterprises and home care agencies (*apoio domiciliário*) are largely formalized by the state, and most workers are contracted as permanent workers through a labor contract. Some home care agencies are formalized by the state, others are private organizations, and some are public-private hybrids; the state-run agencies offer union access. Institutional cleaning workers also have access to a formal contract, but their actual access to unionization is also inconsistent. Both forms of work are "live-out," rather than the more restrictive full-time "live-in" arrangements, and permanent workers are entitled to paid family leave, workers' compensation, vacation, daily breaks, holidays, and public subsidies for services such as childcare. Though regularized and native-born African women's legality in Portugal helps them secure certain rights and avoid more obviously exploitative arrangements, they still face barriers to entering more secure and higher-paying jobs, including racial discrimination, gender expectations, and the reproductive labor responsibilities imposed as family reunification expands their households and communities.

Though home care and institutional cleaning work are by and large gendered occupations, Portuguese labor statistics make it difficult to determine the precise percentages of workers in these sectors who are Africans and African-descendant women, case studies document an overrepresentation of immigrant women of PALOP origin.[116] Most of the people I met who worked in institutionalized home care and cleaning service settings told me that, in their estimation, African or African-origin women comprise well over 50 percent of these workforces. Increases in the flow of immigrants from Ukraine, Romania, South and East Asia, and Brazil in the last decade have not disrupted employers' perceptions of Cabo Verdean women as particularly "hard-working," "gentle," "humble," "committed," and "accepting of any sort of working conditions"— stereotypes clearly informed by the intersection of expectations of gendered femininity and the racial paternalism of Portuguese colonial rule.[117] Within the wider field of capitalist social reproduction, *certain* bodies are racialized and gendered as "appropriate" for care service work; however, in the remainder of this book, I prioritize Cabo Verdean women's experiences and assessments of their own work as well as the ways they contest the naturalized association of "women like them" with "jobs like these." As it happens, we will find that the racialized division of stigmatized and precarious reproductive labor is as much global as it is local.

2

Converging Differences

• •

Stories of Migration

The Cabo Verdean women whose voices animate this book came to Portugal in the context of relentless economic insecurity. Their stories, however, touch on multiple aspects of living in the shadow of empire in contemporary Portuguese and Cabo Verdean society. As migrants living within the larger context of colonial and postcolonial global inequalities, they raise critical points about uneven development, stagnant social-economic mobility, and neoliberal policies that benefit some families more than others. Their experiences migrating, finding work, and laboring within Portugal also prompt questions about the politics of belonging in a country that has formally severed ties with African colonialism, that claims to be an antiracial society, yet remains deeply entrenched in the shadow of empire, where hierarchies based on race, gender, class, and nationality pervade. Taking African-descendant women who labor in low-paid care service jobs in the formal market as my focus opens new ways to see and understand the intersectional inequalities structuring contemporary Portuguese life.

On average, the women who opened their lives to me for this study were forty-one years old. About half were, by the time we met, Portuguese citizens, while the rest were legal residents. They recalled attending primary and secondary school in Cabo Verde, often while living with relatives or family friends because their parents, siblings, and extended kin so commonly migrated (mainly to Portugal but also to the United States, Italy, England, France, and the Netherlands). The remittances sent by far-flung relations sustained life at home, where the economy had floundered for decades, even generations; by the time these women left, more Cabo Verdeans lived outside the islands than on them. Following well-worn migration pathways, most of these respondents arrived in Portugal through family reunification or holding tourist or student visas and with the help of those who came before. Parents, older siblings, aunts and uncles, godparents, and cousins who began to work in Lisbon and other urban areas in the 1990s now assisted in myriad ways: some sponsored, organized, and paid for my respondents' travel, while others helped them access and fill out the necessary migration documents, provided temporary housing, or helped them find their way in the new labor market of Portugal.

Regardless of when they arrived in Portugal or whether they were more heavily influenced in their journeys by "push" or "pull" factors (push factors being those that compel someone to leave their home and pulls representing factors that entice them to do so), most of these women migrated to better support their families. They aspired to achieve more economic stability than that of their mothers, grandmothers, and other women kin and friends who often labored as domestics, in informal sales, or as fieldhands, a sentiment also captured in Celeste Fortes's research on Cabo Verdean students in Portugal.[1] But they also appreciated the opportunity to gain a sense of personal independence from the embeddedness of their family systems in Cabo Verde. Indeed, many informants admitted that their departure had been difficult, but at times they felt glad to avoid the watchful eyes of the same families they sought to support through migration.[2]

There were nine main migration patterns followed by my study participants (see table 1). As mentioned, family reunification was the most common overall, but Cabo Verdean migration paths are as diverse and multifaceted as Cabo Verdeans themselves. Among those who labored in home care, student migration was the second and tourist visas the third pathway; those patterns

Table 1
Migration patterns

Mode of entry to Portugal	Home care (%)	Institutional cleaning (%)	Overall percentage of sample	Average age (overall = 41.7)
Family reunification	29.7	28	29.03	35
Student visa	21.6	12	17.7	31
Tourist visa	13.5	24	17.7	48
Native born	8.1	12	9.6	26
Medical*	5.4	12	8	50
Labor migration	8.1	4	6.4	56
Decolonization	8.1	0	4.8	47
Marriage	2.7	8	4.8	46
Political refugee	2.7	0	1.6	36

* Visa for Cabo Verdeans who wish to visit Portugal for medical treatment. Persons accompanying applicants for their treatments are also eligible.

swapped for institutional cleaning workers, for whom medical migration was the fourth most common entry method. (This could be because home care is regarded as a semiprofessional opportunity by women who hope to eventually continue their studies or secure employment in a credentialed occupation, such as nursing.) Table 1 also shows that the youngest groups of workers in this study are the native-born Portuguese citizens of Cabo Verdean descent and Cabo Verdean educational migrants who labor in home care and cleaning work; the labor migrants are the oldest on average, their twenty-first-century trajectories closely resembling the transnational women migrants' pathways documented in past literature. These women often migrated abroad, then ended up working as domestics in middle-class Portuguese households, unlike the more common trajectories in this study, predominantly shaped by formalized migration pathways.[3]

All study respondents worked directly for their employing organizations: most home care workers (or *apoio domiciliário*) worked for state-funded not-for-profit organizations; a few worked for private, for-profit agencies; and institutional cleaning workers (or *limpeza*) were employed by independent firms that contracted with building owners by sending in teams of cleaning workers. Against the background of a twenty-first-century "new economy," home care and institutional cleaning work both similarly tend to outsource the work of recruitment by drawing on regularized workers who rely on social networks—a sister, friend, or cousin—to access work. This reliance on an intermediary via gendered networks in turn fuels existing labor needs.

Indeed, study participants often told me that home care and institutional cleaning work were agreeable alternatives to the possibilities available back in Cabo Verde. They frequently knew relatives or friends working in these fields, and they could see the benefit of entering a formal market in which contracted labor provided a degree of benefits and protections. In their estimation, regularized, "live-out" work in home care and institutionalized settings offered access to benefits and the ability to reside with their families—in this way, they at times felt lucky to find their way into this labor sector.

Nonetheless, several study participants were ambitious, seeking opportunities for new careers in more stable, higher-paid, less-stigmatized sectors. Home care and cleaning were considered entry-level, low-skill jobs with wages at or only slightly above minimum wage—factors that could thwart workers' upward mobility. When there are few paths to advancement, many pointed out, the best route to economic mobility seemed to be occupational mobility, or a move out of home care and cleaning work altogether. At the same time, the resources, time, and money needed to increase education to secure a higher-paying job with built-in pathways for mobility were in scant supply among the low-skilled care and service workers, many of whom had immediate family responsibilities.

Another difficulty of home care and cleaning work is that the professions are unskilled and stigmatized, and they rely on maintaining hierarchical relationships with employers, workers, patrons, and/or care recipients. The Cabo Verdean workers who filled those positions were entrenched as subordinates, racialized and gendered as Black, African, immigrant women, within but always marginalized by Portuguese society. In her study of Filipina domestic migrants, Rhacel Salazar Parreñas coins the phrase "dislocations of migration" to describe the interplay of limited legal status and reproductive labor divided along the lines of race, gender, and nationality among Filipina domestic workers.[4] In Portugal, my respondents' dislocation stemmed from the racialized inequities inherent in their new, postcolonial, ostensibly postracial setting; from the way Black women were both marginalized and deemed "appropriate" to perform care service work; and from their sense that their labor market inclusion could only ever result in a sort of partial Portuguese citizenship.

In this chapter, you will find, as I have, that Black women's stories are vital for exposing the ways intersecting oppressions structure everyday lives in the shadow of empire. The accounts shared with me coalesced into roughly five patterned experiences, each of which is typified below. First, there is Ana, who, as a child, accompanied her parents to Portugal on the eve of decolonization. Then we meet Lucinda and Carlota, who entered Portugal in the period between the early 1980s and 1990s, before and at the start of immigration changes intended to regulate the foreign population. The third pattern, as exemplified by Dilza and Manuela, includes those who migrated starting in the late 1990s, often through sponsorship from family members, and have finished some postsecondary schooling. Lilian, who migrated to Portugal on a student visa in the early twenty-first century and labors alongside a diverse group of care service employees, represents the fourth pattern, and Jandy, a native-born Portuguese citizen whose parents migrated in the early 1980s, illustrates the fifth most common pattern of migration. Under the label "Cabo Verdean care worker," I met a diverse array of women with diverse experiences of migration, family life, and inclusion in Portugal. By examining their stories, I offer insight into how structures of oppression work together, sorting this group of legalized, formal labor market participants into positions along a continuum of privilege and precarity. I also uncover how changes in their relative positions over time shape their subjective feeling of belonging in the shadow of empire.

Ana

Born in São Tomé to Cabo Verdean parents, Ana was just five years old when she came to Portugal in 1975. Her parents, like many others, left Cabo Verde for São Tomé amid the intense famine and drought of the late 1940s. These "lost" workers' journeys are reflected in a famous *coladeira* song, "Sodade," written long ago but revived in 1992 with Cabo Verdean singer Cesária Évora's chart-topping rendition. Évora's melodic query, "Who shows you that long road, that long journey to São Tomé?" captures the deep feelings of longing, despair, and separation embodied by the forced or coerced migration of laborers from one Portuguese colony to another—the sense that finding a way out may mean never finding your way home again. But Ana's family was different: her parents, who migrated from Cabo Verde separately, met and had children together in São Tomé and then, in the uncertain days of decolonization, made the difficult decision to relocate permanently to Portugal. With the help of a network of Portuguese businessmen in São Tomé, Ana's father secured housing so long as he agreed to work for them in construction once they made it to Europe.

Many study respondents had heard from family and friends about the trials and tribulations faced by Cabo Verdeans who migrated to Portugal in the early and mid-twentieth century. They shared vivid tales of single men promised adequate lodging but instead shunted into substandard housing by their employer-sponsors. Others described living in locals' room shares or with members of their extended kin, shocked when they were obligated to pay well over market rates for their room and board. As these migrants were priced out of the housing stock, illegal settlements sprang up, offering their families alternative living arrangements and the solace of a growing Cabo Verdean community. Ana, who by the time of our interview lived in a public housing complex on the outer fringes of Lisbon, emphasized her family's luck in this regard: her father's employer paid the patriarch's way to Portugal from São Tomé, and he provided high enough wages that her father was eventually able to send for his family.

To Ana, Portugal is home now. Though her housing complex is frequently invoked in media accounts of gang violence and poverty, Ana speaks passionately about the strong sense of community and home in this multigenerational Cabo Verdean haven. Yes, many issues plague social housing. The infrastructure, if not crumbling, is in sore need of repair, it is subject to overpolicing, and the housing seems far from the locations where immigrants can find work, but this is a place buoyed by neighbors' strong, kin-like relationships. On the weekends, Ana can be found hopping from one apartment to the next, spreading the word about a neighbor who has a freshly made pot of *catchupa* (Cabo Verde's national dish) or another selling bundles of plums picked from an urban garden. Families have asked her to be their children's godmother. For others, she provides assistance with eldercare, administering medicine, helping with personal hygiene, or simply keeping them company between her work shifts and on her days off.

Like many Afro-descendant workers in the shadow of empire, Ana found work in the service economy in the late 1990s. She was a mother of two with a high school education, working in restaurant services and in cleaning roles at the airport. After years, she was tired of working nights and yearned for more time with her children, many of whom would become adults in the blink of an eye. In 2009, a friend connected her to a home care employer (friend connections being an intermediary employment pathway shared by nearly all the study's respondents). In our interviews, Ana called the pay in this sector a "misery," a feeling exasperated by a recently added responsibility—providing financial help to her eldest child, who recently gave birth to a joyful baby girl. Many years in, she still lived paycheck to paycheck and had little expectation that she'd be able to retire anytime soon. In fact, unlike respondents in other studies on migrant care workers, Ana had no plans to permanently "return" or retire to Cabo Verde. She admitted she felt less connected to Cabo Verde than to Portugal; more precisely, perhaps, she was connected to her local Cabo Verdean community in Portugal. Still, her impressions of living and working in Portugal tended to convey indifference, if not downright resentment. When describing what led her to her work, for example, Ana was emphatic: "It wasn't that I *chose* my job. It wasn't a choice. I began to work because I needed a job, and there was someone who worked there, she arranged this job for me. It wasn't a choice. We do not have choices in this country."

In other words, migrants like Ana felt a distinct lack of control over the paths their lives would take. Choices were not only constrained but often described as nonexistent for a Black African woman like her. With a subtle sigh of resignation, she described Black immigrants' work in Portugal as "dirty work" (*trabadju sujo*):

> There was a journalist who interviewed people recently, and she exposed
> how the Portuguese are very racist. They have no *pessoas negras* [Black people]
> in parliament . . . yet. You go to France, you go to London, they have *pessoas*
> *negras* in parliament. You go to a bank in France, and you will see many
> *pessoas negras* working there. *Negros!* You go to London and you see the same
> thing, *negros* working in banks. Here, in Portugal, there is not one single *pessoa*
> *negra* working in the bank. Or it's *very* rare. There are doctors, yes. But in those
> sorts of jobs in offices, they aren't there. There's a lot of racism. It's very hard to,
> very hard to find work due to the *cor da pele* [color of your skin]. Very hard.

Talking about job opportunities brought up Ana's sense of blocked opportunities. Her piercing remarks reflect what scholar Stephen Small has referred to as the "ambiguous visibility" of Blacks in Europe[5]—that is, how their overrepresentation in "dirty work" makes them hypervisible and easily identifiable within a given society, though they remain relatively *invisible* in occupations that could offer wages above the minimum, occupational prestige, and opportunities for advancement. Ana thus points to a racialized labor barrier that further marginalizes those who live at certain intersections of occupational status and skin color. Just as her parents' sojourn to São Tomé was shaped by racialized hierarchies of labor endemic to the Portuguese colonial experience, she sees herself as beholden to replicated hierarchies that persist on Portuguese soil. Care laborers straddle an invisible-visible social location that belies the country's claims of racial equality and color-blindness.

Lucinda

A native of Tarrafal, Cabo Verde, Lucinda was ten years old when she joined her mother as a domestic worker in a wealthy family's home in Praia, Cabo Verde. Today, at sixty-two, she is a lively and energetic mother of two and grandmother of three—one of those people who is so clever that they have a witty response before you can finish your sentence. Yet her playful disposition tightened when our interview discussion turned to her childhood in a coastal community hugging the outskirts of Tarrafal. The timelines blurred in Lucinda's memory, a swirl of strenuous labor and subsistence living:

> My mother sent me to work as a domestic worker [in Praia] because her boss was the richest man in the area. I was like a slave really. Because I had to get the water, I carried the pails and hay and wood. And then I would have to go by foot to the house and do things there. I prepared all the food, cook[ed] all the beans to serve the home. That's what my work was like. I cleaned. Then my mother had me stay in the home with her. We worked together as domestics. Just like that. Sometimes we would go to the countryside to harvest things. That's what work was like. I went to Assomada to my grandfather's house. Then from my grandfather's house, I went by foot at night to Tarrafal, right with the people that went to sell things. I didn't have a car, so I would go by foot. Then I eventually had a child at seventeen years of age. By thirty days after giving birth, I was up working already. I worked, washed the floor, did the laundry; I worked in the bedrooms, as a domestic.

Lucinda has labored long and hard throughout her life. As she explains, when she moved on from domestic work alongside her mother, she participated in Cabo Verde's woman-led *rabidante* sales economy,[6] combining domestic work and informal produce sales to sustain her family over several years:

> I began to sell things. I used to buy beans, grain, and animals. Hens, eggs, things like that. I sold them. Then all the money you made left again. Because if you have kids, it all goes. I would work in the homes of people, ironing, washing by hand. There were no machines. Sometimes once a week or twice a week I also made pastries at home to sell. I gathered used clothing to sell. I gathered rice to sell. And that's how I passed my life. During those times in Cabo Verde, it rained in July, August, and September. In the other months, it's very light. Those three months are the only months of water you have in Cabo Verde. So people go to the countryside to earn money—ten escudos per day—just so that you can take care of your children. I hear a lot of people say, "What tiring, hard work in Portugal!" I say, "The work that I have already completed in my life without any results!" By the time I arrived to Portugal, I was really a grown woman.

During conversations with Lucinda, she playfully mentioned her working hands, as she called them. She hoped her children would never acquire the deep crevices that adorn her own palms, slashing from wrist to fingertips like tree roots. Those sons were her connection to Portugal. In fact, when her youngest son migrated to Portugal in 1990, Lucinda remained in Cabo Verde with her second son, weathering economic stagnation with remittances from the first. After the arrival of a new grandchild in Portugal, Lucinda made her decision. We sat below a shady tree in a park as she explained how she migrated in 1997 out of necessity: "I was working there in Cabo Verde in cleaning services for a building for about two years, and then it closed. And after it closed, the only solution was to immigrate. I wanted a better life for my family."

It was not only her son's entreaties, nor the floundering Cabo Verdean economy, that drove her to migrate; she needed medical treatment that was not available at home. So while she noted that her impression of Portugal, having visited for three months shortly after her eldest son's migration, was that the weather was bad, the lifestyle too fast paced, Lucinda would move. Once in Portugal, her son helped her apply for a three-month tourist visa. She outstayed it, leaving her youngest son behind with her aging mother in Cabo Verde. With courage and fortitude, she embarked on her journey as an undocumented transnational migrant and transnational mother, settling on the outskirts of Lisbon. During her first year, she picked up informal domestic work, providing much-needed care for a few hours for a *patroa* (a Portuguese woman), her son, her daughter-in-law, and their two young children.

Lucinda eventually regularized her status through a short-term program that granted Portuguese resident status to previously unauthorized migrants who acquired a labor contract. On top of picking up hours with a *patroa*, she has since worked in various urban institutional cleaning services. Her work having taken her to restaurants, offices, private homes, malls, and commercial centers throughout Lisbon, Lucinda's son and grandchildren jokingly call her a "human GPS," with city bus lines and rail systems committed to memory. She describes the skill as a natural result of "cleaning the city," first as a domestic worker, venturing in the 1990s to neighborhoods that were both inhospitable and financially inaccessible to African migrants like herself, and later as an institutional cleaning worker toiling within the deluge of people flowing throughout the city's urban infrastructure.

Now a Portuguese citizen, Lucinda keeps a photograph of her aging mother hanging on the wall of her son's apartment. In it, a woman with a shiny dark complexion sits in a wooden chair, dressed in a white linen blouse and a pair of thick silver braids, beside a painting of the Virgin Mary. Deep wrinkles press into both cheeks, and the woman sits with a slight hunch. One evening, as we discussed her family photos, Lucinda glanced at the picture of her mother. I asked, "Are there things that you would have liked to know about living and working in Portugal before you left Cabo Verde?" Silent at first, she responded in an uncharacteristically somber tone: "No, I just wanted to leave there because I wanted work so that I could sustain us and, if I could, help my family, if it was possible. It was the only thing that I wanted. But unfortunately, I can't help in the way that I would like to because it's a bit complicated here."

Lucinda, who has labored in the informal domestic markets in Cabo Verde and Portugal, prefers institutional cleaning over domestic work, in which she was personally subordinate to a surveilling employer. Yet while her job provides benefits, full-time hours, and vacation time, she does not feel that the pay is commensurate with the labor it requires. Her occupational location today certainly reflects her status as a low-skilled worker with few convertible educational credentials as well as the contours of the long-standing sociopolitical relationship between Cabo Verde and Portugal. Similar to the stories commonly found in the literature on domestic work that looks at workers' occupational trajectories, stunted opportunities are common in the life stories of Cabo Verdeans who migrate to Portugal. Lucinda's early exit from schooling and entrance into domestic work occurred during a period of drought and in the midst of Portuguese colonialism. Like others, the persistent economic precarity that gripped Cabo Verde after independence spurred in her a yearning to migrate. And like others, the continuity of colonial-era social hierarchies and the shift in demand from familiar, informal domestic work to commercialized service work in the shadow of empire patterned the opportunities available to Lucinda—a dark-skinned Black woman immigrant from a former colony—in Portugal well after her arrival.

Manuela

By the time Manuela migrated to Lisbon in 2012, she was twenty-seven years old and had seen three different applications for European entry visas denied. Twice she applied for a visa to Portugal, where her oldest sister had lived for several years, and once to France. It wasn't until her youngest sister (age twenty-two), suffering from failing vision and gastrointestinal issues, needed medical treatment in Portugal that Manuela got her chance. Her visa lasted only three months, and it did not authorize her to work, but Manuela left the countryside of Santiago planning a more permanent stay.

Manuela wanted to migrate, she shared, for several reasons. For one, João, her long-term partner and the father of her two children, had migrated five years prior. Their frequent phone calls and video chats left her pining for a reunion with her childhood sweetheart. His presence in Portugal was a powerful "pull" factor. The difficulty of life in Cabo Verde, of making ends meet in Manuela's fishing port community, provided a "push." In her teen years, she had begun working—when she had days off school—beside her mother, using her hands to *apanha de areia*, or forge construction materials from water, sand, and stone. After several years, she worked in cleaning services in a capital-city hotel, then found work as a library attendant, which she supplemented by cleaning in a private home on the weekends. From 1,700 miles away, João sent money to help cover the costs of everyday expenses like food and schooling supplies, but the economic strain continued. As unemployment rose on the islands, tightening the screws for Cabo Verdean families, Manuela felt sure that the best option was to migrate.

Thus, early on a Tuesday morning in April 2012, Manuela left the capital city of Praia with her ailing sister. Her plan was to traverse the Atlantic, reunite with her partner, care for her sister, and eventually find contracted work that would allow her to send for her children (who remained in her mother's care):

> We ended up coming here and staying in another sister's house in Portugal who was younger than me. Then because João was already here, I left my sister's house and moved here [to her partner's apartment] to stay with him. Because I came here with my sister who was sick, I was sad because my sister was always in the hospital. It was a hard time. I had to go there every day to see her, and I would return home with low energy. That was the hardest thing. And then I was sad because my children were far away. They were in Cabo Verde, my two oldest children. Then my sister who was here for medical treatment returned to Cabo Verde about a year or so later. She died there in Cabo Verde within a year. But I stayed in Portugal. Why did I stay? Because João was here. When I first arrived in 2012, I didn't work at all; I couldn't work because of my visa. It was in 2013 that I connected with a *patroa* in Benfica and worked in her house. But then I became sick, so I couldn't go to work. It wasn't that I left my job. I called them to let them know I wasn't feeling well enough to go to work that day, and they didn't accept that. And that was that!

Though Manuela had been able to extend her original visa by an additional ninety days, her sister's departure left her in a precarious position. To reunite with her children, she would need to prove she had paid sufficient taxes in Portugal for a fixed amount of time, but her experience working for a *patroa* had left her with a bad taste in her mouth. As reported by the scholarship on irregular global domestic work, the informal market often provides scant to no protections for domestic workers—as she learned when she was fired for getting sick.[7] She could easily find work with another *patroa*, yet to get better hours, benefits, and stability and to enter the formal labor market as a step toward reunification, Manuela had to look for work elsewhere. About that time, she remembered, her eldest sister was preparing to leave Portugal for France and connected Manuela with her employer, a nearby school. Thus, after a year of first caring for her sickly sister and then working for a *patroa*, Manuela eagerly accepted a contract position as a school cafeteria worker. A year later, Manuela finally acquired a visa for her and João's eldest son. After another year or so, they got one for their youngest:

> My children were also worried about me—they asked me how I was, how is Dad, they asked about my sister who died in Cabo Verde, and the youngest one cried

all the time. But my older son didn't. He was older, and he understood what was happening. But not the baby, noooo. He didn't understand, and he kept asking, "Oh, Mom when are you coming to get me?" The thing is this, though. I wanted to go get them, the two of them, but I couldn't because I only had documents for one year. And then I started to work, and I started to pay into taxes, but it was too low. But combined with their father, we could only get a visa for the eldest. So I kept working there at the cafeteria. But then a year or so later, I had been working for a longer time, I had a higher level, and then I was able to bring my youngest in through my own sponsorship. I had documents for two years, I had work, paid more taxes. I was finally able to do it.

Today, Manuela and João are permanent residents living on Lisbon's outer edges. They share their home with their sons as well as a baby girl born in Portugal and an older woman who lost her home to one of the city's campaigns to abolish informal housing settlements. Manuela leveraged her friendship connections to move, after working in the cafeteria for two years, into a job with a cleaning agency. At first, she was just covering hours while employees were on vacation. She gladly picked up three weeknight evening hours for a month, which added much-needed wages to her two-days-a-week supplemental income from her employment as a domestic. When the agency's manager offered her a full-time day shift, Manuela accepted. It was a relief to combine her employment into one block of time as opposed to working at the cafeteria in the morning and then relocating across the city to labor at night. Although she and João say they still struggle a bit to satisfy their family's material needs, Manuela is glad to have secured relatively stable, if stigmatized, work:

Oh, there's too much racism here. Racism! In the buses, everywhere. Sometimes you will be back-to-back with people on public transport because it's packed, and a Portuguese will look at you with that face [*makes face of disgust*]. You see these things, you feel it. Sometimes they tell us, "Vai para sua terra" [Go back to your country]. There are whites that say, "Oh she is a cleaning lady," so they don't treat us well because of that work and because we are *mulheres negras* [Black women]. Which is wrong, because it's work! Whatever job you have is dignified. Working hands are always dignified! But just the act of working in dirty work—whether it's cleaning, restaurants, nursing homes—it's a symbol that the world doesn't appreciate you. It provides that sense, that feeling, or maybe a reflection of how the world sees you. And then it's amplified by your Black skin color. That's where the world really begins to marginalize and cast you aside, because of your work but also your skin color on top of that. Both of them together. We suffer a lot.

With round, bright eyes, Manuela recounted the racist and xenophobic comments, insults, and looks she and other cleaning workers endured in their jobs. Manuela and other respondents suspected most of the city's society held their labor in low regard—indeed, caring work has, throughout history, been unspecified, undervalued, and seen as menial.[8] Yet these women also locate the stigma associated with their *type of work* as being attached to the *type of workers* who fill those roles. In Manuela's view, it's her intersectional status as a Black woman "cleaning lady" that marks her as Other. This fits well with narratives captured by anthropologist Cati Coe, who reports that African immigrant women in the United States frequently come to understand themselves as racialized via their entrance into home care work. The Cabo Verdean women respondents in this study, too, recognize that their care work is arduous, underpaid, and perceived by others as "dirty work" and that dirty work is allegedly only fit for Black, immigrant, and therefore exploitable women. None was unaware that the intersection of race, gender, class, and migration status shaped employers' conception of women like them as the ideal worker in the caring sector, nor that the same intersections dehumanized the care workforce by racializing it and rendering it exploitable.

Carlota and Dilza

In Cabo Verde, Carlota lived in Praia, Santiago with her partner Adilson, their two children, and three stepchildren from her partner's previous relationship. Carlota had worked several jobs in Cabo Verde, beginning as a domestic in an uncle's house at the age of fourteen. As a young adult, she worked in a restaurant in the capital city before opening a small hair salon in her home. In 1996, when she initiated her migration, economic distress was just one motivation. Her mother and sister, living in Portugal, both fell ill, and Carlota felt obligated to visit to care for her nieces and nephews during the recovery. Besides that, she explained, the temporary migration would offer a reprieve from the "drama" and gossip surrounding her shaky relationship with Adilson, who had recently started a relationship with a new woman. She wasn't sure whether her stay in Portugal would be permanent.

Carlota's mother died a month after she arrived, and Carlota returned to Cabo Verde when her visa expired. Half a year later, her sister in Portugal suffered a brain aneurysm and passed away too. Though it would mean leaving her own children behind with her estranged partner, Carlota felt her only option was to permanently settle in Portugal; otherwise, her nieces and nephews would be without a caretaker. This time, like other Cabo Verdeans who entered Portugal in the 1990s, Carlota outstayed her visa. Her arrival coincided with the growth of Portugal's middle class and their newly disposable income, and Carlota found live-out domestic work cleaning and cooking for several families in the city. She eventually secured contracted employment as a live-in domestic worker for a single family in a coastal community near Lisbon. Her nieces and nephews went to stay with their father's family on the other side of Lisbon, across the Tagus River.

Her path toward regularized status, Carlota detailed, was a tough one. Her first contracted employment, in the Portuguese family's house, ended badly when Carlota became ill. Though she said she regularly suffered constipation and gastrointestinal problems, these normally cleared up on their own. Her *patroa*, however, fired Carlota the moment she heard her symptoms. As she remembered, "The woman of the house told me that she didn't want me to work there anymore because I was sick, and she didn't want me to contaminate anything." With indignation, Carlota continued: "She told me that they didn't want to catch anything from me. And so then they told me to go back to *my country*, that they didn't want me to stay here in Portugal. That I didn't belong there." Carlota's words reinforced my sense of Cabo Verdean domestic workers' legal precarity as well as the social consequences of being racialized as a Black woman, sought for her labor yet othered to devalue the worth and dignity of that labor. Her summary firing triggered a long stretch of informal jobs—four years spent working, unauthorized, in the domestic care market:

> And when I went there to foreign services to ask, "Why is it that the whole world comes here, and they have residency, and I have been here for four years and still don't have it?" And they told me that I only had one more month to stay here in Portugal. And so I started to cry. How is it that someone who has been here for four years in Portugal going on five years has no residency? How can that be? How is that just? And I was working that entire time. Fortunately, the woman who I was working for at the time went there and said that I work for her, that she likes me a lot, that she likes my work, and then she signed the paper there to give me residency. But I ended up here with no residency for four years. I suffered a lot. But listen, thank God I have never been without work ever since I've been in Portugal. I worked then and I work today.

Carlota's changed status allowed her to send for her children, though the process was so costly that she had to borrow funds from a distant cousin in France. In 2003, she sent for her eldest daughter, sixteen-year-old Dilza. Two years later, it was her fourteen-year-old daughter Jamilah's turn. Carlota set down roots. She gave birth to a son with a Cabo Verdean man she met through local friends (he has since migrated to London), and she secured Portuguese citizenship in 2007. During this time, she earned a livelihood by combining several sources of income, often working during the day as a domestic, selling Cabo Verdean pastries to friends and neighbors for extra income, and working in the evenings as a cook in a small café in Lisbon's tourist district.

In 2011, Carlota was desperate for work again. The café had closed. A friend found her a night-shift job at a nursing home with paid holiday and vacation time. So three mornings a week, from 7 a.m. to 1 p.m., she continued to perform domestic work for an older woman who lived alone. When her shift ended, she changed into her nursing home uniform and commuted by bus to arrive at the nursing home by 6 p.m. Later, when Carlota read in the newspaper about a company seeking home care workers, she used her now three years' experience in the nursing home to get hired.

Where, for many Cabo Verdeans, their migration was rooted in a lack of opportunities at home, Carlota's eldest child, Dilza, helped me understand that the younger informants, who came as teenagers, chafed at the lack of opportunities they perceived in Portugal. Unlike Ana, who you'll recall arrived in Portugal as a young child on the eve of decolonization, or Lucinda and Carlota, who were adults and mothers when they entered independently in the 1990s, Dilza arrived in the twenty-first century, through family reunification, and as a teenager. She told me that as she prepared for her flight to Portugal on a sunny afternoon in July, her mother assured her over the phone that it was just a quick summer vacation. But when Dilza arrived, her mother shocked her: Dilza, she hoped, would not return to Cabo Verde at all. Her feelings vacillated between allegiance to her mother and longing for her father:

> I cried so much! I went to Portugal to be with my mom. When I came, I wanted to return after one week! But my dad didn't know that I was going to stay. My story is really sad! Because I came to stay fifteen days and then return [to Cabo Verde]! But my mom, no, she was like, "I miss my children. My children are going to stay here. We can eat bread every day, but we are going to be together!" And I, I just didn't like Portugal. It wasn't what I thought it was going to be; I had this marvelous idea of Portugal, and it just wasn't what I thought it would be! When I cried, oh, I used to cry every day. I would wake up crying, and my dad would call. I couldn't even speak to him because of the tears. And my dad even said once, "I'll go to the airport and pick you up!" and I knew that I couldn't go. Oh, and my mom was so angry! She would give me a passport and say, "Well, go now! Go!" [*laughs*] Because my dad wanted me and my mom wanted me, I just wanted to die. And my mom, she never stopped being my mother. So, I had this feeling, in my conscience. It's like you want to leave and then you can't leave. Even today she says, "Oh, I helped you, I was the one that brought you here." Which is true. But I struggled.

At eighteen, Dilza was able to apply for citizenship. She secured a job at a clothing store, and she enrolled in a technical certification course in geriatric care that fit with her schedule. It wasn't long before she received a call from a hiring agency regarding a position in hospice care, nor before she accepted the job and realized she wasn't emotionally prepared for the work. It was emotionally and psychologically demanding working with patients close to death, and weight melted off Dilza's frame before two months were up. Eventually, Carlota notified her of an opening at the company where she was employed, and her mother's reference got her the job.

Today, Dilza is a naturalized citizen. She lives in a multigenerational apartment in a bustling area with her mother, Carlota; her fiancé; her three-year-old son; and her fiancé's parents. She regards her current work in home care and her geriatric care courses as potential springboards into the nursing profession, but without the time or money to further her education with a rapidly growing toddler at home, she has no timeline. Further, like others, Dilza knows full well the opportunity barriers that people like her face within Portugal. With a touch of indifference, Dilza noted the limited occupational landscape:

> The white Portuguese are very racist. They rarely think that the African immigrants come here as students, in administration, in clerical work. That is difficult for people to think. Oh, in cleaning services, watching over older people, in social services. *Yes*. But in the work that is "allegedly" more dignified, within quotes, there really is not a lot, and you don't see a lot of opportunity there. There's opportunity if you want to work in cleaning services, to work two jobs in cleaning services. You will have to wake up at four in the morning to go to work, and you only return home at ten at night. That's one thing. But things like office work, I don't believe that there is a lot of opportunity here. Not here in Portugal. Not for us.

The racialized employment market makes the care and service sector feel essentially inescapable for African immigrants. Young people including Dilza expressed considerable bitterness about how few opportunities they had for upward mobility. When, in another moment, I asked Dilza whether she believed African-descendant people had different experiences if they were Portuguese-born versus naturalized citizens, she replied, "On the one side, finding work is easy because as an immigrant you subject yourself to any type of job. You don't have a choice, you take anything. On the other side, it's not easy when you are competing with another, when there are two people. One of one color, another of another color [*slaps arms*]. The same educational background, the same experiences, but the preference is for the one who is of the same color of the employer, a Portuguese. Of course, *we are in their country*."

A naturalized citizen with professional aspirations, Dilza attributed her decision to enter eldercare to both interest and racialized closure and her inability to continue her nursing degree to her obligations as a mother and daughter-in-law as well as her sector-constrained income. Reasoning that "some work was better than nothing," she had been able to use personal connections to secure home care work, despite its often dead-end prospects for advancement. But her use of phrases like "their country" underscored the frustration that came with feeling like a visible outsider in Portugal. Dilza's story is a profound reminder of how the aggregation of everyday practices and social relations embedded in the racialized division of reproductive labor lays out divisions that reinscribe inequalities in the shadow of empire.

Lilian

Lilian, then seventeen, migrated to Portugal to study nursing in 2006. She knew opportunities for "good" work were scarce in Cabo Verde, and as a high-achieving student, she was awarded a scholarship to study abroad. Eager to follow the transnational footsteps of several of her cousins and siblings, Lilian went to Praia's city hall to apply for a student visa to Portugal. Her eldest brother provided money, an enormous help because the visa required Lilian to demonstrate a bank balance that could convince officials she had the means to travel and live independently abroad. The visa was granted. When she arrived in Portugal, Lilian acquired temporary residency as a student, and she moved in with a cousin who had migrated several years earlier.

Lilian enjoyed the independence of her collegiate life, though she bristled at being under the watchful "eyes" of family members. Like many of the Cabo Verdean women who migrated through student visas, she mentioned having family in and around Portugal and her dependence on her sisters in Portugal and her parents residing in the United States for financial support. They all had opinions. After two years, Lilian met a Cabo Verdean man and, despite her family's objections—they insisted she should focus on schoolwork—started an intimate relationship with him. When she became pregnant with her first child, she remembered,

> I had to stop studying; I wasn't working. During those times I depended a lot on my family members, my mother and father's family. I depended a lot on my older sister, Maria, who was here in Lisbon, and my mother and father who are in the United States. They always helped me. So I had to choose. Do I work, do I study, or do I take care of my son? And I couldn't study there anymore. I didn't have any money anymore, and my parents and my sister were not supportive of the pregnancy, or let's say they weren't happy about it because I came to study and I became pregnant. It was something that they didn't take very well.

Lilian was a new mother in a new country, young and getting little support from her baby's father or her own family, who were still upset with her for getting pregnant and quitting school. Her difficult situation led her to her first care service employment. She moved out of her cousin's apartment in the city where her university was located and relocated to Lisbon to live with her older sister and aunt. She knew her connections there, and the city's greater opportunities for finding work boded well. The move was also strategic in the sense that Lilian knew, however much they opposed her pregnancy, that her family members would help her with childcare. Six months in, her sister's husband found Lilian a temporary job as a domestic worker, keeping house and nannying for a vacationing couple. But when that job ended, Lilian returned to Lisbon and remained unemployed for nearly a year and a half. In due time, she became pregnant with her second child. She was dating a new man, but her family's dismay was the same as it had been the first time around:

> I became pregnant with my second child. And then time passed, and some complications emerged because my aunt *really* wasn't happy about the fact that I was pregnant; she didn't like my child's father *for nothing* [emphasis hers]. Family drama, you know? When I left the hospital after giving birth, I never returned to her house. I went to my now mother-in-law's house. After staying at my mother-in-law's house, I ended up leaving to live with my youngest child's father. . . . Then I started working in Lisbon, it was an electrical company, but I worked in cleaning there too. It was eight hours of work per day. I was there for two or so months. My partner's aunt was the one who found that job for me, contracted work. I went there to cover for someone who was on vacation, so that was about two and a half months or so. Then the vacations were over, so I had to leave. And from there I arranged that job in the mall, full time. My cousin found that job for me.

Today, Lilian is a permanent resident and resides with her live-in partner and two young children on the outskirts of Lisbon in a neighborhood accessible by bus or car. While she and her partner are happy to have steady work, she would like to find something with higher pay and more flexibility so that she can manage the demands of her work and family life. In the long term, the family hopes to relocate to France or the United States, but they are not yet in a financial situation to make that leap. Complicating matters, her youngest son and partner have Portuguese citizenship, but Lilian and her eldest son do not, so it can be difficult for them to travel abroad as a family. Still, they know that Portugal, a country steeped in economic crisis, presents few possibilities for changing their current situation, and Lilian's eldest sister is planning to leave herself.

After thirteen years of working and raising a family of her own in Portugal, Lilian is deeply frustrated that the country does not allow immigrants like her to feel included:

> Sometimes, white Portuguese do not consider or perceive African descendants as truly Portuguese because they weren't born here, or even if they were born here. Of course, if you're *pr-to* [Black], you have to be *pr-to* [Black]! It's that mentality. Here in Lisbon, there are Cabo Verdeans, Angolans, people from Guinea-Bissau, São Tomé. It's a country with a lot of diversity. But there are people who don't like that diversity. There are people who say that people are invading Portugal. But they also invaded our countries! It's hypocrisy. And who helped Portugal today as a country that exited the economic crisis? *Os negros* [the Blacks] were the ones that always worked.

Many participants' narratives featured similar indignation. Lilian migrated to Portugal with hopes of carving out a bright future, yet as her dreams shifted to accommodate her Portuguese-born children, the gendered and racialized economic terrain only hardened. Indeed, as other scholars have found, the birth of babies amplifies *and* exposes structural issues in host societies.[9] Likewise, Lilian's exit from schooling speaks to the gendered constraints borne by new mothers in general, but her frustrations in the years since stem from the limited opportunities available to her and others in a country that so plainly relies on Black people's labor. Lilian's postcolonial migration can be understood within the context of uneven development and the postcolonial endurance of mechanisms that maintain economic vulnerability in the shadow of empire, while her continued ambivalence toward the closed bounds of full belonging is also sustained by the way whiteness and Portugueseness seem to structure social as well as economic exclusion for immigrants and Afro-descendants like her family.

Jandy

Jandy was born in Portugal in 1991, and she grew up in the Lisbon suburbs. Her eldest sister had always lived away from their family, in England, with a paternal aunt who migrated before Jandy was born. The girls' parents, however, had gone to Portugal, leaving Praia, Santiago, in the early 1980s. Under Portuguese nationality law 37/1981, which restricted citizenship for immigrants' Portuguese-born children, Jandy was not granted citizenship at birth; her parents were not, at the time, legally in the country, nor did they have valid work permits. However, as Jandy finished high school in 2006, she took advantage of another immigration policy: children of immigrants who had gone through the Portuguese educational system and whose parents had been in the country legally for at least six years could apply for retroactive citizenship. Unusual in my respondent sample, Jandy's story is nonetheless intimately bound up with the legacy of Cabo Verdean migration.

In our interviews, Jandy recalls a childhood marked by community and challenges. She and her siblings were raised in public housing in a complex predominantly populated by fellow immigrant-origin and African and African-descendant families. Thinking of it brings a fondness to her voice, though it's been years since she relocated with her husband to the other side of Lisbon. Gesturing to the streets below her aunt's apartment window where we conducted the interview (in a block of apartments her aunt had lived in for over a decade), toward a nearby school, Jandy told me that the neighborhoods that hug Lisbon itself are where she feels a strong sense of belonging and community:

I went to that school there, and there's a lot of *negros, Africanos*. But not only *negros* but also Indians, Ukrainians, gypsies. So, I always felt good in school. I didn't start feeling the difference of my skin color really until I began to work. It was a nice community. And our house was always full. We were about eight, my aunt and uncle, my parents and my cousins and siblings, it was all of us together. Till this day I think back on those days and can see my aunt or uncle standing in the doorway, calling us all to come in from the streets from playing outside with all the kids from the neighborhood.

However warmed she is at the thought, Jandy remains ready to rattle off a list of struggles and challenges her family faced throughout her childhood. Her father was sick with aortic valve stenosis, or AVS, for much of her youth, suffering from partial paralysis, and Jandy and her eldest brother cared for him on weekends and after school. After her father died and Jandy turned sixteen, she went to work alongside her brother in food services. Their restaurant shifts in a large commercial center provided financial support for their mother. In later years, Jandy worked in retail, and today she works in institutional cleaning services.

That her co-workers are overwhelmingly migrant and other women of African descent reinforces Jandy's understanding of service work as an extension of slavery, servitude, and racial separation. In everyday interactions, she saw the legacies of long-standing associations of some people with power and others with, well, animals: "I believe the white Portuguese think that we are just here to work. That we are 'slaves,' within quotations. That we are animals. I'm not saying all of them. But the manner by which they treat us. Colleagues, clients. They believe that they are our boss and that we have to do what they say because we are here because we need to be. That's what they think." Later, Jandy alluded to the way the barriers separating African descendants into some kinds of work (and not others) also shape her more general assessment of social inclusion and exclusion:

JANDY The situation of race, or, rather, *racism*, didn't emerge until it was time for me to work. Because it's a bit difficult for us to find work here. Even if we are talking about cleaning services, or other places, you really have to look for work.

CELESTE When you say "us," who are you referring to?

JANDY I am referring to Africans in this case. I, for example, am privileged because I have documents and all that. But I know a lot of people who don't have documents, and so everything is more complicated for them, it really is. But even if you have documents, it remains complicated. Unfortunately, there's a lot of issues due to skin color here. Sometimes we must show that we know how to work, that we know how to do things, so that *they* [emphasis hers] give us opportunities. They enter the interview with this preconceived notion that *negros* don't understand anything. But for example, if they must choose, they will always give the jobs to Portuguese people first, and then they give it to us, maybe eight or nine times out of ten. And this makes it a bit difficult because the so-called real Portuguese are looking for work and we are too, and then, well, we end up staying in as the second plan.

Jandy makes a key distinction here, locating her experience of *racism* in the period in which she was compelled to seek opportunities to provide for her family. Her sense that employers have hidden biases stirs insecurity among Afro-descendant immigrants and citizens alike in my data. To Jandy, a racialized conception of a "real" Portuguese person as white and white only leaves everyone else outside—and that means even she, born and raised in this country, feels adrift in Portuguese society. Indeed, Jandy's remarks illustrate the variation in African descendants' situations in Portugal. Undocumented African workers sit at one end of the spectrum, all but totally excluded (save in informal and stigmatized work sectors). On the other end are those whose Portuguese citizenship helps them compete for jobs within the formal market and provides them with a claim to inclusion but whose race stubbornly prevents true inclusion. Somewhere in between the "lost workers" who migrated in the 1940s and those, like Jandy, born in and now citizens of Portugal lay a range of respondent experiences intertwined with race, gender, and citizenship and the labor through which each aspect of their intersectional identity comes into focus.

Conclusion

Over and over, the women I spoke to characterized their roles as workers in Portuguese society with palpable ambivalence. They and their families left Cabo Verde not only to escape the vise grip of economic stagnation but because they dreamed of a better life, of better opportunities. However, when they arrived, they found their friends and extended kin clustered in care and service occupations they came to see as "dirty work." From subtle to blatant, the everyday racism they encountered as they set down roots taught them that white Portuguese regarded Black women as "appropriate" to that work—and it shaped these women's shared feelings of injustice. The intersection of long-standing racialized and gendered colonial hierarchies and the cycle of global inequality have created bulwarks between "bona fide" Portuguese citizens and racialized migrant Others. Their stories, as diverse as they are, thus illustrate the emergence of a shared subjectivity alongside processes of gendered racial formation, molded by the way Portuguese society circumscribes opportunity structures for Black, African-descendant women in particular.

Indeed, for the Cabo Verdean women I represent in these portraits, there is a clear desire for dignity and respect in their work. But to understand why this seems out of reach in the shadow of empire, one must fully understand Portuguese society and how racism is experienced every day. In the following chapters, I therefore center the heterogenous manifestations of the everyday gendered anti-Black racism Cabo Verdean women face. They are at once racialized and gendered as hypervisible "Others" in public space, yet the inherently racialized and gendered dimensions of home care and institutional cleaning work also simultaneously render them socially invisible. Together, these chapters highlight the convergence of racialized divisions in reproductive labor with particular—and seemingly *immobile*—social locations in Portuguese society.

3

Confronting Everyday
Gendered Racism
in Portugal

● ●

"I used to work at an ice cream stand near a park, and a white Portuguese man approached me," Sheila began. "So, as I would do normally, I asked him what he would like." She was surprised when he responded, as if they were both enjoying a shared joke, "Vanilla. I detest anything that's *pr-ta* [Black]!" The man's response stood out in Sheila's memory not because of its casual racism, nor because it was so direct and tinged with a racially charged, sneering misogyny, but because of her own pointed retort: "Well, *I* don't like vanilla because I detest anything that's white." She seemed proud to have subverted, in that moment, any tacit acceptance of herself as the punchline: "I said that in front of everyone. He immediately looked at me with that face of surprise, and he said, 'Are we still talking about ice cream here?' And I said to him, 'Of course, isn't that what you were talking about?'"

This service interaction, in a public space in Lisbon, was supposed to be all about ice cream, yet Sheila understood the man's unsolicited distaste toward anything *pr-ta* had little to do with his relative preference for chocolate or vanilla. The word itself cannot be separated from the historical and social context of their interaction: a white Portuguese man approaching a Black woman service worker in a public space in an urban area of Portugal. He is a customer; she is to serve him. In a labor market where ethnic minority women are often deemed suited to low-status service jobs, where their race, gender, and assumed foreignness are read as signals that together subjugate and dehumanize, their exchange was loaded with power dynamics. In this context, Sheila's response to his *everyday gendered racism* (in the words of Philomena Essed, who notes that it contours quotidian interactions with racial hostility[1]) was disruptive, subversive, challenging.

Scholar Grada Kilomba locates everyday anti-Black racism at the intersection of the colonial past and the not-yet-postcolonial present, writing that it serves as a violent, if common, shock that "places the Black subject in a colonial scene where, as in a plantation scenario, one is imprisoned as the subordinate and exotic 'Other.'"[2] Structure and ideology are so intimately bound that buying ice cream can be used to shore up power, to leverage gendered anti-Black ideology in service of subjugation. The white man's interaction with Sheila is no isolated practice but a barbed lesson in the enforcement of Portugal's racialized and gendered social system. Everyday anti-Black racism naturalizes hostility in the service of protecting white supremacy.

That Sheila pushed back is itself telling: Essed's and Kilomba's work, for instance, recognizes how the margins are a place of relentless subversion. Sheila did not acquiesce when the man attempted to signal dominance, sealing her position as subordinate. Her quick and incisive retort—that she "detests anything that's white"—reflects a keen awareness of the microaggression as well as her rejection of the legitimacy of her subordination. In other words, by talking back, Sheila holds the man accountable for his attempt to put her in her place. Both she and he knew what was going on in their quick interaction, and Sheila refused to play along. Throughout my fieldwork, I would meet so many Cabo Verdean women who, like Sheila, were well aware of the burdens everyday racism placed on their shoulders. They understood how it unfolded in public spaces as surely as it did at the highest levels, how dominant white regimes tried to maintain power by marginalizing and othering people like them. And they frequently resisted.

Recall that Portuguese antiracial and lusotropicalist ideologies paradoxically claim that contemporary Portugal is multiracial—in fact, that it is a society entirely free of racism. Certainly, as we saw in chapter 1, those in power boast that their country remains unscathed by the mechanisms that reproduce racial inequality. They claim a country free from race-related police brutality and systemic racism in housing, education, and work. Yet the braided ideology of antiracialism and lusotropicalism sustains deep inequality. Antiracialism suggests it is impossible for colonialism to remain powerful via the manifestations of systemic racism, and lusotropicalism that Portugal's supposedly "closer" or more intimate relationship with its colonized subjects belies the idea that it ever perpetrated racialized and gendered violence in the service of empire. This is a pernicious form of power because it denies the racist hegemony made evident in the everyday lived experiences of African descendants like Sheila.

Scholars, in fact, have long spotlighted how white supremacy is buttressed by ideological systems that reinforce systemic denial. In his classic text *The Racial*

Contract, philosopher Charles Mills argues that white supremacy involves an *epistemology of ignorance* that requires white people to understand and know the world in profoundly distorted ways. This epistemology of ignorance, what Gloria Wekker incisively calls "white innocence," safeguards privilege by denying both racial privilege and oppression at all their intersections within society.[3] As Wekker argues, this deep-seated cultural denial divorces the present from the colonial past, allowing white Dutch Europeans to see themselves as enlightened and unburdened by the ramifications of ongoing colonial violence. To Alana Lentin, this structurally pervasive white perspective is evident in a European phenomenon she calls "not racism."[4] This dominant Eurocentric conception of racism goes beyond color-blind logic, leaving no room to "encapsulate the effects of racial rule and the logic it bequeathed on social structures and consequent individual lived experience."[5] This epistemology of ignorance neutralizes racism only by deferring to whites' insistence that racism is a bygone relic, wholly rejected in contemporary Europe. As a result, the roots of contemporary patterns of racial inequality, along with the everyday racism that protects those patterns, are made as discordantly invisible and hypervisible as the women in this study feel. Whites can be presented with the same evidence of racialized patterned opportunity and outcome, and they can credibly assert the data point to anything *but* racism.

In this chapter, I prioritize the accounts of Cabo Verdeans, who understand that their own experiences of both subtle and aggressive forms of xenophobic, gendered anti-Black racism are not outliers, exceptions, or counterfactuals but the fabric of everyday life in the shadow of empire. By rejecting the dominant lens, I argue that in addition to specific structural constraints typically deployed to explain the existence of anti-Black racism in Europe and beyond, powerfully symbolic, quotidian forces work to maintain white supremacy and racial dominance in this allegedly antiracial context. I organize my argument around several themes related to informants' social positioning. For one, Cabo Verdean women's intersectional location within a racialized and international division of reproductive labor informs a labor market–driven understanding of everyday racism in Lisbon, connecting their contemporary experiences of work discrimination to long-standing colonial hierarchies. Second, and relatedly, African-descendant care workers' labor market position requires that they leave residentially segregated neighborhoods and move through public space on their way to and from work. Thus, they are especially vulnerable to racist harassment in public spaces, not only because they must traverse the city for work, but also because gendered anti-Blackness reserves feminine innocence for white women—meaning that Black women are seen as appropriate targets for insult and control. Finally, their role as residents of the greater Lisboan community places women like Sheila in various interracial settings, where the underlying epistemology of ignorance allows the racialized interactions of daily life to unfold as if they are "normal" and "not racist." Entitlement racism—another form of everyday racism in the twenty-first century, according to Essed—allows whites to say what they wish without fear of sanction, in the name of freedom of expression.[6] The heterogenous manifestations of everyday gendered anti-Black racism in this analysis are not isolated events. They are unified by repetition and acquire meaning in relation to other experiences of everyday racism, whether covert or overt. These *cumulative* aggressions reveal the ideological and systemic racism behind each instantiation.

The Everyday Racism of Finding Work

As in many postindustrial contexts, the individuals I met in Portugal made sense of their broader social inclusion or exclusion vis-à-vis their positions and experiences in the labor market. Indeed, in chapter 2 I introduced several Cabo Verdean care workers who linked the ongoing labor exploitation of their wider African and African-descendant community to what they saw as the restriction of their own substantive citizenship in contemporary Portuguese society. Those study respondents who had resided in Portugal for a number of years were particularly vocal in this respect, perhaps because they located their personal work experiences within a longer historical view acknowledging the extension of long-standing colonial hierarchies around reproductive labor. Eva, a fifty-three-year-old home care worker who arrived in the early 1980s as a domestic worker, insisted that Portugal's current occupational landscape carries colonial history into Africans' and Afro-descendants' present-day marginalization:

> There are many Portuguese that think that slavery still exists. There are a lot of older [white Portuguese] people that lived in Africa; they enslaved a lot of people. They had domestics serving them too. And so they think this still exists. . . . And so, the immigrants, the Africans . . . in the past their role was to serve as domestics inside of a woman's house. White women never did these things, because in the past you had to wash everything by hand, wash uniforms by hand, wash clothing by hand—everything by hand. And it was only the *Africans*, the immigrants that came here, [who] were the ones that did that. The Portuguese from here did not do that. And today the truth is that African immigrants, Black people, even if we or they have schooling and experience, we do not find jobs at the same level as the Portuguese do. We cannot compete.

Eva is a naturalized Portuguese citizen, and her verbal elision of "immigrant" and "African" made it difficult to discern whether she was referring to racial or immigrant status alone. I asked her to clarify:

> CELESTE So do you think there are the same opportunities to find work
> for an African immigrant and a white Portuguese? Or how [about]
> a Portuguese of African descent and a white Portuguese? What

about children of Cabo Verdeans that are Portuguese, born here ... compared to children of white Portuguese, would you say they have the same opportunity here?

EVA No, no, no. It's not the same. Priority is given more to the Portuguese. Even when talking about the immigrants that came here and are now Portuguese ... employers will look for the roots of the person. My daughter, for example. She is Portuguese and was born here. They [the hiring managers] will look for their roots and will see "This is a Portuguese woman but she's of African descent." Later [a] person that is of Portuguese descent and *Portuguese* [white] is given more priority. It is easier for them to find work. This is just how it is. *It's their country.*

Employment gatekeepers' biases were a topic of great concern for the women I interviewed. Consider Marcia, a thirty-nine-year-old mother of three Portuguese-born children. In 2014, she graduated from a Portuguese university with a degree in business but was unable to find work in her area of study. She ended up working in food services in a large commercial center. When she was laid off, her eldest sister recommended Marcia apply for a job at the company where she worked, leading Marcia into home care. In our discussion, Marcia linked her initial experiences of searching for work when she first emigrated on a student visa to the everyday forms of racism she and others encounter in Lisbon day after day. She spoke as if disabusing me of the antiracist ideology: "Celeste, racism is something that we all must go through every single day. Racism exists here in Portugal. Eh, when I first came in 2001, I came here to work and study. So, I went to look for a job in the commercial center, Colombo, and that woman said to me, naturally, 'No, we don't accept *pr-tos* here.' I responded, 'Well thank you. And I am very proud to be Black!'" Even then, having run up against blatant racial discrimination, Marcia refused defeat and refused the woman's "natural" deployment of anti-Blackness. Faced with explicit forms of everyday anti-Black racism in the shadow of empire, she reasserted her dignity with a sort of everyday resistance.

While Portugal has instated legislative directives regarding equal treatment in employment, regardless of ethnic or racial origin, Marcia's account of discrimination shows the difference between policy and practice. The woman's casual manner was shocking to Marcia in that it highlighted a difficult, but until that moment not personal, truth about immigrants in Lisbon. Under the veil of multiculturalism, the expressions and practices of white dominance remained unrelenting. Anti-Black ideologies and resource restriction—the bases of systemic racism—were embedded in the ongoing practices of everyday life. "What they think is that, 'Oh that we come here to ruin their country, to steal jobs.' This is why she did that," Marcia said with an air of indifference. "But the reality is that here in Portugal, it's the immigrants [who] are the people that work the most; we have the heaviest, the dirtiest jobs. But in the Portuguese's heads, it's not like that. That's not *their* vision. In their vision, we come here to ruin their country, that's the discourse. We come here to steal jobs. Why? Because the Portuguese are racist."

Amid the normalization of racism in Portugal, Marcia never bothered to notify authorities about this incident. Who would take her complaints seriously? "*We know* it's racist," she remarked, "but to *them*, it's like any other day. [White Portuguese] don't believe they are racist because racism is normalized here. They behave racist but they think their behavior is OK, is normal; they are so racist that just the idea of racism is not *conceived* of by them . . . it's normalized!" Marcia added, resolutely, that today she would report the incident. She felt antiracist political consciousness was on the rise and that people's "eyes are wide open." Indeed, accounts of public incidents of everyday racism have increased dramatically in Portugal, and Marcia is correct that counterpressures can open spaces and opportunities for contestation.

"Racism is reallllly hard. It really hurts, Celeste. I went through this," Belita said as she told me of a run-in a decade before, just after she migrated. It shook her to her core: "I was in front of a white man, I went to ask him something, for some information [about a job]. A person ignores you, or they look at your face and spit on you. He spit on me." Belita paused. "Celeste, that is something that hurts! It really hurts! That's one of the worst thing[s] that someone can do, spit on someone. A person comes up to you just to ask for some information and that person looks at you and spits? That is the worst thing of all." Belita's eyes blazed intensely as she associated that long-ago interaction with the current of racial injustice *and* dehumanization that permeated her early experiences as a migrant in Portugal. The distrust, anger, and even violence demonstrated by the Portuguese against Blacks were burned into her memory. So, too, was the fact that none of the Portuguese bystanders had spoken up when a man spit on her, so provisional was a Black woman's social standing.

When I asked Casey whether she believed there were equal opportunities for "people like herself" to find work in Lisbon, she was indignant. Her "roots," she said, despite her light complexion and light eyes, had been weighed by prospective employers. Now a home care worker of six years, Casey recalled a scenario in which her ability to work as a bank teller was reduced to her ethnoracial heritage, not her qualifications:

> It's not the same for others, Portuguese of African descent or African immigrants. If you interview a [white] Portuguese person, they will say that, yes, that the opportunities are the same. But the truth is that it is not. No, because I already experienced this when I was looking for work. I had my residency card, but I didn't have Portuguese citizenship. I went to look for work as a teller. I went and the interview went really well, and they offered me the job. And when the time came to sign the contract and I took out my residency card because it was needed for the contract, when they saw I was a foreigner

from Africa, they didn't accept it. Because at that level, they only accept white Portuguese women.

Casey's experience stands out because it was not her phenotype that cued the racist discrimination but the revelation of her statuses as African and foreign (albeit with legal residency) at the last stage of hiring—timing that made the rejection starker. Notably, Casey immigrated to Portugal in 2001, well after Act No. 20/98 (see chapter 1) amended the Decree-Law No. 97/77 so that an employer could hire any worker residing *legally* in Portugal, regardless of nationality, pursuant to the 90 percent Portuguese workers requirement imposed on businesses previously. It follows that her experience contributed to her racialized identity and thus subjectivity as *a foreign Black woman in Portugal*.

Like Belita, Casey chose not to seek legal recourse. And like Belita, it was not because she accepted or was defeated by racial discrimination. Casey chose instead to frequently recount her story to others as a way of calling out systemic injustice.

Taken together, these stories reflect the process by which meaning is constructed through my informants' interactions with society's gatekeepers. Hiring managers taught them, for instance, that eldercare, cleaning, and domestic work were the types of jobs available to Black women like them. This message was reinforced in the way women told me they could easily get references for reproductive service work, due to the African and African-descendant community's disproportionate representation in it, and in the way these Black women's occupational location seemed inescapable. The racialized and international division of reproductive labor, buttressed by everyday anti-Black racism, shapes individuals' feelings of belonging within society.

Racial Subtleties

Everyday anti-Black racism encompasses overt actions as well as more subtle practices in which people are left wondering about the other person's intentions. For example, in Sheila's story at the opening of this chapter, she understood there was a pernicious racial and gendered disgust lurking within a common service interaction. In this sense, everyday racism is really a more complex web of what Essed terms "interrelated instantiations of racism"; singular events gain meaning in relation to a larger set of covert and overt practices.[7]

"In Portugal, as the small country that it is, racism here is. . . ." After a pause to consider the right word, an informant of mine finished, "controlled." At other moments, she called it "subtle" and an "expected type of racism," noting, "It's always there. There are situations where racism comes out." Study participants understood the twin levels on which the everyday anti-Black racism they faced operated: they knew the overt racism was one thing, but the subtle racial inflections they sensed when putting in applications, inquiring at storefronts, and responding to newspaper ads were insulting in a different way. "Something wasn't right" about their exchanges with hiring managers or the infrequency of their callbacks. "It's a general attitude you sense," said one home care worker I spoke to. "You go there and you talk to them [hiring managers], but you know that they aren't really listening. And the manner by which they speak to us, you can sense the racism." A cleaning worker added, "People notice that something was wrong during the interview. You can feel it."

Ariana, a Portuguese-born woman of Cabo Verdean descent, recounted, in her strong Lisboan accent, how pleasantly a manager spoke to her when she called to inquire about a clerical opening and then how dismissively he responded to her in person, when she came in for her formal interview: "He saw that I was Black, and I'm sure that's why he wasn't interested. He treated me with this attitude before we even started the interview that was like 'How dare you even try?'" Other gatekeepers probed indelicately about her racial background. "Imagine, when we send in our resume, they don't see photos or anything, so they review it and then call a person. Then they look surprised, you know, wide-eyed, and they say things like 'Oh here it says you are Portuguese, but where are you *from*?' And I say, 'I am Portuguese, just as it says there. I was born here.' 'Oh, no, no, but where are your parents from? Where did they come from?' And there I have to explain, 'My parents are from another country, but I was born here.'" As argued by Trica Danielle Keaton, the "where are you *from, from* question" is a familiar form of everyday anti-Blackness experienced by members of the African diaspora who "are twice demonized as immigrants and by race."[8] Indeed, this familiar question in Portugal inadvertently tells Ariana that she and her family do not belong.

For several years, Ariana worked in cleaning services and at a hair salon before securing an entry-level job at an electricity company (supplemented with part-time hours for a cleaning service firm). That was its own journey:

> I went to be interviewed, and when the time came to be interviewed in a group, I saw that the way that they talk to you is different. They treat us like we don't know anything. For example, when they talk to a Portuguese woman or man, they ask them about their schooling, but the manner in which they speak to them shows that they already have that notion in their head like "Ah, she knows what she's doing, without a problem. She already knows this." But with us, no. It's a lot of that feeling like they are thinking or even saying directly, "Ah, you shouldn't know this. Ah, you don't know this." And then I say, "No, I know. I have done this already." And then people become all surprised, like "Wow, you know that!" And I respond, "Yes, I know, I studied too. I also went to school." [*laughs ironically*] I could see that, when it started, they didn't appreciate me, but then they saw, finally, that the other woman is white, but she doesn't know anything and that I, *a mulher negra* [the Black woman], is knowledgeable. So that happens a lot, in everything; it's everywhere.

Ariana, in taking note of white Portuguese people's negative assumptions about Blacks, points to the "controlling images" of Black people that circulate throughout Portuguese society and construct an idea of Black bodies as incompatible with intelligence.[9] Some interactions may exemplify "covert" racism, showing how seemingly nonracial incidents and implications crystallize into a durable racialized social system. They are normalized in the sense that they are widespread and rendered benign by the principle of antiracialism, yet they are also easily detected by informants, who see them as reminders of their shared subordinate position.

Public Spaces

As countless scholars have argued, spatial exclusion is a core aspect of the gendered anti-Blackness confronted by Black women.[10] Concentrated in a narrow set of gendered occupations and relegated to the ethnic enclaves and public housing populated by African descendants, Romani, and immigrants from Africa, South Asia, East Asia, and Brazil on the outer fringes of Lisbon, the Cabo Verdean women I came to know actually experienced a great deal of solitude. They traversed racialized and spatialized boundaries as they moved between home and work, and they spent a lot of time indoors in their workplaces and in elders' homes. That they frequently relied on public transit to cross boundaries for the business of daily life exposed them to a significant pattern of racist interactions. Some were overt, shocking incidents that occupied their minds for days, and others were mundane hassles that could be swept aside or forgotten by day's end. Ligia, a sixty-year-old institutional cleaning worker who had lived in Portugal for more than half her life, described hearing a common refrain as she moved through life: "Racism is everywhere. 'Pr-ta da merda!' That's what you hear. Bus stops, trains, commercial centers, supermarkets, there are things like that that occur constantly around here. Places where people go and there are all types of people, of all different races. It always happens when you go to a place, an office building in the city where we have to go retrieve some paperwork, something like that. Always."

Pr-ta da merda, which means, roughly, "Black shit," is an unavoidably racist and dehumanizing phrase, here deployed in an ostensibly interracial (therefore antiracial) country. Ligia's remarks highlight the Portuguese controversy around the use of the term *pr-to/a*. To Black people, *pr-to/a* is a racist, derogatory, and dehumanizing term, but many of my informants insisted it is so widely used that many white citizens seem to see no harm in it and dismiss alternatives such as *pessoa da cor* (person of color) as nothing more than overzealous political correctness. Though some Cabo Verdean informants have claimed this word as a way to signify racialized belonging in their community, they too recognized the biting, aggressive charge it carries when uttered by whites. Organizations, some of them mainstream, as well as Africans and African descendants continue to publicly denounce the use of this term, yet many whites, my informants insist, disregard these messages. Thus, whites' continued use of the word is an extension of the broad epistemology of racial ignorance. For many people, whites' ongoing embrace of the term is a clear expression of colonial processes of Black dehumanization and their commitment to white supremacy.

Indeed, given that the "Europeanization of Europe" is a racial project that frames all whites as European and racialized minorities as outsiders (or, in Stuart Hall's words, "in but not of Europe"[11]), *pr-to/a* carries violent accusations of nonbelonging. It is no different from whites who tell Africans and African descendants to "vai para sua terra" (go back to your country) or accuse them of theft and job stealing. It also strips away Africans' and African descendants' personal identity when whites use it to refer to colleagues, alleged "friends," and passersby and in critique of public figures. For example, one informant remembered meeting a friend for lunch in a busy café and hearing a white male soccer fan, glaring at a television, hurl the term when a player on the screen fumbled.

One evening, I found myself telling a Cabo Verdean informant, Diana, about how I had been called *pr-ta pretinha* by a white man as I exited a metro station. It was my first month visiting Lisbon, in 2015, and the older man, who appeared intoxicated, stood up from his place among several other men on a bench to fiercely yell from the other side of the road and ask if I was lost: "Estás perdida, pr-ta pretinha!" I quickly turned the corner and made my way to my apartment share. Diana pointed out how it fits with the normalization of racism in Portugal: "They don't see racism. . . . They are really, really in denial. If there's no racism, then why do they yell out to you *pr-ta pretinha*!" She added, as if to teach me how to react to racism in her country, "To say *pr-ta*, it's like saying *n-----* in the United States, but to a woman! Next time, you scream out to him, 'Do you know me? No! So shut up!'"

Another conversation about the use of *pr-to/a* unfolded as I joined Regina, an institutional cleaning worker, for dinner at her home. We were joined by her niece, daughter, and son-in-law and her son and his two toddlers as we settled in the living room to watch *A Única Mulher*. The show is a popular Portuguese *novela* (soap opera) about the economic downturn in Portugal and Angola that at times addresses racism, xenophobia, and political unrest. While Regina sat on the sofa, her twenty-three-year-old niece, a restaurant worker named Iliana, also sat on the floor between her aunt's legs so that Regina could braid her shiny, textured hair. As we watched, she talked about incidents at work: "They call me *pr-ta* at work," she said with frustration. "I don't like it. It's not right . . . like, people just look at me and say, 'Oh *pr-ta*, do this.' Or 'Oh *pr-ta* come here. *Pr-ta*, go get that!'"

Regina stopped braiding. She turned to Iliana and told her she must demand otherwise: "No, *fidju*,[12] that isn't right! And you need to tell them that." Regina's son piped up, "The *only* people that can call you *preta* are your own people. Only *pretos* can call you that." Iliana sighed. "It really makes me mad. I am more than just the '*preta*.' I'm a person. But they're—the Portuguese—they're brutes!"[13] Contrasting *pr-ta* and *person*, Iliana's comment demonstrates the way her colleagues' very words assert a form of anti-Black dehumanization.

A year later, I was with a friend in downtown Lisbon, during the height of tourist season, when I heard a white Portuguese retail worker use this word with her colleagues. With Nelida, a local Cabo Verdean friend who worked in cleaning services, and her teenage daughter, Zeni, a dark-skinned sixteen-year-old with a voluminous Afro, I was enjoying the exuberance of the narrow streets, thronged with tourists and the swirl of their many languages. Zeni convinced us to duck into a popular clothing store. As she ran ahead to rummage through a nearby rack of bathing suits, I pointed out to Nelida that there was a sales attendant, a Black woman, standing against the wall. She appeared upset. Soon, though, we were distracted: Nelida's daughter picked out a colorful ring of hair scrunchies, and Nelida handed over her wallet, instructing the girl to go pay. The white woman behind the register handed Zeni the receipt as she called across the room to the sales attendant I noticed earlier: "*Pr-ta*, go to the back to get the. . . ." I did not discern the rest of the message. The beginning was more than clear. Zeni looked away, but the white sales associate looked at her, smiling, and addressed her directly: "Don't worry, I have nothing against you." That's when Nelida and I sprang forward. That word was racist, we told her. We wanted to speak to her manager. But the sales attendant maintained her air of indifference. "This is how we play," she said nonchalantly. "We are *friends*. I treat her as though she were my slave!" Stunned and outraged, we realized people were staring. I looked around the room, but the Black worker was nowhere in sight. We stormed out.

It took time and effort, but we followed up on this incident by registering a complaint with the store's manager and with the company's headquarters. Yet often, these everyday experiences of racism are waved off, no matter how painfully they sting. Who has the time and effort to spare just to point out white ignorance, manage the excuses, amplify the burdens?

This personal experience illustrated the lengths to which whites sometimes would go to bypass racial awareness to reestablish their own innocence— and reinforce their racial superiority. The clerk eschewed accountability and attempted to neutralize the master-slave "play" of her everyday anti-Black racism, both denying her colleague's right to a welcoming workspace and side-stepping contemporary gendered white supremacy entangled in her nostalgic pantomime of slavery. As argued by Trica Danielle Keaton, whites in Europe often use "disparagement humor" to dehumanize Black people for the price of a good laugh. When questioned or called out for their anti-Black violence, the perpetrator often resorts to white innocence by projecting the race problem onto the targets of racist humor themselves.[14] This fantasy role-play that distances memory from legacies of racism and violence also alludes to the nostalgic reenactments of antebellum life taken up by U.S. whites who participate in heritage and plantation tourism in the U.S. south.[15] Indeed, practices of everyday anti-Black racism are predicated on dominant white processes of ignorance, yet they also reproduce knowing; Blacks *know* that racism structures their lives because they experience the weight of racist denial and everyday racism. In the evening, Nelida and I discussed the complex dyad of knowing and ignorance and denial we'd seen and felt in the store:

> NELIDA We have a history; we know that people often call others *pr-ta* to offend them. That's the truth! Now, perhaps it's how they "play," but that is between them, but . . . this is a professional place, so she has to act professional! As a customer, I think in my mind, "She treats people like that—like slaves, *like pr-tas*." And to her, it's a game.
>
> CELESTE It's not a game.
>
> NELIDA It's not! We know that because you, we, already have that history; we know that when people say that, it's meant to offend. And so that always stays in our head; even if they are playing with us and acting like they are playing, we are going to always think . . . "How can she treat someone like that?" And principally, in the job, that's strange. For a person who is white and Portuguese, it's simple to say, like, "a joke," because she hasn't suffered due to her skin color. And now we, who have grown up and already seen this happen . . . it's offensive. And she says they are friends. But it wasn't the Black woman who said they were friends, right? It was she who said that, so we have no idea if that is true or not!

For Nelida, words matter. History matters. She is a Black Cabo Verdean woman, and histories of racial enslavement resonate with her own personal history. Words like *pr-ta* or "slaves" have no place in friendly conversation between interracial colleagues, she believes, nor do so-called games that cast Black women as "slaves" in order to psychologically carve out racial dominance in an otherwise stigmatized service position. Yet as a central logic of everyday racism, an epistemology of ignorance shapes the white woman's alleged racial inculpability, divorcing her racial practices from their white supremacist origins. Insidiously, the white woman's investment in racial innocence merely inverts the problem onto the Black people who take issue with her behavior.

The clothing store situation is only part of an intricate web of racialized experiences in this urban context. These situations unfold in spaces that are themselves structured by racial and gender inequality. On another occasion, I joined Nelida and her family for *bifanas* (grilled pork sandwiches) at a busy restaurant during the festival of Saint Anthony. Nelida left the group in search of an unoccupied table while the rest of us, including myself, Zeni, her aunt and uncle and their children, and a few of Nelida's friends wedged ourselves in to wait. We were patient as (white Portuguese-appearing) men waiters rushed back and forth, but no one seemed to take notice of us. Annoyed by the now uncomfortably long wait, Nelida went inside the restaurant to order on her own. When she reappeared, she looked exasperated. A waiter, who followed her, informed us, "If you paid inside, [then] we can't serve you here. Your bill has been settled. Your bill is not with the waiters out here." Nelida was clearly, and rightly, annoyed: "We waited to be served; we were ignored. And there's nowhere to sit inside now. The other waiter did not say anything to us at all, so now we are sitting here. Can we order drinks or what?" Interrupting in *kriolu*, Nelida's brother-in-law asked her what the problem was. The waiter angrily pointed to a white family standing nearby, waiting for seats, then bellowed at Nelida, "What you are doing is not right! Can't you get up and give others your seat, woman? What you are doing is not right!" Reflexively, a firm "humph" slipped, almost in unison, from Nelida's sister's and my mouth. "'Humph' what!?" demanded the waiter. "Can't you all just act civilized? Act like civilized people, at least this one day! *Civilized!*"

That our table of customers was dismissed by a swirl of waiters in a restaurant, rushing between the aisles, tidily showed how African descendants are rendered invisible within Portugal's public spaces. Blacks are constructed as individuals unworthy of service, right here in a bustling restaurant in the heart of Lisbon—the same place that hosts the country's largest population of African descendants. Systemic racism is embedded in the urban infrastructure, and so the Black residents of the racially segregated suburban parishes enter this space on unequal terms. They may be treated as unwelcomed "outsiders," even surrounded by tables full of tourists. The spectacle that ensued when Nelida raised even the mildest resistance, however, made our group suddenly hypervisible. All eyes and ears focused on the heated discussion, witnessing the waiter's biting but decontextualized invective: "Can't you all just act civilized? Act like civilized people, at least this one day!" He activated colonial and racist imagery that frames Blacks—that framed *our group*—as nonhuman and primitive.

Yet the moment she heard his utterances, one of Nelida's friends rose from her seat. A dark-skinned Cabo Verdean woman, she declared loudly, "Well, *today WE* are staying *here* and acting *un*civilized!" As she sat back down, she regarded the table and let out an emphatic "*Neh!*" Her voice was bold, almost triumphant: "Today we are real Amazonians, huh!" At this, Nelida looked to the waiter, lifted her arms like a gorilla, and began to laugh. Her actions directly called out the man's allusion to colonial racist images of the uncivilized, inhuman African. They showed we weren't ignorant of his intentions, nor were we leaving. Eventually, the waiter gave up and stomped away while another finally tended to our table. Of course, this was not without cost. Resisting the waiter's behavior took up time and emotional energy, and it also risked escalating the dispute in addition to being publicly stereotyped and scorned.

The Everyday Gendered Racism of Public Transport

Because Black women like my respondents so frequently traversed the city, moving from segregated neighborhoods at the city's edges to workplaces in often predominantly white neighborhoods and lively commercial centers, they spent a good portion of most of their days using public transit. The claustrophobic spaces of train cars, platforms, and bus stops were rife with everyday racism. One Saturday afternoon, as my husband and I rode the *comboio* (city commuter train) along the Lisboan coast, I spotted a Black woman on the opposite end of the car. A younger Black man held her from behind as she exchanged what appeared to be heated words with a seated white couple—I couldn't hear what they said over the cacophony of the train terminal as we pulled into our stop. Seconds before we stepped out onto the platform, I looked over my shoulder and saw the white man rise from his seat, shouting in the Black woman's face. In that moment, his words were as clear as could be: "Pr-ta da merda!"[16] The doors slid shut, and the train cars became a blur as they whizzed away.

Another time, a few weeks earlier, we were on a bus out of downtown Lisbon. It was packed, so we made our way toward the only empty double seats—a row toward the back of the bus that directly faced the row across. As we settled in, I made eye contact with the white woman who was sitting across from us. The woman visibly, performatively scowled and sighed, then stared at us: a medium-brown-skinned Cabo Verdean American man and a light-skinned Black American woman. Sensing her anger and disgust, I stared out the window for the brief, extremely uncomfortable ride to the next stop. There, many people exited, while a woman hand in hand with a young child entered the now less densely packed bus. The child—a joyous, maybe five-year-old in a Spiderman T-shirt—skipped down the aisle, tugging the hand of his dark-skinned mother. As they approached our seats, the white woman took notice of the mother in her blue-and-white floral wrap dress and matching headdress, scowled, and placed her leg across the open seat beside her. Where we had earned only a scowl, this much darker-skinned woman, in her traditional African clothing, and her happy child were entirely shut out. My husband and I moved, sitting instead near the woman and child.

Public transportation proved an emotionally and politically charged space in which the salience of race was palpable. Informants told me these interactions with whites and other ethnic groups were both fleeting *and* common. This was especially the case for home care and cleaning workers whose race, gender, and occupational status (made visible by phenotype and/or uniforms) may evoke particularly negative images in the minds of whites. "People think we work with feces or poop. The Portuguese think we are dirty. People think bacteria and viruses," said Diana, a home care worker. "They may not sit by us in public transport, or they move to a different seat if we sit down by them. I notice these things a lot. I feel that people think we haven't cleaned ourselves properly, we haven't washed our hands well enough or at all. We are just associated with shit and filth. All things dirty."

The seemingly monotonous, everyday habit of "Traveling While Black" was frequently punctuated by scrutiny and aggression from "rank and file" white commuters:

ROSEANY There's always something that they [white Portuguese] don't like. Sometimes in the transportation, when there are a lot of Africans, [there's] always someone who gets up and goes to sit in another seat. I have been told that I smell bad, directly. And I have been told to go back to my country, just like that. "Vai para sua terra!"[17] They told me that when I was on the bus.

FATIMA They already said that to me, "Vai para sua terra!" I was at the bus stop, waiting for the bus. You have to respect the line, who was there first, second. They come and pass you and you say, "What, you can't respect the line?" They respond, "Vai para sua terra, Vai para sua terra! Pr-ta da merda!" That has already happened to me many times, in many places!

A major mode of Portugal's everyday gendered racism is seen in white citizens challenging the general right of Black women to "be" in certain spaces. As Katherine McKittrick has argued, anti-Blackness has persistently denied the spatial legitimacy of Black people. In her view, the colonial violence of slavery and labor regimes that historically profited from spatialized violence left Black bodies marked as being "without Euro-centric history narratives, without land or a home, without ownership of self."[18] Fellow urbanites on a public bus may not be as directly connected to the state as law enforcement or immigration officers or public officials, yet they still wield social power when they treat the very presence of Blackness as a problem. The structuring ideology of everyday anti-Black racism empowers them by providing a sense of racialized group membership—belonging—to whites in Portugal and deputizing them to police that group's bounds.[19]

Aline asked, in an interview, a poignant rhetorical question: "So where is *my* country?" Aline, a forty-eight-year-old woman who worked in cleaning and relied heavily on transportation, was born in Angola to Cabo Verdean parents. There, though her parents had darker complexions, she explained that she was commonly mistaken for mulatta: "I was in Angola, and you know what I felt? . . . My friends were very Black, and I was lighter, and people would tell me to go back to my country! And . . . that was my country, where I was born." While her experience in Angola could possibly be connected to colonial-era sociopolitical relationships between Cabo Verdeans and colonial administrators, her experience in Portugal was specifically linked to race and the assumption of migrant status: "But in Portugal, oh, there's too much racism here. Racism! Sometimes [white Portuguese] tell [Black women], 'Vai para sua terra!' especially when we encounter them in public transportation. I will be sitting there, and someone tells me, 'Go back to your country' and 'This isn't your country.' And that is horrible, because think of this: So where is my country? Angola isn't, because they would tell me I was mulatta, but I am not. And then I come here, and they tell me I am Black, and it's the same thing." In the Portuguese metropole, colonial distinctions between different groups of lusophone

Africans are, at times, elided into a broader racialization and all the gendered, work-linked stereotypes it carries.

This brings us back to the way that multiple systems of oppression operate simultaneously in any given society. Emilia, a thirty-year-old cleaning worker, spoke at length about how everyday gendered anti-Black racism shaped white Portuguese people's ascribed understandings of racialized femininity. When she was pregnant, Emilia told me, public transit had become particularly difficult in that respect. While patriarchy, in general, frames women's role as their ultimate moral obligation and, relatedly, gendered assumptions frame visibly pregnant women as vulnerable and in need of protection, Emilia recognized how *her* status as a pregnant *Black* woman was excepted from the "rule" of respect and protection. "When I was pregnant, I suffered a lot of racism," she said bitterly. "People don't respect. They push or pass you when you enter the metro, the bus. They don't care if you're pregnant." She recalled an instance that made her exclusion plain: "I once asked a white woman if I could take her place, and she looked at me straight in my face and said, 'Go ask that woman over there for her seat, that woman who is of your color. In fact, why don't you go back to your country?' And I asked that white Portuguese woman for her seat because she was sitting in the space *reserved* for pregnant women." Emilia was denied the "privileges" of motherhood by a white woman who took the fleeting opportunity to exert racial dominance.

Talking Back

Commonly, when study participants shared their stories of everyday racism, I asked in Portuguese, "And did you react?" Everyday racism is a pervasive microstructure in the shadow of empire, and Cabo Verdean women engaged in a number of strategies to reject the legitimacy of their subordination, just as Nelida's friend had in declaring our group would stay in the restaurant and—worse yet for the racist waiter—that we would, in fact, be just as *uncivilized* as he imagined. Indeed, while a major instantiation of gendered anti-Black racism involves white Portuguese people challenging Black women's "right" to presence in certain spaces, the same racial and gender demography creates room for both exclusion *and* resistance. When I asked my standard question in Portuguese, some women responded in *kriolu*, "Nu papia pa tras." They *spoke back*—and more to the point, they expressed this resistance strategically, avoiding the Portuguese phrasing, *eu respondo*, meaning "I *responded*." To *responder* to someone's verbal attacks, in Portuguese, would signify a two-way relationship, but to *talk back*—to *papia pa tras*—signifies an unexpected response—it reveals, in the words of bell hooks, that the speaker is daring to disagree with structures of power and authority.[20] Everyday gendered anti-Black racism attempts to marginalize, subordinate, and silence, but speaking back as a *Cabo Verdean woman* highlights and rejects the assumed hierarchy of the interaction.

Most study respondents told me that they contested these microlevel acts of domination as they traversed. Some directly yelled at perpetrators, while others used sarcasm or logic to challenge the absurdity of the scenarios. They also responded to verbal assaults on their dignity by expressing pride in their Blackness and their womanhood. Marissa, a Portuguese citizen, is a dark-skinned Black woman with flowing braids who rightfully linked everyday racism to the racialization of Africans and African descendants in Portugal:

MARISSA That thing about racism, it's not going to end, even for people who are born here. They look at our face and say what they so frequently say: "Go back to your country! You are here to steal what is ours!"

CELESTE And how do you typically react when you hear people say things like that?

MARISSA Sometimes, I don't pay them any mind. You know why? Because they are also in *my* land! But also, I play around. I tell them with so much pride that I am so proud to be a Black woman, because they wish they could be Black like me, but they could never! I think that sometimes it's a matter of jealousy. They see us, happy, dressed well, hair perfect, working hard. They think we are vain, but really it's [their] jealousy. So when they say these things, I tell them, directly, "I am *so* proud to be a *mulher preta*" [Black woman].

In a world where gendered anti-Blackness pervades, Marissa speaks back rather than remain silent and in "her place" within the social hierarchy. She goes further, too, in demanding recognition of Blackness and all that it encompasses in a world where racist colonial ideologies attempt to narrow its scope and possibility.

Nilda, a fifty-five-year-old cleaning worker, also described responding to microaggression with unmistakable pride. In this case, on a bus ride, it was not what was said but what was *not* said—Nilda was accustomed to what she described as the "cold" nature of the white Portuguese, and she was unwilling to stomach it. "One day I was sitting on the bus," she remembered indignantly. "The seat was empty, so I went there to sit. A man entered and was looking for a seat, and the seat beside me was open, so I told him, 'Sir, come sit here.' He responded, 'No, no, no.' He stayed there leaning on the door. I said to him, 'You say no, because I am a *mulher preta* [Black woman], but I am extremely proud to be *preta*!'" She smiled at the memory: "He looked away, in complete shock." Everyday racism is perpetrated by people who uncritically occupy a dominant place in a particular hierarchical representation of reality; Nilda challenged that "reality" and the idea that Blacks are inferior to whites, and therefore suspicious, instead presenting her alternative worldview—one in which she could confidently affirm her pride in Black femininity.

Nearly thirty years younger than Nilda, Roseany was a twenty-eight-year-old home care worker who had been in Portugal just over one year when we met.

She, too, told me she talked back when she encountered everyday anti-Black racism, though her response took a different form. "When they tell me to go back to my country, I speak back!" she exclaimed proudly. "Because they are also in Africa, in Cabo Verde, in Angola. . . . There are many [white Portuguese who] end up staying there because they love *our* country [and] because Africa doesn't have the same discrimination like here in Portugal. They are very well received in Africa. And so, I tell them, they have always been in Africa and remain there to this day!" If her harasser is so upset with Black women's border crossing, in other words, Roseany points out that the "Portuguese" have long done the same. Further, by pointing out how the Portuguese are "very well received in Africa," she also squarely addresses their hypocrisy. Portugal is a former colonial empire that violently enforced its presence in Africa and maintains economic ties with former colonies after flag independence. Yet in contrast with African nations, Portuguese national belonging constructs the category of "citizen" (and therefore belonging) in opposition to (assumed) immigrant status *and* Black Africanness.

The Many Facets of Silence

As African and African-descendant women traverse the Portuguese urban environment, their undeniable presence squarely challenges Portuguese antiracial ideologies that attempt to other them as invisible in a racially hierarchical society. Yet there is a face to this invisibility on streets and sidewalks, in public transportation and other public spaces, within educational institutions, in national sports, and in workplaces. Indeed, in the words of Afro-feminists Akwugo Emejulu and Francesca Sobande, for Black women in Europe, "to exist is to resist."[21]

Everyday practices of contestation, however, come in many forms. Some women I met explained to me that silence was the best response to everyday anti-Black racism. These women said they recognized how people's ignorance blinded them to reason, and they figured acknowledging everyday racism with their words would further empower their harassers. "I used to react," said Emilia, fifteen years since her migration. "I used to fight with others on the bus, on the train, everywhere. Now I don't. I simply ignore them, because I am so accustomed to it! I am so accustomed to it that it doesn't affect me that much anymore because I feel bad for those people! Because here they are, in the twenty-first century, acting and thinking this way. Ignorant people. It's like . . . this is a woman or a man who is below my level; it's not worth arguing with someone like that." Emilia described herself as loving and kind to others but found it pointless to respond to the sheer ignorance of racists, whom she characterized as pathetic, unreasonable, and beneath her. Silence was her preferred way of "talking back."

Ariana thought much the same. For her, silence was a suitable nonverbal response that conveyed the idea that she stood way above her harassers and their actions, which, to her, revealed ignorance and a lack of education: "And when a person is ignorant, I don't attempt to talk. Because they will never understand. And so, silence is sometimes my response. I stay quiet and continue on my way." Ariana finds it more appropriate to carry on with her journey because she believes racialized ignorance goes hand in hand with an unwillingness to treat the so-called Other with basic respect. She did, however, add, "When it's something that happens right beside me, then I *will* say something, but it's usually not toward the person who is doing it, but more so to the person who it's being done to. I say, 'Listen, ignore those people and don't stoop down to their level, because that person is ignorant. We are better than that.' . . . Sometimes that's better than arguing with [white Portuguese directly]. They don't listen." By diverting her attention to those who are on the receiving end of racist practices, Ariana is able to offer them solidarity and support while also backhandedly responding to the perpetrator.

Noble intentions aside, Ariana remarked that her silence was also about offsetting the emotional toll of being subordinated by performing an unbothered, stoic demeanor. She later admitted, "I don't speak because I also feel nervous. But then I end up thinking about those things all day because it's disgusting to see that—disgusting." Not commenting was never about ignoring the racism, because that wasn't an option. Ariana's strategic silence remained embedded in a complex relationship of power in which the subordinated may feel *compelled* to remain silent, even if that silence looks to the oppressor like acquiescence.

Samira understood that whites could regulate public spaces on their own accord—and that they could summon the power of the state. Thus, she decided to remain silent when subject to racist harassment because she had a legitimate fear of violent retribution: "Sometimes I remain silent, because sometimes if we respond, maybe they will attack us. And so that ends up being bad for us because we must defend ourselves in some way. And imagine they call the police, and the police will think it's *our* fault." As time passes and more visibility is attached to the everyday practices of racialized violence in Portuguese society, it paradoxically makes Black people in Portugal more aware of the likelihood of police intervention should they raise the stakes of an interaction through direct resistance. For example, one video was heavily shared on social media the summer I met Samira. In the bystander footage, we see forty-two-year-old Cláudia Simões, a Portuguese woman of African descent, and her eight-year-old daughter have been verbally attacked by a bus driver in Amadora, Lisbon, because the girl had left her ticket at home. The bus driver reportedly ordered them to leave and shouted, "This is not your land, you are all here to ruin our country . . . you *pr-tos* are ruining our country, you all think you can ride without a ticket." The bus driver called the police, which led to a video of Simões being violently assaulted by a police officer on the side of the street. Simões reported further that out of view of the spectators, the officer had attacked her inside his vehicle and told her, "Scream now . . . *pr-ta*, monkeys, you are all garbage, shit."[22]

Here, as elsewhere, these violent scenarios reveal the entanglement of everyday gendered anti-Black racism with the power of the carceral state—and the degree to which whites are able to invoke the power of the state in order to regulate racialized belonging.

Conclusion

In a departure from a global epistemology of ignorance, in this chapter I situate knowing as rooted in the everyday experiences of Black, African-descendant women in Portuguese society. The fact that so many of them activate a critical consciousness throughout their everyday lives is a testament to their rejection of their own marginalization and nonbelonging, to the entire falsehood of antiracialism as a sustaining ideological system of racist denial. Cabo Verdean women's contemporary struggles for dignity as they go about their days in the shadow of empire—and their efforts to offer their own conceptions of belonging—are central to how they speak back and resist.

Further, as I have shown, a racialized and gendered demography of space shapes the ontology of Black women's bodies in the shadow of empire. Yet the public spaces I describe throughout this chapter constitute just one container of social action—of the practices of gendered anti-Black racism and resistance. Cabo Verdean women's interlocking identities are also manifested and monitored within more spatially bound contexts, like the private homes in which home care workers tend to the elderly and the semiprivate worksites in which institutional cleaning is performed. In the following chapters, I will dig into the performance of racialized emotional and body labor in gendered care work and how it, too, informs African-descendant workers' experiences, self-conceptions, and understanding of belonging in a country where entrenched colonial, racialized, and gendered hierarchies of privilege and power prevail.

4

Negotiating and Challenging Gendered Racism in Home Care

· ·

Sonia is an exuberant worker who goes to great lengths to ensure the elders under her care are happy. She sings playfully, dancing and joking around with them during home visits. And though she says she really shouldn't answer calls from clients on her day off, Sonia readily answers when Dona Andréia, a seventy-five-year-old widow whose one child has emigrated abroad, calls to check—will Sonia be visiting the next day? With a smile, she assures the woman not to worry; she'll be there. "She treats me well," Sonia explains sympathetically. "We have something special." Later, Sonia noted again that she was particularly fond of Dona Andréia because she treated her with "respect": "I never felt that she treated me differently because I was Black. At that level, I think we were simply friends. She needed me and I think, in a way, that my skin color didn't matter more than the love I could give."

Perhaps Dona Andréia seemed special in contrast to some of Sonia's other clients. When I met the care worker after her shift one evening, she was visibly flustered. Sighing, she told me the agitated elder she'd just visited had snapped at her, calling her a "dirty *pr-ta*":

I didn't really react, although I should have. I sat in my friend's car after work. I didn't enter my house. I guess I should feel bad about it. I sat there for a while and thought about him. The anger in his eyes. But I guess this is a pain you must overcome. I know I am a Black woman, and I am proud to be, you know. But . . .

it's hard sometimes. And they need to understand that we are the ones that are there to take care of them.

As a dark-skinned Portuguese woman of Cabo Verdean descent, Sonia is accustomed to encountering racist epithets on the job. In fact, so were most of my participants. As I delved through months of field notes and interview transcripts, it was clear to me that gendered anti-Black racism was not a fleeting and rare occurrence for participants but rather a fundamental component of Cabo Verdean home care workers' lives as they labor in the shadow of empire. As sociologist Pei-Chia Lan argues, the "construction of social boundaries—drawing lines between 'us' and 'them'—not only requires the political-legal regulation of citizenship and national borders but also involves symbolic struggles and local negotiations in the daily interactions between employers and workers."[1] I similarly argue that home care work offers a lens to understand how broader intersectional identities and oppressions of Portuguese society are experienced, perpetuated, and resisted by Cabo Verdean women in their everyday work interactions and experiences.

Indeed, while many studies have explored the intimate bonds developed between eldercare recipients and caregivers, my participants described a lot of these relationships as less than warm.[2] They spent so much of their time at work caring for elders, and nearly all respondents provided vivid examples of racist incidents with elders, colleagues, managers, and elders' families. Not only did they endure racist taunts; they noted in some cases that their white managers, supervisors, and frontline colleagues—almost all of them women—evaluated their work unfairly and treated them with a lack of respect. Together, these descriptions pointed to another of the many contradictions negotiated in workers' daily lives: these women feel marginalized because this society devalues both Black femininity and care work, yet for this reason, Black femininity is constructed as uniquely appropriate for performing paid care. In this chapter, I consider respondents' successes and failures in their quotidian negotiations of identity and labor, demonstrating how their racial and gendered political consciousness forms as they try to make a living and retain dignity in an allegedly "raceless" postcolonial state.

Forming a Gender and Racial Consciousness

Home care in Portugal is primarily live-out, meaning workers do not reside in the homes of their care recipients. It includes several teams of workers, including frontline employees, managers, and supervisors. Within any given team, the supervisor or supervisors delegate responsibilities, communicate information to workers, and manage employees' scheduling concerns. Each morning and in weekly meetings, workers are in contact with managers and agency directors, and they can call them on the phone as needed. Generally, however, workers enter elders' private residences alone or with just one co-worker.

A home care worker may visit up to eight elders in their private homes to provide a scheduled set of services each day. Workers engage in a great deal of "body
labor" associated with the daily care of the elderly: ranging anywhere from
checking vital signs and changing diapers and rubbing lotions, medicines, and
ointments on the body, to dressing, bathing, feeding, moving, carrying, shaving, and cleaning the body.[3] And in cases in which an individual needs intensive
round-the-clock care, a worker may have to wait to leave until the next worker
arrives. Workers may also drop off keys with a colleague scheduled to open the
next day, and workers who are scheduled to work a late-night shift also complete
certain tasks—like cleaning the home and changing the elder's linens—on time.
Some elders live alone and have little to no interaction with their family members, but at times families are present, and eldercare workers interact with the
elder's children, siblings, spouses, nieces and nephews, grandchildren, or visiting friends. Thus, while some elders have more autonomy and can delegate tasks
to the care worker, others communicate their needs and instructions through
their family members. Either way, home care workers labor across several occupational hierarchies, none of which is clearly organized. Workers interact with
several parties who can prescribe their work, which varies from one home and
client to the next.[4]

Home care workers also disrupt the racialized pattern of urban space because
they so frequently enter white Portuguese citizens' private spaces and interact
with their families. Of note, though they perform invisible care labor beyond
the purview of the public's eye, they are hypervisible within the confines of
elders' residences due to the intimate nature of their work. This invisible and
hypervisible social location, in turn, has made them especially attuned to detect-
ing the everyday gendered anti-Black racism amplified by the proliferation of
"superiors" in their work. As illustrated in the research on domestic workers in
the United States and Europe, the subordinate worker in a racialized and gendered caring arrangement like domestic work has always been associated with a
level of political consciousness on both counts. This research finds that the fundamentally different positions occupied by care workers and their (often white
women) employers provide a source of situational knowledge for workers who
came to understand the various levels of subordination and privilege embedded
in their work.[5]

Indeed, home care acts as a gendered and "racialized organization" where
routine everyday interactions among colleagues and "routine organizational
processes, racial schemas delineating racial sub- and super-ordination," mediate
the reproduction of material and social resources and rewards.[6] Consequently,
several respondents developed an intersectional political consciousness through
which they made sense of their working relationships as they navigated the gendered and racialized organization. Their reflections on gendered anti-Black racism focused centrally on interpersonal relationships with their white Portuguese
women colleagues. They described these interpersonal dynamics as particularly
challenging, emphasizing how white women colleagues treated African and

African-descendant workers with less respect than others and regarded their work as inferior. Solange, a twenty-eight-year-old woman of Cabo Verdean descent who had labored in home care for nearly five years, had a lot to say on this topic. Solange valued her work and expressed a deep passion for helping those in need, though she was clearly perturbed in her interview when she described the tension between her and her white women colleagues.

> We have colleagues that . . . perhaps it's not racism, but it's a feeling that they [white Portuguese women] show. They show us differences. They have different personalities and treat whites differently than they do Blacks. They are two-faced, that's how I can describe it. They treat us differently by race. It's a subtle difference, but it exists. Even among colleagues . . . there exists some type of prejudice. For example, sometimes they treat Blacks like they are more stupid. Like we don't understand, it's in the way they talk to us. . . . We are supposed to be professional, within quotes, but I don't feel it.

Solange's choice of the word *feel* here conjures the centrality of racialized affects in home care, or the sensations, emotions, and bodily reactions that reflect and reaffirm power relations.[7] As Encarnación Gutiérrez-Rodríguez suggests, affects evolve from material conditions and within a historical and geopolitical context "haunted by past intensities."[8] Black women like Solange labor within a context where gendered anti-Black racism pervades and where Black women's labor has been historically devalued such that this reality imprints a corporeal sense or feelings of devaluation among Black women workers. These *feelings* Solange and others describe stem from the subtle, yet apparent, dynamics of their working relationships: the quiet sigh from a white woman worker who silently changes shifts with a Black woman colleague, slyly condemning her five-minutes-late arrival; the white women who seem to distrust Black women workers' judgments regarding elders' health concerns; the frequency with which white women reprimand them for speaking *kriolu* with their Cabo Verdean co-workers. These moments and so many more, respondents insist, reflect unreconciled racialized and gendered tensions simmering among workers.

Solange's reference to "professionalism" also reflects important dynamics of modern work. In this team-based care sector, respondents were found to be increasingly pressured by managers to institutionalize what they referred to as "professional standards" of behavior among interracial staff—standards they understood as a blanket covering white colleagues' (and others') unreconciled animus toward Black people in general. Self-regulation is key to the professionalism push, becoming particularly consequential in a context where the state's antiracialism collides with organizationally prescribed workplace standards. Flora, a twenty-seven-year-old home care worker with four years' experience, argued, like Diana in chapter 3, that *pr-to* is akin to "n-----" in the U.S.

context, and so professionalism now dictated a different term: "They [managers] say 'of color' when referring to us. The people there, that's what they say when referring to us. So they don't say *pr-to* because they don't want to offend us when we have our meetings. The majority of workers are African now too. So that's why they use 'people of color.' We have to be professional."

This sort of professionalism, the use of respectful identifiers when referring to ethnic and racial minorities and the directive to maintain friendly and amicable relationships with co-workers, makes sense and feels useful for fostering a comfortable and professional working environment. Yet it still requires self-regulation. Race, per se, is not mentioned by respondents' managers and supervisors because, theoretically at least, race does not exist in Portugal. But to the respondents, the professionalism mandate is merely a coercive ideological norm preventing those most impacted by racism from discussing race even though they all understand its everyday salience. Here, as elsewhere in the world, the postindustrial appeal to professionalism acts as a micro-, interactional-level disciplinary mechanism that particularly impacts the most marginalized, demanding "self-control" in line with organizational definitions of what is and is not appropriate behavior and speech.[9]

Respondents became particularly passionate when they spoke about the quotidian work interactions in which white colleagues judged Black workers too harshly. Simple workplace problems were attributed to Black women's alleged stupidity, tardiness, or ignorance. As my respondents explained, they felt that their white colleagues adhered to gendered and racialized images of Black women so that no matter what words they used, bias still colored their normal everyday interactions. After all, colonial images have often framed Black women as unintelligent and careless.[10] (Studies find Black women in the U.S. workplace consistently describe being placed, by virtue of their race and gender, under intense scrutiny by colleagues who assume they are incompetent.[11]) Past research has centered the experiences of Black people who labor in white spaces, but the narratives I collected also show that white colleagues who are numerical minorities in the Black spaces of reproductive labor draw on stereotypes of Black African women as an inferior group as they typify their behavior, skills, and abilities. For example, Eva, the fifty-three-year-old Cabo Verdean home care worker we met in chapter 3, realized even after nearly ten years in this occupation that one of her white Portuguese woman colleagues discreetly speaks to the manager to reconfirm morning instructions. She does not trust that Eva has correctly communicated these instructions to the rest of the team: "There are certain jobs that they think a Black person, a person of color, is just not capable of doing, that only white workers are the ones that have that capability, that has enough intelligence to do that. I don't know why she would do it. She thinks I'm not smart enough to understand the message. That's where you feel the difference in the way whites treat other Black workers—in the treatment."

Carina, a Cabo Verdean worker of light complexion, was often misclassified by co-workers as white, and she told me that it made her privy to conversations her Black colleagues were not. Her eyes blazed and then her face hardened as she called out her white Portuguese colleagues during the interview:

CELESTE Do you feel that people that work in home care ever suffer from prejudice based on skin color or nationality?

CARINA Yes, yes! Yes, yes! I've heard of it already. I *know* that in our agency there are some white colleagues that constantly speak bad about "os pr-tos." And that's racism right there. Racism! White Portuguese colleagues constantly speak bad about Black people and use these words, constantly . . . those people are racist! They speak bad about "os pr-tos," "these damn *pr-tos*," "these damn *pr-tas*," "All they want to do is rob, ruin the place, they are all drug traffickers, that they smell bad, that they work beside us, don't know how to work, they are lazy."

Importantly, Carina's sharp testimony corroborates the "feelings" of unfairness and stereotyping described by darker-skinned workers. Amid management preaching about professionalism, Carina's story and others like it make it clear that daily interactions communicate to Black workers that they are regarded by white colleagues as part of an inferior group, typified by lower skills, abilities, and knowledge. Significantly, in my respondents' view, establishing criteria for professional conduct does little but create a tense environment in which Black women are subject to common, subtle, and elusive othering while also feeling compelled to stay quiet. In this way, professionalism may control white workers from engaging in explicitly racist behaviors, yet patterns of marginalization remain intact.

Who Has Authority?

In this tense working environment, Cabo Verdean women believe they are unable to openly criticize the inequitable treatment, lest they be perceived by management as "difficult" and noncompliant with professional standards. In this way, professionalism serves a disciplinary function, helping white women perpetuate domination by controlling the behavior of workers who occupy marginalized social locations within their workplace—and to do so without being questioned.[12]

Certainly, authority is complex. In classical sociological theory, it often refers to the power that one person, or *one group*, theoretically and practically has over another. To this, classical theorist Max Weber adds a refinement: authority carries an element of *legitimacy*. Actions and forms of domination carried out by those in power (or in relatively more powerful positions) are considered *legitimate* when the subordinate believes in the legitimacy of those in power. In fact, there is always a degree of denial or refusal of that legitimacy, necessitating that there are negative consequences to refusal. The essential conditions for authority thus include having a role that enables the authority figure to give orders in the name of the group and to back those orders with rewards for compliance among the subordinates.[13]

Critical race and feminist scholarship extend this understanding by emphasizing the historical racing and gendering of the cultural notions of authority and power: the dominant group is associated with whiteness and maleness, in many contexts across geography and time, and men and women of color are assumed a priori to be not only subject to that group's authority but *without* any authority of their own.[14] Classic social theorist William Edward Burghardt Du Bois famously argued that whiteness serves as a "public and psychological wage," whereas economically exploited working-class whites reap social status rewards that are bound to their characterization as non-Black.[15] These refinements are especially relevant with regard to care labor, since women of color in postindustrial societies are framed as "appropriate" to roles including reproductive labor, as the work and the women are both considered subordinate. It is no surprise that Black women in care work feel unjustly criticized by their white frontline colleagues, unequally tasked, and vulnerable to their white co-workers' assertions of authority.

At fifty-six years old, Constança remembered that when she arrived in Portugal, she worked overnight in a white Portuguese family's house, caring for the *senhora*'s children. After a few years, she found a job in cleaning services at an airport, then at a new nursing home near her neighborhood. When we met, Constança worked in home care and picked up part-time cleaning work. All along, as she has labored alongside white Portuguese and African-descendant colleagues, she has been fomenting a political consciousness:

CONSTANÇA I think that the *mulher branca* [white woman] always has it easier than us. Because for us . . . for the most part, we are given the most [*pauses to think*] . . . the most difficult jobs to do. They always give whites the easier jobs, and they give us the harder work. Or the work that is most filthy.

CELESTE Like what type of work?

CONSTANÇA [*Pauses to think*] An example is . . . there could be . . . some vomit on the floor. Sometimes they would be like "Oh, leave that there. I'm not going to send her [a white woman] over there because I'm going to send that *mulher pr-ta*."

CELESTE And who does that? Your manager? Supervisor?

CONSTANÇA It depends on who is there in that moment. You go and do [the filthy task] because it's what has to be done. You aren't going to say no to whether it's your supervisor or manager. It's *your* job and you have to do it. So you do it. But you feel anguished because it could have been anyone that could do it. Not just me . . . because I am *pr-ta* [Black woman].

The word *filth* was frequently applied to the work associated with Black women by white Portuguese (also recall that whites use the dehumanizing racist insult *pr-ta da merda*, as described in chapter 3). Cabo Verdeans told me, over and over, that white supervisors and colleagues reserved the heaviest, dirtiest, and simplest jobs for Black workers. A ten-year veteran of the care industry, Mafalda, summarized: "They [white colleagues] think that a person of the Black race doesn't have enough intelligence to complete certain tasks. Sometimes my white colleagues treat Blacks like they are donkeys. More ignorant and stupid. Like we can only do certain things, things that they typically do not want to do. Like clean filth and diarrhea, things like that." Cultural norms and capitalist exploitation stigmatize caring labor, as it is associated with femininity, yet Mafalda's incisive comments speak to the intersecting demonization of caring work and of Black femininity through the assignation of anything filthy to Black women. In a gendered occupation like home care, task delegation plays into a racial and gender hierarchy of being: white women's superiority in this gendered, devalued occupation is reaffirmed by assigning the most taxing labor—the dirty work—to Black women.

Interestingly, a few respondents told me that their hiring agency only allowed white Portuguese women to prepare food. Black women, however, were the ones to deliver the meals to elders. Though it is common for Black women to work as cooks in restaurants throughout Lisbon, this distinction here is significant. In her study on occupational segregation before 1970, Enobong Hannah Branch finds that white women were the only ones allowed to handle and prepare beef in the meatpacking industry because Black women were considered unclean.[16] It was thought that their hands would contaminate or "spoil" the products. Cabo Verdean home care workers shared that they, too, were told by white Portuguese elders that Africans were dirty and unclean. Thus, it could be that the racist and anti-Black colonial ideologies that associate Blackness with dirtiness (again, recall how common respondents were referred to as *pr-ta da merda*) subtly shape the segmentation of tasks surrounding food preparation in some workplaces.

Overall, these stories cue researchers like me to turn to the notion of what Melissa Wooten and Enobong Hannah Branch call "appropriate labor," or the imagined perfect, fit laborer for the job at hand. In this case, we see how race collides with gender to shape conceptions of the ideal care worker: a Black woman is the normative ideal worker for specific service needs of white Portuguese citizens.[17] But while she is appropriate to carry out certain tasks, she is racialized and gendered as a Black woman, and she finds the division of caring labor and legitimate authority in her workplaces is itself racialized and gendered. Rosalia, a forty-eight-year-old home worker with nine years of industry experience, reflected,

This [a Black woman being unable to give orders] always happens. It's racism, and I have experienced this. There's racism here. The women, the white women, they don't like Africans. Our skin color makes a big difference to them, like this.... I'll ask a white woman, "Hey, can you go over there and get this for me? Or can you take on this one woman, and I'll complete your home visit?" And she dismisses, "No, no, I can't!" But they are quick to not ask but tell us what we need to do. They want to control, but they can't be told what to do by Blacks.

Here Rosalia's comments draw forth how her white woman colleagues may exert racial dominance as they labor in a low-paid gendered occupation like home care. Rosalia truly felt disrespected and systematically excluded by her white women colleagues, even those doing the same low-status, low-wage work. Women like her did not recognize a shared status of subordination among African and African-descendant and white Portuguese workers but continual clashes between white and Black women with differing racial, ethnic, and cultural identities. This particularly appeared to crystallize around the cultural conception of control and authority, a reminder of how legitimacy itself is so often racialized and gendered.

Aside from one case, all the participants working in home care said they were exclusively managed by white native-born Portuguese women, who, in turn, often privileged white Portuguese women in filling the teams' supervisory roles. Interestingly, a few respondents reported that they did have foreign-born Ukrainian supervisors, a reality that further sedimented their belief in the depth of gendered anti-Black racism in their workplaces. In other words, though white women do find themselves in devalued occupations, working alongside Black women, white managers may still afford them higher-status roles. Belita, a thirty-six-year-old worker with a long tenure in home care and nursing homes, pointed out, "In terms of qualifications, the immigrant or resident or citizen can have better qualifications than the white Portuguese person, but the white Portuguese person will have more power or conditions to progress in the field or occupation while others do not. They will advance more in the same job alongside others [Black women] that are more qualified. I don't know why. Maybe racism, maybe xenophobia. Whatever it could be, I'm not sure. But I have experienced and observed this firsthand in my institution."

Belita herself had been with her agency longer than many of her supervisors, and she was unsure whether to attribute the differential allocation of resources (like job status) to racism or xenophobia. Scholarship similarly spotlights how racism and xenophobia are entangled via the discrimination directed against foreigners in Europe, or what Inês Maria Calvo Brandão refers to as "xeno-racism" in the Portuguese context.[18] Yet the difficulty that Belita expresses, I argue, also relates to how Black people in Portugal (as in much of Europe) are often assumed to be foreign, regardless of legality.[19] That is, their racialization (based on, but not limited to, their phenotype) excises them from the Portuguese body politic, and thus, their foreignness is assumed *because they are Black*. This may translate to differential rewards within workplaces; Belita is a Portuguese citizen, but she comments that her managers promote and prefer white Portuguese women over Black women, regardless of the Black women's citizenship. In this sense, it is the same gendered anti-Black racism that limits the advancement of citizens like Belita and shapes the privilege of women citizens that are racialized as white in this predominantly Black work setting where citizen and noncitizen Black women labor. Importantly, because intersectional inequalities are relational, the promotion of white women is systematically paired with the devaluation of Black women.[20] They are symbiotic, as if one simply cannot exist without the other.

So how do white women end up occupying the modal category of superior workers even in a care sector where Black women are framed as ideal workers? I have already discussed how pervasive images of gendered Black servility might impact assessments of Black women's labor performance. The consequence is that Black women may find it difficult to establish bonds with white colleagues and supervisors. Respondents further reported that white managers gravitated toward and aligned themselves with white women workers. They registered all sorts of subtle yet apparent dynamics in workplaces, perceiving managers directing more eye contact toward white women colleagues during team meetings or walking side by side and chatting with white staff during breaks and on the way to team meetings. They *feel* the braided effects of racialized feminization subtly operating within interpersonal dynamics in workplaces where white women may also be rewarded with a psychological wage. And as research shows, the difficulty in forging collegial, congenial relationships means that they are less likely than other workers to be treated with respect, let alone elevated into leadership roles.[21]

Thus, in home care, everyday organizational practices like task delegation and performance evaluations exacerbate social inequalities and construct differences among otherwise equal employees because they import racialized and gendered power hierarchies at many turns.

Family Members of the Elders

An excerpt from my field notes reads:

> Constança and I enter a small corner café located on the outskirts of Lisbon. A bell rings as we open the door and enter a familiar setting: Delta coffee posters and dishware, a Portuguese comedy talk show plays on a television that hangs above a polished metal counter with Sagres and Super bock draughts on tap. An older white Portuguese man sits at a table in the back of the café and calls over to Constança in a familiar tone. "Menina, tudo bem?" Constança looks over at him, smiles, and goes to the counter to order her usual afternoon espresso. The man seems to be in his seventies, he wears a small black cap, a gray wool vest, and a pair of black slacks. A metal walker sits just beside his table. Constança approaches us holding carefully onto a small porcelain saucer with a white espresso cup with

one hand as she carries her purse with the other. "How are you today, feeling well? Everything is well?" The man, nodding in agreement, responds, "I'm the same as yesterday. I'm OK."

The man's wife eventually enters the café and sits beside her husband. Without making eye contact or greeting Constança directly, the woman asks her whether her husband had anything to eat. After calling over to the café attendant to take her order, the woman turns and looks at me and asks me if I would like anything to eat. Constança quickly answers for me and tells the woman that we ordered earlier, though we actually didn't. We sit a few tables behind the couple and wait as they converse. Constança whispers, "If I don't go, they will tell on me. His wife gets angry. I am supposed to walk around the block with him or just sit here as he gets his little coffee, maybe a piece of bread. But today he just sits around." After fifteen minutes or so, the wife gets up from her seat and tells us that they are ready to go. Constança immediately walks over to the older man and helps him out of his chair; he holds onto Constança's shoulders and lets out a slight grunt as she secures him from his waist to help him keep balance. Then Constança secures his hands on the handles of the metal walker and holds tightly onto the man's arm as they slowly make their way out of the café. All the while the wife stands close by and observes the entire exchange but does not participate.

Elders' families are often central fixtures in the lives of home care workers, whether they live with the client or not. This can create a sense of being watched or monitored, creating tensions just as easily as it might spur everyday conversation. Edna, a thirty-four-year-old who told me she had been with her agency for four years, attributed her recent decision to leave the organization to the vigilant criticism of her elder clients' omnipresent family members—particularly their daughters, sisters, and wives. In retail work, she felt, it would be easier to complete her work. Other respondents said similarly that they preferred working with people who resided alone, though they might become more emotionally attached to workers as quasi-family members, as their solo living provided more autonomy for care workers to do their jobs.

Of course, the vigilance respondents noted relates to a well-examined issue in the literature on care work: women relatives (given the fact that care labor is, in societies attached to gendered familialism, associated with women—female relatives like daughters and wives especially[22]) may feel guilty about outsourcing the gendered and familial work of eldercare and attempt to overcome this feeling by appointing themselves as supervisors of paid women care workers, as it were.[23] However, while the guilt of not performing one's gendered duties might explain some of the tension they felt in their interactions with women family members, the Cabo Verdean workers I spoke to also surmised that it was their status as Black women that fueled the hostility they felt when interacting with men and women family members. To them, it seemed elders' family members lobbed overt gendered anti-Black racism toward African-descendant care workers and went to great lengths to surveil and control Black women's labor and bodies.

Workers sharing such observations often expressed what seemed a somewhat contradictory sentiment regarding their appropriateness for performing care. On the one hand, they understood their social location as being determined by systemic race and gender inequality within the labor market and how it naturalized cultural conceptions about who was appropriate for performing reproductive labor. The role of care worker is essentialized as something that Black women are suited for—and there is a cycle wherein the job is both stigmatized and stigmatizing.

On the other hand, their relegation to care work thrusts them into the private homes of white Portuguese elders, many of whom had never engaged with Black people at such an intimate level before. They found that elders' relatives sometimes refused their labor because they associated white women with superior labor performance and African-descendant women with long-standing "controlling images"[24] of illness, filth, and criminality. In the context of home care, family members drew on these images to occasionally outright refuse Black women's care in the private space of a vulnerable senior. In this sense, Cabo Verdean women experience the effects of conflicting discourses. They are hypervisible as "appropriate" care workers even while the conflation of whiteness with Portuguese identity renders them invisible in Portuguese society. Their entrance into elders' homes also remains subject to suspicion and regulation given their gendered racialization as hypervisible Others. In this way, care workers negotiate multiple forms of quotidian invisibility and hypervisibility, straddling a precarious social location where the intersection of their race and gender means they are at once preferred *and* scorned simultaneously.

A number of the Cabo Verdean women I spoke to also recounted scenarios in which family members assumed, when something went missing, that they had stolen from their clients. Indeed, the literature on domestic work similarly illustrates how frequently employers accuse workers of theft.[25] In her now classic work on Black domestic workers in Boston, Massachusetts, Judith Rollins argues that employers' accusations of *or* even tolerance of stealing serve an important ideological function, as they justify the material and psychological exploitation of Black women domestic workers by their white women employers. While families who seek eldercare support from agencies represent a more socioeconomically diverse group than those who typically hire full-time domestic workers, the latter being more collectively affluent, the fact that accusations of stealing remain frequent suggests that the racialized and psychological dimensions of caring labor remain intact.[26] As caring labor has long been bound to racialized, gendered, and classed notions of servility and deference, and stealing supports the negative stereotypes of Black people, accusations of stealing recounted by participants may relate to how care recipients and their families attempt to carve out power in a context where authority has to be negotiated among the three parties: the worker, the employing organization, and the care recipient and/or family member.

Consider Aleida, a thirty-two-year-old eldercare worker of Cabo Verdean descent, who was among the participants who recounted stories involving accusations of theft. She had worked for the company for six months when a client's daughter called her supervisor with a serious complaint: 180 euros, previously stashed under a mattress, had disappeared on a day that Aleida and a white Portuguese colleague entered her mother's home. The woman was, she claimed, certain that Aleida had stolen the money. In fact, an investigation turned up evidence that Aleida's white Portuguese colleague had committed the theft. As she recalled, the suspicion made her work "terrible":

> So she [her supervisor] tells me, "Money disappeared. It was underneath the mattress. It disappeared. 180 euros." I mean, I turned pale! The woman's daughter called my supervisor and told her that she was certain that I stole it. And the other colleague was white. . . . But it wasn't the elder that complained. It was the elder's daughter. She was someone who would often complain over who was coming to the house. Who is entering the home, who is there? She never accepted new people, especially if they were African. She says she isn't racist, but if the worker is African, everything is different. If it's a Portuguese woman, everything is fine. But if it's an African, she follows you around. To have someone there following you around your first days of work, watching you as you work . . . it's terrible! I know I went to the home with her [the white Portuguese colleague]. And also, it was the first time that I ever went there, so she had to show me around. At one point, she asked me to put something in the kitchen. It was at that time that my colleague went into the woman's bedroom, and that's where the money was. She was a pig because she knew I didn't have any way to defend myself. Right? As a Black woman . . . the Portuguese just think that we are always doing something wrong. That we are criminals.

Aleida's positioning—referring to herself "as a Black woman"—revealed how her politics of race and gender consciousness have led her to see herself as doubly disadvantaged within Portugal's hierarchical social and power structures. Her account speaks to the way a white peer could take advantage of the power differential, assuming lesser surveillance and the racialized scrutiny that would come to her Black woman co-worker as family members of elders also draw on negative stereotypes regarding Black women's criminality. Thus, family members *and* white co-workers could use the presence of the alleged "inferior" Black woman to reinforce their position of power within home care, where authority is redirected from the household to the organization.

The gendered and racialized surveillance of Black women's bodies and labor performance topped the list of complaints for many respondents when it came to their relationships with the family members of elders in their care.

Eldercare work, certainly, is a specific case: it involves relationships of care, vulnerable clients, and stakes no lower than life itself. Women in my study told me they sometimes became emotionally invested, going to great lengths to provide supportive and altruistic care, especially to those who were ill or dying. However, they insisted that elders' vulnerability was often utilized as a justification for family members' racist behavior and unfair scrutiny of the Black women hired to provide that care. Alongside family members, workers expressed feeling traumatized or distressed should a person under their care slip away, yet their intimate proximity to the family rendered them the most visible, readily available scapegoats for absorbing families' frustration, anger, and grief. In such intense moments, family members' biases against Black women seemed to surface. For example, Ana Paula, a home care worker with a three-year agency tenure, said, "When things are hard, we also feel it."

Ana Paula, at the time of our interview, was caring for Dona Maria, who had begun to show visible symptoms of Alzheimer's disease. Dona Maria's children hired the agency to help their father cope with the ups and downs of caring for his wife through her last days. Ana Paula still recalled the first time she met Dona Maria and her husband, Nuno, who at that time seemed to simply overlook her. He made eye contact with her white colleague, but, Ana Paula said, "He treated me like I wasn't even there. I was no one to him." But over time, as Dona Maria got worse, Ana Paula's invisibility shifted, and she became a focal point for Nuno's frustrations. She described how he was "always in a bad mood": "I think he called to complain and spoke to the managers. He screamed something like, 'Oh, your *pr-ta doesn't know anything*!' I think he did the same thing to another worker, he screamed at her, '*Pr-ta*!'" In other words, for Black women care workers, invisibility and hypervisibility are two sides of the same coin in the shadow of the empire, each a punishing condition deployed according to the variable salience of race, gender, and everyday anti-Black racism throughout their working relationships.

Marginalized by the Vulnerable

The vulnerability of the older population, which care workers repeatedly referenced in our interviews, is an especially well-circulated narrative in Portugal, where the population is aging and fertility rates continue to slide. In the small neighborhoods of Lisbon, this "graying" of the population is evident: the patrons of buses, cafés, markets, and city squares are predominantly groups of older individuals. Gray-haired men spend entire weekends chatting, playing cards, and reading newspapers in neighborhood parks and public spaces. It's enough to make Portuguese citizens, gripped by the remnants of the economic crisis, fret, *Who will take care of the vulnerable elders?* One informant, a former nanny and recent entrant to the field of home care, put it this way: "There are a lot of older people abandoned in their homes within the center of Lisbon. There are a lot of vulnerable old people. You see it on the news. Portugal has a very old population; it's aging drastically. So they need us." Another reflected similarly that the elders "are like children, very vulnerable. We need to listen to their complaints, and we need to act like we understand because they *have* to trust us. Sometimes, we are all they have."

This framing of Portuguese vulnerability serves a dual purpose. While it encourages workers to perform what they determine is good care, it also positions Cabo Verdean women as morally superior to the families of the elders they care for. Pierrette Hondagneu-Sotelo finds that Latina domestic workers in the United States engage in this "oppositional framing," blaming the mothers of the children they care for for being neglectful of their children.[27] Tamara M. Brown finds a similar dynamic among the West Indian nannies and childcare providers she interviewed in Brooklyn, New York.[28] The Cabo Verdean home care workers I interviewed in Portugal at times saw the "choice" of these families (the children, grandchildren, or siblings of elders) to outsource elder responsibilities as just that—a selfish choice shaped by what they described as the Portuguese people's lack of desire to spend time with their relatives.

Constança, whom I introduced earlier, frowned as she discussed an elder woman's son. "She has one son," she forcefully stated, "and he's basically a neighbor because he lives very close to her, but he doesn't go every day. Only during the weekends, only Saturday." Constança juxtaposes the woman's son with her own family members, stressing that in Cabo Verde, an expansive set of family members and friends take care of the elders. She believes the Portuguese are selfish and individualistic rather than family-centered like African families more generally:

Celeste, I think in general that the Portuguese here don't really like having the elderly in their homes. Not like Africans. Because her son is married now, he has his wife and his kids. I think that the man's wife doesn't allow his mother to live there with them because the older woman always says, "I don't know why my son doesn't come and live here with us" . . . because her house is big. She has a big house, but she lives alone! She has a house with three bedrooms and two bathrooms, but she's alone. And her son . . . well. She's always saying, "Why don't they all come here to live with me? We all fit here." I don't understand that, but I think in general the Portuguese don't like to live in the same house with their parents, they don't like it, they don't like their elders!

Interestingly, Constança's remarks overlook structural conditions (employment) or cultural conditions (gendered care expectations) that may help explain why the woman's son may not provide direct care to his mother. Yet this narrative appeared to provide workers with a sense of value and meaning in the important work they performed daily, setting them in contrast to their care recipients' own family members, whom they viewed as morally inferior.

It is also implied that Constança was referring not solely to the *Portuguese* per se but *white Portuguese*, given that she herself held Portuguese citizenship. In contrasting Cabo Verde and Portugal and the white Portuguese and African descendants like herself, informants like Constança also articulated a collective ethic of care as they described their work as a community responsibility. In doing so, they emphasized their fulfillment of an important social responsibility as they pushed back against the indignities of performing so-called devalued, stigmatized work within a society that is far from inclusive of African and Afro-descendant families. They affirmed the importance of their *visibility* as caregivers of the most vulnerable.

Even so, the oppositional framing picked up by workers does tend to occlude the role played by care/welfare/migration regimes that shape racialized and international divisions of reproductive labor, and the public discourse of vulnerability is not applied equally to African migrants and their families. As Portugal attempts to combat an ongoing economic crisis through the partial retrenchment of the welfare state, its society is exacerbating the disadvantages facing those marginalized by their race, gender, class, and national affiliations,[29] meaning that the vulnerable elders, regarded as "deserving," are helped by caregivers who are themselves in need of significant care. The occupational hazards of nurturant home care work—stunted social mobility and economic insecurity along with the physical hazards of performing strenuous body labor—reflect how bodies carry different amounts of social worth. As in the United States, European societies' anti-immigrant sentiments intersect with systemic racism to build a consensus around the unequal distribution of the state's rights and responsibilities, including concrete provisions like financial aid alongside more enigmatic, boundless resources like dignity and belonging.[30]

This situation suffused relations at the organizational level too. Several respondents noted that their organizations' emphasis on white Portuguese clients as *vulnerable* subjects essentially neutralized any recognition of workers' own precarity and vulnerability. While they experience an onslaught of racial slights while caring for aged citizens, for instance, these incidents are routinely ignored or dismissed by management and non-Black colleagues. Aleida, mentioned earlier, was both angry and resigned as she said of her profession, "The prejudice and racism are always there; it's always there. It's part of the work." She and others noted that elders might call the agency to urge them to send a white care worker (as they feared a Black woman's touch could make them sick), or they may treat them rudely, disrespectfully, and with distrust. They commonly endured being called *pr-ta* by the seniors in their care. Again and again, they faced the consequences of stereotypes as they interacted with clients and their families—as has been documented in research on care work in other countries.[31]

The comments workers shared served as stark illustrations of the everyday anti-Black racism they encounter, as well as how carefully my respondents must manage their own emotions as they are routinely devalued.[32] I noticed that during our conversations, many respondents stressed that elders were *racist by nature*, socialized in an increasingly outdated society that overtly normalized Black servitude and dehumanization. In this way their overt expressions of racial hatred and disgust could be regarded as not only incorrigible but also understandable. But those expressions could be shocking:

> We have elders that clearly say in our faces that they don't like *pr-tos*. (Mafalda)

> Sometimes they say things like "Oh, I don't know who that is, because you all have the same face. You are all *pr-tas*, you are all the same to me!" (Solange)

> They have their prejudices—because, on the day to day, they say things in my work like "Oh, even though you are African, you are still a good person." Because for them, [normally] if you are an African person, you just *can't* be a good person. (Adriana)

> At work we suffer from a lot of prejudice. For example, there are a lot of elders that say, "Oh, it was that *pr-ta*!" if something disappears. (Flora)

> Yes, [the elders] call us *pr-ta*! Scream at us, "*Pr-ta*!" ... "*Pr-ta* whore!" (Marcia)

As this narrative constantly surfaced during our conversations, I began to understand how "generational differences" served as a coping mechanism for workers enduring a barrage of slurs and stereotypes. So, too, did their simultaneous affirmations of pride in being Black women and descriptions of maintaining equanimity in these situations to reconfirm their dignity as they performed devalued work. Adriana discussed how, to her, refusing to validate everyday racism means ignoring it in her work:

> But I also think that prejudice also depends. It depends on who acts in a prejudiced way and who feels discriminated against. When an elder tells me "Oh, I don't want you because you are *pr-ta*," I don't valorize that. Because I feel like "This, that person doesn't know me. Perhaps if he or she knew me, and didn't base everything on appearance, they would see that I'm not like that." That's what I would do. I would say, "Listen, unfortunately and fortunately for you, I am here to provide a service." I have the mentality of an employer. "If you don't want me to provide you this service, then, well, you will have to call my manager and tell my manager that. Because I am here to represent an institution." I don't valorize that. Why? Because I feel like this: they are old, and I am here. I have to live here too. I need to live my life as easy as possible. So, I am not going to live in racism. I won't allow their ignorance to affect me. If you valorize it, then it becomes sort of real, you know.

Adriana's remarks highlight how she employs the language of the organization to offset the emotional toll of being devalued by clients. (Of course,
workers who labor informally, contracted directly by the care recipient or their
family, have no ability to do the same.) They also importantly show another
dynamic: how workers use nonreactivity to limit elders' power over them,
their self-conceptions, and their lives. When Adriana spoke, her whole counte-
nance changed. She sat upright, nearly proclaiming, in a proud and explanatory
style, that she doesn't "valorize" racist remarks. Sociologist Adia Harvey Wingfield's important work on tokenism in the workplace is instructive here in that
she finds Black male workers in predominantly white U.S. workspaces spend an
enormous amount of energy on "emotional labor," or the effort to bring their
visible emotions in line with institutionalized feeling rules, practicing restraint
and concealing their frustration with race-related dynamics and issues on the
job rather than risking unemployment.[33] In line with my earlier discussion of
professionalism, Lisa Ruchti also reports that women nurses experience a
slew of racist and sexist comments from people under their care, yet they may
worry that their responses to those scenarios may paint them as unprofessional
in the eyes of other charge nurses.[34] Ruchti refers to these tense encounters with
patients as "intimate conflicts," as they reflect the work nurses must carry out
as they attempt to forge trust with patients. Though the Cabo Verdean workers I interviewed may labor within more ethnically and racially diverse settings,
they too encounter institutional and economic pressures to suppress their emotional states and discount their vulnerability to raced and gendered aggression
from clients.

Other institutional pressures undeniably shape the ways workers respond
to racist incidents at work. Jason Rodriquez's research on certified nursing assistants also illustrates how reports of clients' negative treatment are
often dismissed by leadership, who attribute elders' violence and verbal slurs
to Alzheimer's disease or dementia as if they have no real effect. This framing,
Rodriquez argues, not only strips elders of their agency; it naturalizes violence
as an assumed, and relatively harmless, occupational hazard.[35] Like Rodriquez, I
found that respondents' rhetorical framing of elders' racism was both a coping
mechanism and the result of organizational impulses. Bianca, a care worker of
two years, described her agency's use of illness and vulnerability discourses to
brush off workers' complaints of racist aggression:

> BIANCA There is one elder that one day said to me, "Oh, . . . so and so . . . ,
> 'vai para sua terra, *pr-tá*'" [go back to your country, *pr-tá*]. But some-
> times people don't respond and let it pass, because even though it's
> happening, sometimes people feel "Oh, it's a sick person, so that's why
> they are saying that."
> CELESTE Why do they say that—*Oh, they are sick*—and who says that?
> BIANCA Because that lady has Alzheimer's disease, and she also is a bit
> slow mentally. And because of that, they . . . our managers tell us not

to respond because she's so sick. I guess it's the feeling that "they don't know any better."

Bianca chuckled at my naïveté when I asked whether she had been warned by managers about the potential for racist encounters with elder clients under her care: "It's Portugal, Celeste. What do you expect?" No one had warned her because everyday racism in Portugal is normalized. It's a no-brainer that the marginalization Black women like Bianca experience in public will be present—if not amplified—in private. But in this sense, the characterization of similar actions within a working relationship as a matter of illness or age minimizes the reality confronted by African descendants in every sector of Portuguese society. The power of Portuguese antiracialism is that it denies the reality of racism while naturalizing and downplaying it. The dominant group simultaneously endorses the nonexistence of racism and maintains it as a commonsense way to understand the world around them.[36]

In one heated interview, Solange, who you'll recall had five years' employment in home care, shared an experience in which she seemed to wrangle with the problem of whether a client's racism was evidence of mental illness or, well, being a racist person:

CELESTE Is it difficult sometimes when you work with someone that is sick or old? So, they say something racist, but they are also ill with things like Alzheimer's sometimes.
SOLANGE Well, for example, I remember there was a situation. We had a man that was bedridden, and he was sick with a fever. And my other Cabo Verdean colleague and I went there to give him something to eat. He never said anything pertaining to our skin color or anything, but that day he let it escape! "You all do this because you're *pr-tas*! Damn *pr-ta* whores are the ones that do this!" But I don't know if that was racism that always existed in him that he never let emerge. But that day when he had a fever and everything, he let it come out!

Solange was distraught, though this was far from her only story. In fact, over three-quarters of the women home care workers I interviewed indicated that they had experienced overt racialized misogyny and gendered anti-Black racism from elders while they were working. When asked whether they knew what to do in a situation like that, only three workers responded with possible interventions. Three informants indicated that they would talk to their managers, while the remaining felt that little could be done—the clients are old and mentally suffering, and it would be impossible for them to unlearn their racism at this point in their lives. The women often seemed resigned that their careers would always feature racist treatment. My aim here is not to paint workers as powerless but to highlight how workers' choice not to report incidents is itself, in part, an agentic response (akin to the women in the previous chapter who used silence when verbally attacked in public) as well as shaped by the demands of the organization.

The impression that racism is inevitable at work mirrors Joan Acker's notion of "organizational logics," or the taken-for-granted policies and practices that legitimize a hierarchy among co-workers.[37] Adding to Acker's discussion, which primarily centers gender inequalities, critical race scholars argue that the workplace is nowhere near race-neutral, as racial ideology is often a tacit and taken-for-granted facet of organizational life.[38] Cabo Verdean home care workers' stories convey the embeddedness of antiracial ideology in their occupational logic. Racism is treated as a relic (in the antiracial ideology of the country), which explains its remnants among the elderly, and mental illness (in the ideology of elder vulnerability) is used to explain racist incidents because racism is obviously not contemporary; therefore it is as if racism is just another symptom for care workers to manage (in the ideology of professionalism). In this way, organizational logics reflect and reproduce social norms and further conceal Black women workers' experiences. As the challenges that Black women face when interacting with elders are rarely fully addressed by management, the organization reproduces the racially charged relationships between workers and care recipients.

Skin Color

Categories of analysis such as color, gender, class, and race are not sets of essential or fixed characteristics but situational, socially constructed social identities. As such, not all my informants experienced the same treatment, even though each entered a structured environment in which status, the delegation of responsibility, and the valuation of the work all appeared to be shaped by race and gender. Skin color surfaced as an additional marker of structural differentiation among a largely Black workforce including Cabo Verdeans alongside the growing presence of Ukrainians, Brazilians, and African workers from São Tomé, Guinea-Bissau, and Angola.

Deborah was one of those who spoke about the way colorism inflected the racism she experienced in the workplace. A passionate Cabo Verdean eldercare worker with light skin and curly golden-brown dyed hair, Deborah connected her phenotype to the differences in the prejudice she and her Black co-workers endured on the job:

> This is how it works here. The darker your skin, the more prejudice you experience. I suffer less prejudice than my colleagues that have darker skin because I don't have really dark skin. . . . People with kinkier (*cabedju bedju*[39]) hair or darker skin will experience more prejudice. For example, at work they, the old people, they told me, "Oh, you aren't so dark like your colleagues. You don't have such coarse hair either." It's a way they differentiate between one *pr-ta* and another *pr-ta*, though we are all *pr-tas*.

Hazel-eyed Carina, the lightest of all my informants, strongly identifies as a Black woman and detailed a number of overtly racist incidents in her job search yet pointed out that she was commonly mistaken for white. When I asked if she dealt with racism in her eldercare work, she said,

> No, because I think in their minds, I am *branca* and not *negra*. Elders don't realize I'm Black, and so I don't experience any of that with them, but others [Black workers] do. And when I confront this one [white] colleague about her racism, she tells me, no, I'm not Black. And I tell her, no, my race is the Black race. And she tells me that I'm *not* [Black], that it is not my race. But if you are a mixture, you are still Black. My mom is not white, and my dad is not white. My parents are both Black. And when I tell colleagues and elders that I am also Black, they tell me no, that I'm not. Because I'm light and have hair like this [*touches curls*].

Carina was clearly upset as she discussed this dynamic. She felt fortunate that she avoided many of the racially hostile interactions so familiar to co-workers with darker skin yet angry that her white Portuguese colleague dismissed both her complaints about racism *and* her racial identity. She was privileged by phenotype, but colorism meant race and racism remained a source of significant emotional injury. Importantly, I still found that status distinctions (like worker, supervisor, and manager) as shaped by race were apparent across all my interviews, and lighter Cabo Verdean women like Carina and Deborah did not appear to experience immediate advantages in this realm. What workers' narratives *do* suggest, however, is that phenotype is an important day-to-day marker of differentiation used by elders and their families when interacting with workers of African descent. Lighter skin may facilitate positive relationships relative to the hostile ones described by other workers, and that may lead to higher job satisfaction. Simply, workers want to be treated with respect and dignity because they deserve to be treated with respect and dignity. And while opportunities for occupational advancement in care service work are negligible, the mere ability to forge positive relationships with (and avoid complaints from) elders and their families is likely to facilitate more positive relationships with supervisors and managers. Colorist differences in the treatment of Black workers may become even more pronounced as lusophone African workers increasingly respond to Portugal's racially segmented job markets and state expansion of home care services (tied to the graying crisis). Greater levels of segregation may lead to greater reconfiguration of workplace inequalities around social categories of difference and oppression, including skin color.

Talking Back

Despite the strength of Portuguese antiracialism, Cabo Verdean care workers are far from dismissive of the racism evident in their own lives and workplaces.

Respondents frequently activated their racial and gender political consciousness in our interviews, questioning the organizational logic, for instance, that covered for elders' everyday gendered anti-Black racism by attributing it to (and exculpating it on account of) age and illness. Take Catarina, who explained her unease around supervisors and managers who employed this logic. As she pointed out, she doesn't believe that she or her family would suddenly manifest racist attitudes if they became sick in the future. In fact, she recounted a particularly memorable incident when a researcher visited her agency. The researcher was so astounded by elders' constant barrage of racist remarks toward caregivers that he told the director of the institution that the treatment of Black workers by elders was unacceptable. In response, the white director shuffled workers' assignments so that no Black worker would care for one of "the most racist" elders observed by the researcher. However, Catarina critiqued, "If they [managers] know that a worker is experiencing racism, it's not like they throw the elder out of the institution, no. But they take the worker away from that particular elder. And in my opinion, they are doing the wrong thing. Because *that* is racism, in my opinion—to just switch a *mulher negra* [Black woman] with a *mulher branca* [white woman]? That's just accepting racism, that's what it is! Accepting that this happens, well, that's racism."

As Catarina has gleaned, this managerial strategy paradoxically shifts the problem from racist behavior to the "problem" of Black workers representing the organization. When I later asked Catarina what she believed would be an appropriate step for management to take, she articulated a sophisticated analysis that included her understanding of the perpetuation of racism via a refusal to institutionalize mechanisms of support for workers of color:

> I would tell them [elders and elders' families] that racism is not accepted. I would say, "Here we do not participate in racism, we do not accept racism, and we will not accept racism here because we work with Africans here. We have all races working here." So, in my opinion, the management needs to take a strong position on this, and if the elder or their families, or whoever doesn't accept this, well then, they cannot be part of the institution. That's what I would do. It needs to be institutionalized. It needs to be a real statement like "Racism is not accepted here."

Catarina broadened her view of racism from everyday practice to institutional racism and presented an alternative vision of an ideal workspace: one that actively and affirmatively rejects racist behavior while acknowledging the real impact of racism throughout society and within the organization. This is predicated on the idea that the eradication of racism requires active participation by the organization's higher-status workers (who largely control the labor process) rather than the mediation of the visibility of Black workers in certain problem spaces. While overt, sustained resistance to an organizational logic that reinforced the inevitability of racism was not apparent in interviews, narratives like Catarina's show that workers are well aware of the quotidian organizational practices and norms that reproduce racial and gender inequalities, deepening divisions between white and Black women workers even in a predominantly Black work setting.

Overall, it seemed to me that workers went about their days carving out their own private strategies to resist the racialized devaluation of their work, bodies, and identities by managers, supervisors, elders, and elders' families. While these strategies do not fully unsettle the organizational devaluation of Black women's work that remains so consequential in the lives and careers of Afro-descendants in the shadow of empire, they do illustrate Black women's relentless fortitude in carving out dignity in their work.

Conclusion

Participants' experiences highlighted in this chapter illustrate how they navigate the hypervisibility of their racial and gender status as well as the invisibility rendered by antiracial ideologies. In the midst of widely accepted, highly gendered, and racialized controlling images that construct Black women as suitable for yet incompetent in performing stigmatized work, the accounts here reveal that white colleagues and clients discount Black women's labor performance and capabilities. Second, in workplaces in which the modal category of authority and competence is vested in white femininity, the weight of racial dynamics creates a scenario in which Black women's performance of imposed standards of professionalism (a.k.a. silence) obscures the pervasive racism they encounter on a daily basis. The rhetoric of professionalism, along with the institutional adaptation to elders' racism, further reproduces the invisibility of race and normalizes white women, unencumbered by the weight of workplace racial dynamics, as natural leaders. Third, in refusing to engage with colorism or meaningfully address racist work experiences, management upholds the antiracial cultural ideology that adds a layer of irresponsibility and incomprehension to the controlling images that paradoxically contour Black care workers' lives at work and beyond. Because this work is so firmly tied to interpersonal contact via nurturant care work, I turn next to the development of racial and political consciousness among another segment of those who perform the non-nurturant "dirty work" of the city: institutional cleaning workers.

5

Negotiating and Challenging Gendered Racism in Cleaning Work
● ●

On a busy summer afternoon in a Lisboan commercial center, I went to the public restroom. The space, as it often was at the height of summer tourism, was crowded. From inside a stall, I could hear a familiar mixture of semihushed conversations, cries, soft giggles and whispers, and the whoosh of people entering and exiting through swinging doors. Feet shuffled on the tile as I snatched a conversation from the other side of the fiberglass divider.

With a strong Lisboan accent, the first woman asked, "What is all of this? Look at this mess! Toilet paper everywhere. Garbage here, and garbage there. *Caralho*!¹" Silently, I peered under the stall door. I spotted a pair of wine-red leather sandals tightly snuggled around pale, white toes neatly painted with pink polish. A second set of feet provided less information, clad in a pair of undiscerning black shoes. Then the voice connected to the feet spoke up: "These *pr-tas* don't know how to clean these spaces. Go call that *pr-ta*! She needs to come in here and see all of this." When I pushed open the stall door, two startled white faces met my face in the mirror before hurriedly heading for the exit.

I recorded this incident—in which a pair of white women with no formal role in this space felt empowered, even entitled, to call upon a Black woman (in fact, to repeatedly refer to her with a highly charged racial slur) to clean around them—in my field notes in the summer of 2019. Further, they attributed the mess to Black workers' incompetence, not the deluge of customers rushing in and out of a heavily trafficked space (a public bathroom, which has never been associated with scrupulous cleanliness). In this chapter, I turn to Cabo Verdean women to illustrate how these dynamics play out for workers treated as both invisible and hypervisible as they perform stigmatized, often overlooked, and frequently taken-for-granted labor for which they are socially deemed uniquely appropriate. The intersections of their racial and gender identities curtail opportunities, render them subject to scrutiny and suspicion from white (and, at times, other non-Black) patrons and colleagues, and contribute to the formation of their racial and gendered political consciousness in the shadow of empire—all while these working women make sure the institutional spaces for which they are responsible meet the capricious standards of people in power.

Aline, introduced in chapter 3, provided a useful summary of the specific form of invisibility that Black, African-descendant cleaning workers like her face in Lisbon: "There are whites that think, 'Oh, she is a cleaning lady,' so they don't treat them well because of that work. Which is wrong, because it's work! Whatever job it is, it's dignified. You should speak nicely to everyone. So, you go there, to wherever, to work. And nobody says 'Bom dia!'² No, they ignore you. That is racism, you know it. It's like treating someone as though they are invisible, like they don't see you . . . like they don't matter."

The dyadic relationship between invisibility and hypervisibility, as expressed by study respondents, is a central feature of everyday racism in the shadow of empire, because it is this dissonance that allows for the naturalization of racial inequality without admission of racism's coordinated operation at every level—personal, social, organizational, institutional, systemic, national, and more. In Portugal, as in much of the "Fortress of Europe," African descendants are consistently erased from the national imagery. The emotive feelings of invisibility, in this sense, become fundamental to the experience of being racialized as Black in a white supremacist society. Meanwhile, the reality of this oppression marks African descendants as Other, ushering in their hypervisibility—and their vulnerability to systemic racial discrimination in realms including education, housing, and employment. Comparatively, because racism, classism, and sexism intersect to produce gradations of experience, Black working women who traverse public spaces are marked, in their visibility, as deviant in ways that more tightly couple them with the invisible "dirty work" of cleaning labor.³ On top of this, like the eldercare workers in chapter 4, Black women who labor in cleaning services are subject to scrutiny and marginalization long denied through the Portuguese antiracial ideologies of the state.

Beyond the Daily Pleasantries: Invisibility and Hypervisibility

In Lisbon, institutional cleaning (or *limpeza*) typically follows a team-based model of approximately five to twenty or so women. These teams are headed by managers, or *chefes*, in charge of monitoring employees' work performance. These managers are usually working-class white women, and frontline employees who labor under them are mostly Africans and African descendants (particularly Cabo Verdean and Guineense), though they are joined by a number of urban white Portuguese women and others from immigrant groups including Ukrainian, Romanian, and Brazilian. In large stores and commercial centers, employees and managers wear cleaning gowns; the "color" of the uniform is often what separates them.

Initially, many cleaning workers demurred when I asked about their general impressions of their clients and the people who patronized their workplaces. It made sense: like many service workers in gendered occupations, they had internalized the requirements of performing workplace femininity. They knew they were expected to "do" powerlessness by expressing deference and passivity, to navigate the niceties of their workplaces without interacting at length with anyone but their direct colleagues. Those who labored overnight or in the early mornings might only cross paths with institutions' employees, clients, and patrons as they arrived or left after their shifts. Still, they knew to greet others (and how to do so). Their stories painted a picture of social distance and proximity, of not drawing attention and remaining deferent, respectful, and whenever possible, invisible.

Study participants understood the resulting interactions were superficial. Like home care workers, who believed that an ethos of professionalism served the ideological function of maintaining their silence regarding abusive personal interactions, cleaning workers tied the prescribed pleasantries of their work to an indirect mandate to serve, to be docile, and to remain distant. A far cry from the demands placed upon workers in the nurturant care services, these nonetheless imposed emotional, affective, and body labor upon cleaning services workers.

After four years with a firm that manages custodial services for medical laboratories, fifty-seven-year-old Cabo Verdean Josefina said the employees who worked in the building she cleaned were "accustomed" to her—so much so that she could say firmly, "I blend in." In fact, she explained, "I work among clients and employees; typically, the employees are working on their computers while I am working. When I enter, I say, 'Bom dia, boa tarde,'[4] and employees typically all say the same to me." But that was the extent of their interaction. She learned that she was to mold her body in a way that made it both present and absent simultaneously. As she put it, "I try not to interfere." Whereas home care workers' performance of nurturant care requires them to navigate one-on-one intimate interactions with elders, institutional cleaning workers are called to create an "illusion" of invisibility through their labor performance. Paradoxically, many of the institutional cleaning workers I met felt the strongest sting of invisibility when they were in the presence of employees and patrons but were treated as though they could not be seen. In Josefina's remarks and those of others, I understood that Portugal's cleaning service workers are common fixtures of urban infrastructures, yet their service is often "invisible" and often little appreciated.[5]

Indeed, workers tied the prescribed pleasantries of their work to an indirect mandate to serve, to be docile, and to remain distant, if not invisible, but they also connected this mandate to the normalization of everyday racism. Interviews were frequently dotted by stories of patrons and employees who treated the Cabo Verdean cleaning workers disrespectfully, with disregard, or with outright contempt. It was within these interactional dynamics that workers like Josefina located the salience of race and anti-Black racism in their work settings. For example, the *theoretical* amicability of her working relationships withered as Josefina spoke about the everyday racism embedded in her *practical* interactions:

> I know how to coexist with people. I say "olá, bom dia, boa tarde" [hello, good morning, good afternoon]. But you *feel* it. It's not just the way they talk to you. It's the way they act, it's the way they coexist—with us. There's something that is wrong. It's a feeling that something is not right. Racism is always there; it's part of the job. It's always there. Any type of situation, we know it's there. People feel it! But racism is always there.

In a powerful reminder of the racialized affective dimensions of care work inequalities, here Josefina expresses a disconnect between surface niceties and actual behavior. Josefina's "feeling" of racism is more than an emotional exchange. It is an affective exchange of racialized servility, buttressed by the coloniality of labor, which reflects power relations between bodies. Indeed, as Josefina peels back the sterile interactional dynamics of her job, she distinguishes between the niceties and the undercurrents—what she can in fact *feel*—of these brief exchanges:

> JOSEFINA There are some [employees and patrons] there that are racist, but the majority are more secretive. . . . There are only a few that don't say hello; they pass you without saying anything, no "bom dia," no "boa tarde." When people do that to me and they don't say anything, I look at them and say, "Bom dia!" [Good morning], "Boa tarde!" [Good afternoon]. I say it! I say it just like that [*with straight-backed posture and a pointed tone*]. I say it because I think it doesn't harm anyone just to say hello. Sometimes they look at you and don't even respond.
>
> CELESTE Are you referring to employees or people that enter the building but who are not employees?
>
> JOSEFINA Both. The difference is that employees are used to me by now. So, they are usually more likely to greet me and then continue what they are doing. But some of them still ignore what I say. But If I say something today and they don't respond, then tomorrow I won't say anything. I'd rather not say anything than feel bad about it.

Josefina's statement harkens back to home care workers' sentiments in chapter 4, though institutional cleaning work is different in that its workers negotiate brief and spontaneous—yet still powerful—interactions with random patrons in commercial centers and other businesses rather than intimate interactions within private homes (see table 2 in the appendix for workplace comparisons). Throughout my study, participants would reference *feeling* the "coldness" of white Portuguese people, with which Josefina's complaints about unreciprocated greetings fit so well. I heard frequent complaints about patrons, especially, who rarely committed to a culture of workplace pleasantries. For example, Marissa, the fifty-year-old dark-skinned Portuguese citizen we last met in chapter 3, worked in cleaning services in a clothing store in a midsize commercial center. While she was happy to have secured contracted work, she felt that she and her colleagues were treated as subservient by patrons and employees alike. Every day, she took note of the patrons disregarding the mess they created around themselves and the employees who failed to tidy up before closing. To her, it seemed "they [employees] do that because it's like 'Oh, Blacks will be there in the morning to clean this up.' And patrons . . . I am sure they think, 'Oh, it's a Black person that's going to come here and work.' I think it's a conscious and subconscious thing. They make a pigsty just because a Black person is coming to clean!" She described being sought out by patrons with complaints about something or other they found less than perfectly cleaned, regardless of her responsibility for the situation, and about employees who, when they were particularly busy, did the same. All this while their work was humiliatingly criticized:

> They [patrons] create a pigsty that nobody wants to see and no civilized person would ever do. That's one of the hardest things. It pains us to wake up at five in the morning and work a whole day thinking everything we did was good. But when we finish, people appear who tell us that they aren't happy. And sometimes, it's all a lie. It's all to provoke us. The complaints . . . it's all a form of humiliation. When someone finishes their work and the other says, "You should have done more."

Marissa's use of the word "civilized" here harkens back to the earlier incident I recounted, in chapter 3, where a white waiter drew on racist stereotypes by framing our group as uncivilized—and therefore unworthy of service. However, here Marissa applies this term to disrespectful patrons. This rhetorical switch allows her to carve out feelings of worthiness in a context where her labor is clearly devalued. Indeed, Marissa said that there was never enough time or enough co-workers for her to complete everything every day, and so the humiliation of quotidian critique was constant. Respondents interpreted these incidents as the mirror image of the invisibility that accompanied the bulk of their time on the job. Thus, it wasn't the criticism that hurt the most but rather the ignorance of the enormous sacrifice demanded by cleaning work and the simple humanity of the immigrants who perform and are socially assigned to that labor.

While this feeling of being invisible was true for respondents who worked in close proximity to patrons and for those who cleaned spaces in the deserted hours of the early mornings, late evenings, and overnight shifts, the latter associated their invisibility with the isolation of their work. Called to clean the infrastructure of the city, they felt their isolation and inadequate compensation were part and parcel of the wider social animus toward African immigrants. Their colleagues who interacted with patrons and non–cleaning service employees in public settings or private businesses emphasized instead that their invisibility reflected the subservience of the work itself.

While a collective feeling of invisibility was apparent among study respondents, their *hypervisibility* resulted from an interplay of structural exclusion and cultural association where Black women have been constructed as appropriate for the menial, or the "dirty work" of care. Djamila, who worked for a firm cleaning in a gym, was typical in saying,

People who work in cleaning services experience a lot of racism, in many ways. Many ways. I have seen this, experienced this. At the gym sometimes clients enter the bathroom, they use the bathroom, and then throw the toilet paper there on the ground. They use their tampons and leave the applicators on the floor, or they leave their dirty pads on the seat, with blood and everything. Or they urinate on the floor. That happens there at the gym. It's a humiliation . . . because at the gym we have some people that take the paper towels and they just throw them on the floor. They leave it there. Because the people who do that do not respect the workers, they don't have respect for the job, they do that *on purpose* to humiliate people! And they do this because the majority of the cleaning workers here are African. It's really hard to find whites in this job—it's like 30 percent white and 70 percent African.

Respondents rightly believed that the racialized visibility of their status as Black women cleaning workers, buttressed by their overrepresentation in a narrow set of care and service occupations, shaped white patrons' and clients' entitlement *and* their disregard for Black women and their work in general. Similarly, nearly all respondents recounted stories pertaining to white patrons who purposely hid rubbish or otherwise policed their labor, assuming the entitlement to authority I witnessed in the public restroom at the start of this chapter. Djamila shared, for instance, "Clients will stick something somewhere in an area that is hard to see. And then the next day they will wait to see if you, as a worker, see it to clean it up. Like a little test to see if I cleaned there. And then they put it there just to tell you, 'Listen, there's some paper there,' or some gum." Djamila reads these microinteractions as impositions of the long-standing coloniality of labor and the controlling images and stereotypes of Black people that associate Black women with servility and uphold labor market segmentation. When these dynamics manifest at work, it is often in service of justifying these women's disproportionate concentration in care and service occupations.

Djamila and others also insisted that the humiliation they felt and experienced also signaled an overall assault on their humanity. In these ways and more, workers understood how patron requests and complaints are not benign but rather reflective of differential levels of racialized power and status.

Ivete, age thirty, had transitioned from four years in institutional cleaning work to laundry services at a hotel. When we spoke, she, too, stressed the way patron interactions made race and power particularly salient in her workday:

> Sometimes there are white Portuguese clients who purposely say things to belittle the workers. They will say things like "Hey, this is dirty!" And they like to say the word *pr-to*. They say, "*Pr-tos* don't do good work. *Pr-tos* don't know how to work." I have overheard them! They go to the store, they throw crap on the ground, and they say it clearly: "Oh, the *pr-tos* are here to clean, so they will clean it up." For example, if we go to a place to eat and you see that they have the center for putting away your trays and throwing out garbage, you are going to do it, right? It's not a question of being raised well—it's a matter of having good sense. But no, people [are] making those [behavioral] decisions based on the skin color of others.

I asked Ivete, "Why don't people respect the work that you do?" Hardly pausing, she retorted, "There are people who don't have respect." Elaborating, she added, "So people do this because they know that there are people who can clean up after them, *but* that's where racism comes out as well." In Ivete's view, the intersection of her occupational and racial statuses compounded the indignities she perceived and felt within her workplace. These indignities were ontological ones and not just a simple lack of respect for the work. She labored in an occupation devalued for the *type of work* performed and the *type of people* who perform that labor.

Higher-Ups' Surveillance and Distrust

Institutional cleaning workers spoke at length about how white Portuguese and non-Black supervisors and managers, the majority of whom were women, drew on racialized expectations of femininity by treating Black women not only as subservient and appropriate for taxing physical labor but also as untrustworthy and devious. This combination is nothing new; historical accounts find these stereotypes and racist ideologies have abounded throughout colonial and postcolonial eras in which African women, whether enslaved or free, were compelled to toil in an exploitative subsistence agriculture and reproductive labor peonage system.[6] The fact that these racist and sexist ideologies surface in contemporary cleaning and home care work illustrates that despite official claims, they continue to fuel the marginalization of and discrimination against Black, African-descendant women in their workplaces.

Consider Susana, a fifty-nine-year-old cleaning worker with nearly thirty years of formal and informal cleaning service experience. Recently, she told me, she had worked alongside her twenty-four-year-old daughter cleaning a large store in a commercial center. Shortly after she left that post, a group of young Black women Susana's daughter knew from her high school days were accused of stealing from the store. Susana specified that one member of the group *had* stolen an item but fumed that her daughter was fired: "It was a guilty-by-association sort of thing," she said. "A person who is treated like an accomplice is treated no different than the culprit." In her new post in the business office, Susana believed similar dynamics were transpiring. The new supervisor's daughter, also an employee, frequently arrived late to work or didn't arrive at all. Yet when Susana came across the time sheets one evening, it appeared the supervisor had failed to mark her daughter's absences. When Susana's manager passed through the building one afternoon and asked why an elevator and corridor had been left uncleaned, Susana had told her truthfully: the person who oversaw that area was the supervisor's daughter, who had not yet arrived to work. The problem was that the supervisors and managers all knew one another and exchanged information. Upon learning Susana had spoken to the manager, her new supervisor targeted her directly:

And so that manager went and spoke to my supervisor. And then my supervisor confronts me. The woman says in front of all my colleagues, "You think my daughter is like your daughter—who is a thief and they fired her from her job!" Just like that. I said, "Oh, that's good. Given that the person who is an accomplice is treated like a thief, I assume that you don't have the right to speak." I said to her, "Because you yourself also steal: your daughter misses work, and you don't report that on the time sheets."

Susana flipped her supervisor's accusations, and she looked back on the moment with a sort of pride. Yet before and after that incident, she felt unfair treatment from her supervisors and colleagues—it seemed that culturally controlling images of Black criminality precluded Cabo Verdean women's ability to be seen as individuals. Instead, they were treated as distorted, discriminatory representations of entire groups. Indeed, Susana learned that her daughter's mere friendly association with a young Black woman who stole a cheap item from a store was used to justify the marginalization and maltreatment Susana faced in her new place of work: "My old supervisor told my new supervisor, 'Be careful with Susana, because Susana steals. Don't leave her alone. And close all your cabinets and everything. If she starts working there, make sure that you follow her every move.'" Like the home care workers subject to racialized surveillance, Susana was frequently suspected of theft, however egregious or petty. A white Portuguese colleague, for example, accused Susana of stealing her lunch container from the workers' locker room one day, leading Susana to refuse to enter the changing room alone ever again. Afterward, she said, "When I entered that changing room, I would tell my supervisor, 'Hey, listen, I have to enter, so you are going to go in with me. So that if something happens, you all can't say it was me!' I wouldn't have a way to protect myself or defend myself. But I allowed myself to enter there when there were two or three people. And if no one was there and I wanted something like a snack or cookie, I would just avoid that by keeping [snacks] in my bag that I carried along with me, just to avoid problems." Susana responded to white workers' distrust and surveillance by adjusting her behavior to limit any potential accusations.

The assumption of distrust was embedded in various types of encounters described by study participants. Those who arrived late to work or missed a shift were not given the benefit of the doubt, they told me, but saw their behavior chalked up to incompetence, laziness, or lack of dedication. None were assumed to be navigating a personal injury or family conflict. Aida contrasted her previous manager, a Brazilian man who inquired after her well-being when her daughter was hospitalized and organized a donation fund for care packages for employees (contributing the largest amount himself), with her current one, a white Portuguese man who had been with the company about a year at the time of our interview. The former "was Brazilian, he was attentive to everyone," and "he understood what life was like; he was also a foreigner! He understood our situation because he was also a foreigner. He is here looking for a better life. Just like me." Their shared immigrant status seemed to strengthen their working relationship and bridge their different ethnic backgrounds. Her voice lowered, however, to a resigned register as she turned to her current manager: "The one that I have now is Portuguese. I can feel the difference now that I have a manager who is white." In her telling, this man participates in favoritism, aligning in obvious ways with white workers rather than the far more numerous African-descendant employees and burdening Black workers with assumptions of dishonesty. By pointing out her managers' nationalities *and* racial backgrounds, she suggests that the difference she feels is, in part, due to the racial barriers between them:

> The person who is my manager [now], he isn't good. He doesn't speak right with his employees. He lacks respect. So, with me, this all started because I twisted my foot the first day that he entered as the new boss. And I couldn't come into work. . . . I was cleaning my house, and I was standing on top of a chair, and the chair fell. And I had broken that foot sixteen years prior. I already had a fracture. So, I hurt myself, and I couldn't get around with that foot. I had to wear a cast. And he ended up upset. And what did he think? "Oh, she probably purposely twisted her foot so that she didn't have to come into work." It's what he told a colleague. Imagine a person purposely hurting themselves to avoid work! There's no logic there. And that's how the relationship started.

Since returning from her week of bed rest, Aida found that her manager continued to engage with her in a way that told her that he didn't regard her as trustworthy or, in fact, as a fellow colleague with a personal life of her own. Aida made sense of this by suggesting the manager lacked respect for workers' utilization of benefits such as sick leave that accompanies contracted work. Indeed, research on paid domestic workers in the regularized market in Portugal does show that the violation of workers' rights by employers is common, particularly with regard to benefits such as holiday time off and sick leave as well as social security benefits.[7] Of course, these dynamics may also reflect how capitalism's organizational logics underlie workplace hierarchies: often, workers are treated as devalued units of labor, with little recognition or support for their personal lives and gendered role as mothers. Yet racial inequality is also embedded in this pervasive workplace dynamic. To Aida, who also surmised that distrust was a racialized dynamic in her occupation (which is culturally coupled with *immigrant* labor), it seemed "whites [like her manager] assume[d] the worst": "They assume that we lie. . . . We are always doing the wrong thing in their minds."

Samira, twenty-eight years old, had a lot to say about her own toxic relationship with a former supervisor, a Brazilian woman. When the supervisor failed to express a sense of immigrant solidarity, Samira reasoned her supervisor had a problem with the Black women who composed the majority of her subordinates. "My boss was very . . . how can I say this? She was *discreet*," Eva said with a sigh. When asked to elaborate, Samira replied indignantly, "Every person needs to respect the other person! We need to know how to accept and coexist. And have a culture of respect at work among us. She lacked that." Samira came to recognize that her supervisor frequently questioned Black workers' honesty and treated them with little respect. When they asked for days off, she questioned their commitment to the job and the company in ways she didn't seem to do with the Brazilian and white Portuguese workers. In fact, where the supervisor was curt and brusque with workers like Samira, she chatted amicably with non-Black workers: "Sometimes she did things that made you realize that she was racist. Sometimes she would argue with us, and she would say things like 'those *pr-tas*'—let it come out! And you could perceive the racism. She didn't do anything else that was blatant, but the person who is smart can see it, perceive it." As I've noted in other chapters, few in Portugal are unaware that *pr-to/pr-ta* is a racist term—hence why Samira contrasted her supervisor's usual "discreet" manner with the term *pr-ta* just *slipping* out. That, in itself, is evidence of an inequitable working environment. Later in the interview, Samira mused on the origin of her boss's racism and colorism, attributing it not just to the social structures of Portugal but to norms the woman imported from her own country of origin: "Brazil has a lot of issues with racism and color. The people from Brazil who come here aren't as dark as some of the people there [in Brazil]. They can come here and bring with them that type of prejudice that exists there." Research does find that Brazilians face racist xenophobia in Portuguese society, adding nuance to Samira's comments.[8] Read this way, they underscore the ways that a person's own oppressive experiences will not automatically forestall their anti-Black racist practices.

Relationships with Colleagues: Linda's Story

When I met Linda, a tall, brown-skinned fifty-seven-year-old Cabo Verdean with a short, loose gray Afro and a sharp smile, she had worked in cleaning for about fifteen years. Before she regularized her immigration status in 1996, Linda worked for several employers in the informal market; later, after she married and moved in with a fellow Cabo Verdean, she picked up live-out jobs for several years. At age thirty-nine, she secured work in a cleaning firm that placed her in a large, centrally located office building. The firm was managed by white Portuguese men and women, and the frontline workers included Ukrainians, white and Black Portuguese, and lusophone Africans. Initially, Linda appreciated the work for its autonomy—she no longer had to labor under the direct watch of her employer's family. When we spoke, however, she had returned to the housecleaning business. The emotional and physical labor of institutional cleaning services had, she said, taken a toll on her mental and physical health over time: "At the beginning, I was OK. But as you age, maybe by the sixth year, you start feeling it, the effects of the physical and emotional strains of the job. And they just did so much to me that was wrong, it's hard to even speak about it. But I just had to deal with it . . . deal with it, because I am not a person like that."

The team-based work had taken place before or after normal business hours, so Linda's most sustained interactions had been with her colleagues and supervisors from her cleaning firm. And those interactions had been rife with what she described as favoritism, bullying, and an unequal distribution of work:

> They abuse you too much. My boss used to go behind your back and do things that were just wrong. And colleagues too. Because I do my work when I am supposed to work, but the boss and colleagues don't start trouble with everyone. Just with some. You have to work like a bull; you are always working, working, working. Without rest. And others are there, relaxing and not doing anything. They sit down, relax, have time on their hands. They could say something like, "Oh, with that age she has been working in this job for a long time," so they could have given me respect. But no, not me.

In her twelve years at the firm, Linda outlasted lots of other workers. The Ukrainians, for instance, appeared able to use the job as a transitional one, while low-paid cleaning and service work seemed an intractable, permanent facet of her own occupational trajectory. Maybe that was why, Linda complained, supervisors favored Ukrainian and Portuguese employees while assigning Black workers the most arduous jobs, such as hauling heavy bins and cleaning large areas alone—a comment that naturally called to mind the accounts of home care workers in earlier pages. Forcefully, Linda characterized *her* work as "slave work." With intensity in her eyes, she explained,

It was a slave's job because my job was to clean the garage. I also had to clean each elevator on each hallway and clean the hallways leading to each elevator. I had to do that on five floors. I was there for twelve years [*eyes widen*]. And I used to be able to stand nice and tall [*motions to her arm and shoulder*], but [not] after all those years of scrubbing, making those movements, and cleaning. And so I twisted this all up [*motions again to shoulders*]. I had to do it all on my own, and it was just far too much work. It was eight hours of work, and they had this huge garbage bin that contained all of the garbage from all of the building, and I had to haul that around. And I am even asthmatic, and I had to clean all of those crates with chemicals. And then, instead of putting the garbage in the crates, colleagues would throw it on the ground.

Institutional cleaning is heavy, physical work, and workers like Linda are used as tools in today's service economy, and this has immense consequences for their own bodies. In line with Erynn Masi de Casanova's discussion of embodied inequality, the organization of cleaning service work expects workers to communicate hierarchies of class, race, gender, and occupation through bodily performances (deference, invisibility, etc.). Yet the physical aspect of the work also uses up and damages workers' bodies in the process.[9] Interestingly, descriptions of bodily tolls from labor were more prominent in the narratives of cleaning workers than among the home care workers. But their nurturant labor was, of course, physically demanding too—it could involve moving elders into and out of beds and bathtubs, up and down stairs, and into and out of their clothing. Indeed, I took note of how workers complained about their bodily aches and pains as I shadowed them—and this was just as true for home care workers as it was for cleaning workers. So what made the difference? It is possible that home care workers failed to describe this work as grueling "slave's work," as was so common among cleaning workers, because nurturant work is explicitly tied to the care of bodies and moral obligations of care as expressed through public discourse regarding elders' vulnerability. Meanwhile, though participants resisted the popular characterization of cleaning work as "dirty work," many still told me that the physical acts of scrubbing, cleaning, and hauling—especially when they were not equally shared across cleaning teams—were assaults on their personal dignity. Linda considered the sheer amount of work she had to carry out an open form of discrimination: "I couldn't complain to my superiors because they would tell me I wasn't more important than anyone around me. My manager told me that if I wanted to make a complaint that I needed to just call my colleagues and tell them directly. And that's when the stress started. When I see something, I try to fix it on my own so I don't have to run into problems. But then it starts to consume you on the inside."

Here Linda illustrates another instance of taxing *emotional* management. That is, she stifles her anger at racial inequality to protect her job and tries to come up with personal solutions to alleviate the effects of that racism. Her manager's insistence that Linda was "no different" than anyone around her compelled her silence. Still, her feelings were validated by Cabo Verdean and Guinea-Bissauan colleagues who agreed that the company created an inequitable working environment and shared her struggle with silence. Whether it was resignation or reserve, I cannot say, but Linda distilled the situation down to the following: "It's because of skin color, that's why people do these things. People know it's racism. People know it's racism, and people don't always say anything because it's just so normal for them to do this, the Portuguese. But what can we do? We are here; we have to work."

Bad pay, physical burdens, and the weight of everyday anti-Black racism were plenty to handle, but Linda's interview comments focused on the emotional burden of navigating interpersonal relationships with non-Black frontline colleagues as a reason she needed to leave institutional cleaning. Having returned to housecleaning with a *patroa*, she told me,

> What can I say? I like the independence [in institutional cleaning work]. *But* any place where there are many people working is full of problems; it's nothing but problems! I feel this way because the world in which we live today . . . for example, white colleagues talk about everyone else, about their lives; they don't work! They just go there because they are friends with the boss and the boss enables them. For example, I used to go in there to work, and let's say I am cleaning here or there. But they enter and don't care. They step right where I just cleaned and throw paper on the floor.

Previous ethnographic research finds that Cabo Verdean women prefer cleaning jobs with public establishments because they experience greater autonomy and less surveillance, but Linda later explained that the degree of interracial interactions in her previous post added to the emotional overwhelm of the job.[10] Where other workers described their rage when clients and patrons threw trash around, Linda's blood boiled to see fellow frontline staffers acting just as disrespectfully toward Black co-workers like her. Race structured the power of individual workers, though they all held the same position. What follows is her response to being asked, "Why do people do that?"

> They already know that I am there to work, but I don't have even one vote; I am powerless. I have the hardest work to do, the heaviest work. We are like bulls. And they [*laughs*], the boss tells them, "You all are going to go clean off the table where people get their coffee, and throw out the garbage, wipe it all down." Then they just go and sit down. And then the boss comes and sits down by them; they end up joking around and chatting. And they don't do anything. But if I went and sat down, there would be a problem because we are not allowed to do anything that they do. Not me. My job is just to work, work, work, work!

At the time of this interview in 2019, Portugal's nascent public discourse on race discrimination often focused on overt practices of hostility, like the police assault recorded by passersby, but in this exchange, Linda described the significance of subtle dynamics, even among people who might otherwise build bonds of solidarity. Her observation that her supervisor aligned with her white Portuguese and Ukrainian colleagues was particularly visible in the "favors" she observed: her supervisor took breaks with her white colleagues, chatted them up in hallways, overlooked their tardiness, and delegated lighter work to them. That conferred a sort of soft power that allowed these colleagues, who similarly labor in a stigmatized profession, to exert racial dominance—and be rewarded with a psychological wage—by treating Linda as second-class too. Taken together, the environment showed Linda and other Black workers that they were seen as wholly *sub*servient, even within a service industry.

Linda reflected, "For a person who is white and Portuguese and hasn't suffered due to her skin and now—we who have grown up and already seen this happen—assume that we are just here to serve? . . . It's offensive." The intersection of Linda's racial and gender identities and the long-standing colonial history underpinning the politicization of this intersection in Portugal further charged her colleagues' behaviors. Philomena Essed refers to the way, for instance, that notions of servility are institutionalized and lead white people to treat others in accordance with their race as a *social practice* based on ideological forms of systemic anti-Black racism tracing to historical processes such as colonialism and labor migration.[11] In this way, everyday gendered anti-Black racism is woven into the social fabric and replicated in its institutions and structures. The situation of the Cabo Verdean cleaning workers I interviewed exemplifies how racist and sexist ideological forms of structural disempowerment invade workplaces through routine and repetitive practices. In the aggregate, these reinforce the racialized "antiracial" Portuguese society. Linda's long-delayed response—quitting—was one of many ways that my respondents resisted.

Talking Back: Iliana's Story

The society's devaluation of cleaning work teaches everyday people to go about their days without significantly registering the workers who labor around them. The agency further seeks to keep workers in the shadows by compelling them to reproduce inequitable work environments through the emotional and physical demands of the jobs. This is compounded by the invisibility of the agencies that corporations hire to manage the cleaning of buildings, which in turn further marginalizes workers. Yet the shadow resists invisibility in that its existence *is* undeniable. Likewise, even while antiracialism denies the impact of coloniality and purports that systemic racism is a contemporary impossibility, respondents draw from their social location within the shadows to speak back and assert their dignity as Black women in Portuguese society.

Like other interviewees, Iliana spoke with pride about instances in which she spoke back to the everyday anti-Black racism she faced in her ten years in cleaning services. Along with her institutional job, she continued to pick up additional hours in the informal domestic market, using evenings and occasional mornings to supplement her meager income. In her friend's living room, Iliana explained that her second domestic job had its difficulties, but she was most passionate about the challenges she faced in the cleaning firm. She was a serious-looking woman in her midforties, her long Senegalese braids swooped to one side and tucked into a large bun. I noticed how Iliana fumbled with her bracelet as she spoke, pushing a series of blue glass beads interspersed with black-and-white *conta di ojo* (evil eyes) pendants back and forth on her wrist. As her fingers fidgeted with the beads, she explained that she, too, had firsthand experience with the inequitable distribution of work:

> In my case, I work in my employers' homes. And that's where I don't see racism. But when speaking about my colleagues I have in [institutional] cleaning services, that is where I have seen many racisms, and it's where I have experienced it directly. And many of my African colleagues and *colegas negros* [Black colleagues] complain about it too, because where there's *mulheres brancas* [white women] working alongside *mulheres negras* [Black women], whether they are *negra* [Black] or *africana* [African]. . . . I am not referring to just nationality, I am referring to color, the difference of color because there can also be Ukrainians or Brazilians or Portuguese. . . . There's always a difference in terms of the work that is being performed. The dirtiest work is for *pr-tas*, the hardest work is for *pr-tas*, the most humiliating work is for *pr-tas*!

Again, we see labor divided by race and gender at the sector level, then again by race and gender inside the organization. In Iliana's experience, Black women are seen as appropriate for "dirty jobs" like cleaning but also for the dirtiest, heaviest jobs within the occupation. Iliana described this as a humiliating division of tasks but notably said she didn't "see" racism in the same way when she worked cleaning homes in the evenings. It was not that her domestic employer was not *racist*, or that domestic labor is not upheld by racialized structures, only that institutional cleaning work made a racialized workplace hierarchy so readily apparent because people like Iliana could observe firsthand how colleagues were differentially treated. Further, Iliana identifies skin color and race as major social markers, often determinants of workers' different labor experiences. This is important as institutional cleaners were far more likely than home care workers to work with other non-Black immigrants, yet processes of marginalization remained intact. In this sense, Iliana points to the *intersection* of gendered anti-Blackness, nationality/immigrant status, and colorism as consequential to the ways Black women's marginalization unfolds in cleaning services. Her conflation of Africanness and Blackness also harkens back to home care workers' remarks, reinforcing the shared othering of African and African-descendant Portuguese women, regardless of their citizenship or nationality status.

That the incomplete belonging extended to women like Iliana was ultimately provisional—and revocable—was repeated each time she saw Black colleagues denied breaks and vacation time or heard supervisors and white colleagues use the dehumanizing term *pr-ta* when communicating among themselves. On one occasion, her manager, a white Portuguese woman, actually instructed her to "work over there with the rest of the *pr-tas*." Whether subtle or blatant, again the suite of anti-Black practices brought humiliation, as they were deployed to put Black women in "their place" within a society where Black people are consistently denied a right to place. Here, too, many women with whom Linda worked chose to remain silent out of fear of reprisal:

> It's humiliating! The racism. People recognize it themselves. We workers in cleaning services, we see the difference in how we are treated, but sometimes we have to stay silent because sometimes, even though it's painful, we can't speak. This already happened in my case. We cannot speak. It's just "bom dia" [good morning] and return to scrubbing the walls. And sometimes, our big boss doesn't know what is going on because in many cases we don't have the courage to tell our bosses, because they [supervisors or managers] threaten us, they tell us that they will fire us. I already have known people who have lost their work for asking, "I don't have the right to take a vacation?" That's injustice.

In Iliana's experience, the failure to speak up painfully exacerbated the emotional repercussions of laboring within a devalued profession while being held to the professional pleasantries she knew were ideological mechanisms of worker control. Referencing the "good mornings," for instance, she brings up the racialized emotional norms and "feeling rules" that regulate interpersonal interactions within cleaning work and require Black women to suppress any anger, frustration, and irritation lest they invite negative repercussions.[12] "And even with clients. If we hear them speaking, all we can do is fake like we are scrubbing the walls. And what are the clients speaking about? About me!" fumed Iliana.

As has been argued by scholars, and as illustrated in the earlier discussion of Cabo Verdean home care workers, marginalized individuals, such as Black women institutional cleaning workers, are often coerced into re-creating inequitable working environments through their own labor performance.[13] The "feeling rules" applied to an overrepresentation of Black women add up to an anti-Black work culture that reinforces the hegemonic ideology that race *doesn't matter*. Given the frequency with which respondents identified anti-Black gendered racism as a persistent workplace reality, one might wonder why respondents did not seek legal recourse. After all, Portugal does have an antidiscrimination policy and has revised this policy in the twenty-first century. Yet both the home care workers and institutional cleaning workers I interviewed generally expressed feeling indifferent about reporting their experiences of racism to higher-ups. Most respondents individualized their qualms instead, noting that they have learned how to "deal" (in Portuguese, *lidar*) with the emotional vicissitudes of the work. Only two respondents indicated that they were aware of reporting mechanisms, such as the Commission for Equality and Against Racial Discrimination (CICDR). Respondents' failure to carry out formal complaints is therefore likely more a result of a lack of knowledge of reporting mechanisms and fears of retaliation or feelings of disempowerment shaped by the intersection of antiracial ideology and an anti-Black workplace culture.

Indeed, when I asked whether she thought anything could be done by the agency to address the racial harm she experiences, Iliana reflected, "I went through all that humiliation," she said with a sigh, "and I told myself not to say anything even though it hurts. I stayed silent because I decided it was better just to leave that work without saying anything. And I needed the money." Thus, as in the case of home care work, the power of antiracialism as it intersects with work demands for deference and powerlessness is that it neutralizes complaints about racist practices.

Iliana's story, however, reminds us that there are always two sides to the oppressive dynamics faced by African-descendant working women. As the history of African-led resistance to Portuguese colonial rule attests, the shadow of empire has always been a place of subversion. At one point, Iliana straightened her posture and took on a tenacious tone, then told me about speaking up—and losing her job:

> [This supervisor] showed us that, to her, everyone from our race is, excuse my language, the same shit. And so I told her I would go to the tribunal because *in this country you can also go to jail for racism.* I told her that I am working honestly, that I have documents and am not a clandestine immigrant, that she has to respect me because I am an employee here at my work post, where I need to be respected in order to respect others! And what did she do? She fired me. She took out her phone and said, "I am going to record your voice and take it to the office. You are fired!" I said to her directly, "You can fire me; I am not doing anything wrong!"

Her silence to that point had been a sign not of complacency but of fear. When she hit a breaking point, Iliana recognized her relative privilege as an immigrant with regular status working within a formal, regulated market and chose to speak for all the women tired of dealing with the same shit. She did not have the leverage to demand respectful working conditions, but she could stop being deferent on the issue of her own humanity. The supervisor's subsequent targeting of Iliana thus illustrates yet another extension of Portuguese antiracialism, in which individuals and groups who speak up about their encounters with racial oppression are silenced, chastised, or deemed ignorant.[14]

It is particularly significant, however, that Iliana stated, "In this country you can also go to jail for racism." She chose to utter these words, in 2019, against the backdrop of a growing antiracist movement in Portugal and an ongoing and highly publicized and unprecedented trial of Portuguese police officers accused of crimes ranging from torture and kidnapping to racial hatred toward Blacks. Portuguese antidiscrimination policy also broadened its criteria in 2017 to encompass indirect and direct forms of harassment, which has been accompanied by state campaigns to increase awareness about reporting mechanisms through the CICDR.[15] In this sense, counterpressures elsewhere can also open opportunities and the willingness to overtly resist.[16]

A few months later, Iliana was working in the informal domestic cleaning sector when she received an unexpected phone call. Her former manager asked that she return, full time, to the company (because, ironically, she had found the labor of a white Portuguese woman hired to replace Iliana lacking):

> She was such a cynic, and I was angry, but I didn't say anything because I really needed the money. The day I returned, I was confronted by my manager and my old supervisor, and I didn't say anything. My manager said hello to me, and so did she [the supervisor], like nothing happened, and my supervisor said to me, "Seja muito bem vinda" [Welcome back]. And my manager congratulated me and told me she was happy that I returned to that job. I only responded to her because I was upset and very sad. I responded, "Thank you, boss. We are in peace." And that was that.

The contradictory conversation confirmed what Iliana had always known: it wasn't the quality of her work that cost her the job but her refusal to accept racist treatment from her supervisor. Iliana has since continued to work for the cleaning firm. And her supervisor does not appear to target her anymore—indeed, as Iliana explained to me, the two of them barely communicate. Before our interview ended, however, I asked Iliana whether she felt that it was worth speaking up, given how the situation unfolded. With bright eyes, Iliana looked directly at me. After a brief pause, she smiled and responded firmly: "When I see something that I don't like, that I think is wrong, I speak. I tell my colleagues to do the same. And I am not the type of person who will just go by quietly." There were solid structural reasons many stayed silent and many risks associated with speaking up. For Iliana, at least, it seemed it had been a risk worth taking.

Conclusion

The last time I spoke with Iliana, she and a pair of fellow Cabo Verdean women joined me, off to the side at a child's birthday party, to discuss the activism that seemed to be fomenting around race and politics in Lisbon. She had not personally attended any antiracism events, but Iliana commented that young people were particularly active and that she would like to get involved. We peeked through the plexiglass oven door to check on the cakes as they baked, lofting higher and higher, and the women spoke about their work. The younger woman worked alongside Iliana in institutional cleaning services, while the older woman noted that she had done domestic labor in Lisbon and France since the early 1980s. "During our *feriados*,[17] Celeste, this is how we are," Iliana laughed, motioning to a line of women sitting outside of the multistory housing projects. Four middle-aged Black women, each with her own skin tone, sat in a row of chairs, laughing and chatting as a woman wearing a purple and blue *pánu di téra* tended to fish sizzling on a portable grill. "During the week, we deal with the Portuguese," she added, this time in Cabo Verdean *kriolu*, "but then on the weekends or the evenings, we talk about how to deal with them! *We know more about them than they know about us.*" The older woman's bright golden earrings shook lightly as she nodded in agreement.

The conversation that ensued encapsulated many of the difficulties presented in this chapter, yet it also highlighted how Cabo Verdean service workers, like Iliana, develop socially informed knowledge about their oppression, including coping and resistance strategies. They do not need to be silent in their own spaces. They can build and share collective knowledge. Just as reported in countless works on women of the African diaspora in Europe and throughout the world, Cabo Verdean women may challenge the nurturement of an ideological atmosphere that is tolerant of everyday gendered anti-Black racism. Cabo Verdean care workers draw from their social location from and within the shadow of empire to construct alternative modes of belonging and resist the systemic intersectional oppression that they and their families face.

6

Spaces and Places of Joyful Belonging

•••••••••••••••••••••••

"From Monday to Saturday or from Sunday to Friday, we have to show them that we are Portuguese," Mirela said as she sat in a café in her neighborhood, sipping espresso from a tiny porcelain cup. Neatly framed photos of famous Cabo Verdean popular figures like Cesária Évora and Amílcar Cabral adorned the four walls around us. "But on Sunday we don't have anyone to answer to, not even a schedule, and so we gather together; it's part of our culture from our country. We sit outside, we're all Cabo Verdean. We are all family in my neighborhood. But we also get together to criticize what they did to us yesterday or what they did to us the day before yesterday."

In so many hours of their lives, African and African-descendant women dealt with intersectional oppression. Overt or covert, interactions left them painfully aware of their "places" within the social hierarchies and labor markets of postcolonial, ostensibly antiracial Portugal. They often felt hypervisible as outsiders, whether in clients' private homes, the office buildings of downtown Lisbon, or the public transit that shuttled them to and from work. Yet they also felt invisible, as women doing the stigmatized work seen as "appropriate" or natural for them, and as Black women trying to speak out about the gendered racism many white Portuguese liked to pretend didn't exist. But they were never without places of respite and resistance, places they had carved out for themselves where they could be unburdened, irrepressible, honored, understood, and seen.

Cabo Verde's Independence Day is July 5, and it is recognized in many of the small peripheral neighborhoods of Portugal's urban areas. Mirela invited me to a gathering in an event hall in her municipality, Amadora, roughly ten kilometers from central Lisbon. Friends, neighbors, and newcomers filled the space with their laughter and conversations—I walked into a welcoming crowd of happy people. Older men and women sat chatting at tables, while teenagers bantered playfully in the corners, their array of hairstyles too numerous to catalog. Straight, curly, and coiled coifs topped Black and brown faces with shiny twists, locks, and braids, smatterings of bronze clips and cowry shells, and Afros of every size. I noticed a cluster of men, just beside the main entrance, unpacking instruments. Three drew acoustic guitars from their cases, two set up keyboards, and in the middle, a man in an Amílcar Cabral shirt sat upon a *cajol*, a wooden box drum. The room became louder, reverberating with a comfortable cacophony of laughter, musical instruments tuning up, tables and chairs scraping, and feet shuffling on cool linoleum.

In the farthest back corner, festively dressed people carried colored basins filled with bottles of water, soda, and beer; carafes of sweet homemade *pontche*;[1] and containers of *toresma* into a kitchen area.[2] Others brought heavy dutch ovens heaped with fragrant rice, *congo*,[3] and *catchupa*,[4] Cabo Verde's national dish. Young adults set up the folding tables while older folks began filing into the kitchen, reappearing with porcelain bowls filled with food. Toddlers tugged at their parents' clothes or romped around in their bright holiday outfits.

Mirela and her friends brought me along as they grabbed empty seats near the band, where we watched as a line began to form in front of an older, brown-skinned Cabo Verdean woman with her own little table near the kitchen. Her hair was tied back in a blue head wrap, and she wore a blue-and-white checkered apron. As she created dozens of small, traditional Cabo Verdean pastries, or *pastels*,[5] by dropping a spoonful of well-seasoned tuna onto a disk of soft, pale dough, I spotted a pair of familiar *conta di ojo*, or evil eye, earrings. With a quick, one-handed maneuver, the cook folded the dough and dropped the pastels into a portable deep fryer. Beside her, a younger woman stood ready to scoop them out just as soon as the pastry pockets transformed into the perfect golden-brown hue.

Eventually, a light-skinned woman with curly, chin-length hair took the microphone, and the guitarists began to play a slow-moving melody. She greeted the crowd in *kriolu*: "Hoje eh dia di celebra. Hoje eh dia di tem orgulho. Nos eh povu bonitu . . . mas importanti di tudo, nos eh forti!"[6] Onlookers nodded and clapped at her words of welcome, the reminder that this holiday was a time to celebrate their people, their beauty, and their strength. Then the woman began to sing the words the crowd knew so well:

Keli é nha vida [This is my life]
Keli é nha storia [This is my story]
Ê si que e nha vida [This is how my life is]

Ê si que e nha storia [This is how my story is]
Cheio de altos e baixos [Filled with highs and lows]
Cheio de pontos e fracassos [Filled with small successes and mess-ups]
Cheio de perdas e vitórias [Filled with losses and victories]
N sabi ma nta consigui [I know I will overcome].[7]

The familiar song, written by a young Cabo Verdean singer named Elida Almeida, is called, in English, "I Will Overcome." At its core, Almeida's song is about the complexity of life, in all its painful defeats and joyful victories—the contradictions expressed by so many of the transnational migrants I had come to know in Portugal. No wonder, I thought, it was so embraced by the Cabo Verdean diaspora.

Given Cabo Verde's ongoing economic insecurity and high mortality due to historic famine and drought, Cabo Verdean migrants and their families often straddle a cultural narrative that emphasizes *hardships* and *resiliencies*. As they migrate to host societies, entering labor markets and interacting with natives and fellow immigrants, they often experience the effects of colonialism, patriarchy, economic restructuring, and globalization. Their shared diasporic identity—connecting Black populations across the world, regardless of their immediate connections to Africa—emerges, argues Paul Gilroy, from this "common experience of powerlessness."[8] Anthropologist Kesha Fikes more specifically describes the diasporic subjectivity among Cabo Verdeans in Lisbon as "temporally shaped by the political economic conditions of life, and hence labour-time in particular settings, which thus shapes the *everyday* forms of expression that are politically possible."[9] Cabo Verdean communities, then, are linked transnationally by constellations of shared conditions of oppression as well as the *localized* social, political, and economic resources that help and hinder their available forms of resistance.

Indeed, though my interview data were filled with stories of turmoil and injustice, they were also full of observations that suggested that the Cabo Verdeans' long-standing immigrant communities in Portugal had successfully constructed alternative modes of belonging that challenged the devaluation of Black African femininity and the naturalization of Portuguese whiteness that were so apparent as they went about their lives. Like Almeida's song declares, as they face the emotional vicissitudes of gendered anti-Blackness *and* the anti-racialism of this society, it seems the communities that welcomed me respond, "N sabi ma nta consigui." I know I will overcome.

In our interviews, it was apparent that Mirela was acutely aware of how her work required her to perform deference and passivity for white Portuguese work colleagues and supervisors, as well as the patrons she encountered in her institutional cleaning work. She approached this as though she wore a mask when she was on the clock. Once she returned to her neighborhood or joined her Cabo Verdean community in places like the café where she sipped espresso

FIG. 5 Quinta do Mocho, a public housing neighborhood in Sacavém in the municipality of Loures. *Source:* https://commons.wikimedia.org/wiki/File:Quinta_do_Mocho_-_181_%2832830340006%29.jpg.

among friends, Mirela and the other Cabo Verdean women could peel away those masks and reclaim their dignity.

Amid racialized segregation and spatial environments plagued by physical and psychological threats, ethnic enclaves become places of respite in which Cabo Verdeans create community, enact critical consciousness, and perform proud Cabo Verdeanness, Africanness, and Blackness all at once. Indeed, the spatial patterning of Cabo Verdean women's work is an extension not only of gendered patterns of caring labor that assign service work to women but also of how long-standing practices of domination and resistance continue to inform, as Black feminist geographer Katherine McKittrick argues, "a Black sense of place."[10] A Black sense of place includes an awareness of the geography of opportunity—labor sectors and working environments, racially segregated neighborhoods, and other boundaries laid by colonial legacies and contemporary white supremacy. Yet it also includes those spaces Cabo Verdeans co-constructed in the shadow of empire, the ones where they could resignify the urban infrastructure and forge a diasporic understanding of identity for their children and other kin. Demonstrating what sociologist Kishi Animashaun Ducre terms a "Black feminist spatial imagination," the women who shared their stories with me had imagined and made places of solace and welcome in an otherwise inhospitable world.[11]

Cabo Verdean care workers may be constructed as devalued units of labor by migration and labor regimes in the shadow of empire, but they relentlessly reimagine and resist that position. As this chapter illustrates, their Black joy stands as a powerful testament to that resistance.

Neighborhood Space(s)

Originating in the 1970s, informal housing developments, colloquially described as *barracas* or *bairros de lata* (tin neighborhoods) sprang up to hold the massive influx of *retornados* (returnees) from Portugal's former colonial territories to its mainland cities. Most were built on unoccupied public land, without permits, and often with whatever materials residents could gather from scraps they found at their construction worksites.[12] The housing consisted of unfinished apartment buildings, often without running water or electricity. Even so, the substandard and at times dangerous living conditions provided immigrants with solace and critical spaces for cultural resistance. Arseana, a sixty-eight-year-old Cabo Verdean woman and longtime resident of a clandestine neighborhood, described her residence as marked by danger, disinvestment, *and* community when she arrived in the early 2000s:

> We were all Cabo Verdean during those times. Saturdays and Sundays were our times. People came and visited because the neighborhood was the only place to congregate [*laughs*]. The buildings weren't completed, so we would just sit out on the streets, we would go and fetch water because the homes didn't have water; it was like we were in Cabo Verde! We sat on the ground, we were just the same, washing clothes by hand, all of it, all of it was like it was there [in Cabo Verde]. *We didn't have help.* So, we went to our neighbors and helped them, and we helped one another. We were all family. . . . But listen. We suffered a lot, too, *fidju.*[13] We lived together, but we suffered together. Children fell from the buildings because they weren't all finished. There was an older man who died from a fall because the buildings weren't complete. My son was two years old and fell from the third floor—almost died. And it wasn't just him. Many of the children from there still have scars and marks from those houses.

After migrating to France to work as a nanny, Arseana had since relocated to her eldest daughter's home in income-based social housing.[14] The movement from a *barraca* to social housing was a common path among study participants who migrated at the turn of the twenty-first century. In 1993, the Portuguese government launched a massive program of social housing that specifically targeted people living in informal settlements. By 2002, nearly fifty thousand housing units were built. Most of these developments were large, low-cost housing developments located far from work and amenities, often in peripheral and suburban areas of Lisbon and Porto. In some cases, a violent practice of eviction characterized the demolition of informal housing, leaving people in the streets without any social support. As emphasized by countless scholars and social commentators, the state-supported eradication of informal urban settlements and the rise of dense, segregated neighborhoods deepened trends of racial segregation, material deprivation, and processes of stigmatization.[15]

Place resignification, or the transformation of city spaces to social landscapes full of symbolic value,[16] was therefore central to how my study informants made sense of their belonging within the greater Lisboan metropolitan area. Arseana and others associate the segregated Lisboan neighborhoods of social housing, or *bairros sociais*, with feelings of home and community as much as they lament the racialized state surveillance, low quality, and mismanagement of some of the oldest social housing on Lisbon's outer edges (qualities they attributed to racism in law enforcement and a state-level disinvestment in Portugal's African and African-descendant as well as Roma communities). Though public commentary may commonly cast aspersions toward racially segregated neighborhoods due to their association with crime and drugs, most respondents reported feeling secure and socially embedded in their neighborhoods. And while some informants did acknowledge problems of crime and the drug trade, they did not see these as *the* defining problems of their neighborhoods.

A range of scholarship similarly finds that residents of racially segregated communities around the world construct a positive association with their structurally disadvantaged neighborhoods because they often provide a social barrier against negative interactions in the broader community.[17] The dominance of racial and ethnic minorities in public housing and segregated neighborhoods in Lisbon, then, also marks a symbolic boundary that contrasts with the spaces where experiences of everyday gendered anti-Black racism and forms of racialized and gendered victimization (physical, verbal, symbolic) predominate. Indeed, scholar Sónia Vaz Borges has explored how informal neighborhoods and those inhabited by racially minoritized groups in Portugal are automatically laden with negative associations and cast by white Portuguese society as dangerous, criminal, and lacking civility.[18] This uniformly negative framing, Borges argues, occludes what these spaces in and around Lisbon also represent: a dialectical relationship between their residents and the broader society, between oppression and resistance, which is shaped not only by exclusion and racism but by quotidian enactments of family and culture, exchanges of ideas and mutual support, and resignifications of belonging. As such, segregated neighborhood communities are a product of the systemic racism and exclusion experienced by racially minoritized communities, yet they simultaneously (and perhaps paradoxically) mitigate experiences of marginalization in broader Portuguese society.

Layla, a home care worker who migrated from Cabo Verde nearly fifteen years before, was one respondent who had lived in her neighborhood for many years. Like other informants, she lamented the fact that life was so fast in Portugal and that she and her co-ethnics were typically too busy to engage in frequent cultural exchanges. "Society is different in Cabo Verde; people were more united with one another," she reflected. "Life was easier and harder. It was harder because of lack of money . . . poverty . . . but the family was more united. It was easier because you could depend on family, neighbors, a community. . . . Here in Portugal, everyone practically lives their own lives. You can't depend on people to help like you could back there." Here Layla expresses a contradiction as she alludes to *djunta mon*,[19] a Cabo Verdean sociocultural economy of mutual-support practices that historically enabled survival. Given the persistent racial, gender, and class marginalization in the labor market, family and community networks are disproportionally concentrated in a limited and narrow set of care and service occupations that demand long, unsocial hours. This results in less time to receive or provide mutual support, a reality that informants like Layla see as remarkably different from their experiences growing up on the Cabo Verdean islands.

Layla had little desire to return to Cabo Verde. Most, if not all, of her close relatives already resided in Portugal, the United States, and Holland. Plus, Layla now felt a strong attachment to her neighborhood in Lisbon proper: "My *bairro* is where I feel the most *àvontade*;[20] it's where I have a little piece of Cabo Verde." For Layla, the *bairro social* is more than a physical housing structure—it is a symbolic meeting point between culture, belonging, and community where she can experience joy and a form of visibility that eludes her in other spaces where white Portuguese predominate. One cool, late-February evening, I was waiting for her to pick me up from a bus stop when I spotted an older man sitting alone. He held tightly to a bulky plastic bag and kept his one free hand inside his coat sleeve, perhaps in an attempt to keep it warm from the damp, cold wind. When Layla pulled up, she looked toward the man for a long moment. "Coitadinho,"[21] she said to herself quietly as she sucked her teeth. She called out to him from her window, "Nho meste boleia,"[22] did he need a ride? Putting on a smile, he hopped into the back seat, and Layla pulled out onto the slightly slick road. Within seconds, the two started chatting. The man was born in Assomada, Santiago, a city about forty kilometers from Praia, the capital. "Nha mae e di fogo e nha pae di praia";[23] Layla told the man that her dad was from Praia, Santiago, and her mother from the island of Fogo. Moments later, at a traffic stop, she looked toward the back seat and added, with a smile, "Ma *mi e* [*emphasis hers*] di praia, *mi e badia*,"[24] as if to emphasize their shared island—their *badia*—connections.

After dropping the man off, Layla commented that she typically wouldn't pick up a stranger, but sometimes made an exception: "I usually don't do those sorts of things; I would typically be afraid. But *I know my own, Celeste. I could tell he was* kriolu. *And we are here.* I feel safe." After a pause, she added, "*Coitadinho*, it hurts so much to see an old man like that, *nha gente*[25] alone in the cold." Layla was a home care worker, so she was particularly sensitive to the needs of the elderly. Like many others I had met who labored in home care, Layla articulated a cultural and collective ethic of care as she described her caring labor as a community responsibility. But here she also connected place ("we are here") and ethnic visibility ("I know my own . . . I could tell . . . *nha gente*") to her feelings of safety and openness to helping an elder stranger. In this way, ethnic identity, place attachment, and a commitment to caring concurrently shaped her willingness to carry out culturally informed support. These are the sort of everyday interactions, shaped by the broader context of living in Portugal as an African-descendant woman, that give meaning to her day-to-day activity patterns and social interactions with others in her community. The Black Cabo Verdean diaspora exists not simply because of migratory departures from Africa—it forms alongside localized desires for connection and belonging.

"Outsiders," Tereza, another informant, said, referencing the white Portuguese perceptions of social neighborhoods located on the outer fringe of Lisbon, "have a lot of images in their heads." At twenty-four, she was wise in assessing, "For example, outsiders think, 'No, they are going to rob you there, assault you there.' And why do they feel this way? Because parents send that message to their kids! 'Oh, don't go there because there's too many Blacks there, they are going to rob you, they cause a lot of trouble, they are all loud.' Then a person goes there and it's nothing like people describe it. It's a place for family." As Tereza resisted the characterization of segregated residential spaces as violent and criminal, she denied the homogenizing effects of such discourse. Later, she explained that *she* associated her neighborhood with a diasporic Cabo Verdean, Black, and African identity, as well as a feeling of being part of a "family" with her broader community:

> In the *bairros*, that is where we feel the most comfortable. In social housing, where I grew up, for example. That's where our friends are, other Cabo Verdeans, *negros* [Blacks] ... but other Africans too. We are all family. And people who come from the outside, sometimes they enter with that opinion that others have, others who don't live there, and they come with that idea that it's a bad place here. But here the Portuguese are more about staying in their homes. We, for example, when a family member comes or a friend visits, we like to go outside and maybe grill a bit, listen to music, and all of that. But people who are not used to that see that as strange. They see a lot of people together, laughing and playing around. And to them, they find it strange. But we are just there, family members, taking advantage of the weather, eating, drinking, singing, dancing. . . .

Spatialized and joyful practices of culture and the broad extension of family shape this young woman's sense of where she belongs, and their absence in other areas of Lisbon, including the commercial zones frequented by tourists, shapes her sense of where she *doesn't* belong. "They don't provide you with that basic level of respect," she said indignantly. "So in those zones, I don't have that feeling of belonging. Foreigners who are there might not feel that way because they are tourists, so they must think that everyone has the right to be there." When she was working or "playing the tourist" with friends, Tereza told stories about white Portuguese restaurant and store attendants who treated them as unwelcome outsiders. To her, a cleaning worker in many of the same spaces, the situation was ironic: "But the white Portuguese, I think they look at us like 'Why are they here?' Sometimes they must look at us and think we don't have the money to pay. I work just like they work, and so I have money to spend too. If I didn't have money, I wouldn't be here, that is for sure. But we like to experience new places, different places; we like to be tourists too. We are Portuguese, and we also like to play the tourist here too." Tereza's remarks make claims of belonging based on nationality ("We are Portuguese") and economic contribution ("I work just like they work"), yet her experiences suggest that her racialized identity prevents her from truly feeling like she belongs.

Even so, a few white Portuguese live in Tereza's segregated neighborhood, and they, too, made their way into her designation "like family." "A white Portuguese that lives in social housing has a different perspective than someone who never entered a neighborhood like that," she explained to me. "And so they treat us better, basically like sisters and brothers, like family. For example, here in the apartment building, I grew up here before moving to another house, and we never had problems with [white neighbors]."

In line with findings from past research, several residents of social housing and racially segregated communities described neighbors in this way.[26] They conveyed a feeling of bonding with one another and a sentimental connection and attachment to the neighborhood in which they lived. In fact, as we strolled around the neighborhood together, neighbors often called out, asking how we were doing. Tereza herself called out to the multiracial group of children that playfully kicked a well-worn soccer ball in a courtyard as we approached her aunt's home, as well as two boys (both Black) running after each other beneath the underpass of the building. "Watch out!" she yelled at the chaser who appeared to be moments away from tripping on his tangled shoelace. "Don't forget to fix your shoes," she instructed. On other occasions, younger informants like Tereza ran up to open windows for a quick benediction on the forehead from an elderly Cabo Verdean woman whom they spotted by the kitchen window taking in a cool afternoon breeze. Tereza reflected, "They [white Portuguese living in social housing] always looked after us, they would always pass and greet us: 'Good morning,' 'Good afternoon,' 'How is everything?' and 'How is the family?'" Family, to her, wasn't an essentialized biological construct but a category she associated with community and mutual respect within this diasporic space. Beyond its confines, in other public spaces of the city, she could not treat others "like family" and have that treatment reciprocated regardless of race. Belonging, then, manifested from the construction of race *through* locality.

Religious Space

Other respondents cited as their spaces of refuge community spaces in which cultural practices rather than racial hierarchies dictated interactional norms.

Religious ceremonies, organizations, and churches met this criterion for some, particularly older respondents. Aside from religious expressions or benedictions shared during conversations or the quick and inconspicuous trinitarian hand motions employed before pulling out of a tricky parking space, religious practices such as consistent church attendance were not common for many of my informants. Few had the time (though some sent their children to church), and respondents were picky about how they would spend the little time they had off—managing family care took up a great deal of it, though they relished the chance to stop by a corner café for a quick espresso or even a leisurely meal with friends. Still, religious ceremonies such as baptisms, weddings, and funerals dotted my fieldwork, and informants (the majority of whom identified as Catholic) actively participated in important cultural-religious practices such as acting as godparents.

Among those who were regular churchgoers, one recent émigré, Nilda, said Catholic mass offset the "coldness" she had found among the Portuguese people for the past six years. Nilda's sister "lived across the river," in Almada, where there is a large African and African-descendant community, but fifty-five-year-old Nilda lived in an apartment complex with her son and daughter-in-law, farther from city amenities such as parks, stores, and restaurants. Never in Cabo Verde, however impoverished the conditions had been, had Nilda recalled feeling as isolated as she did while living and working in Portugal. And so attending church on her days off allowed her to feel like she was "part of something." She reflected,

> When I arrived here, at the beginning, I spoke with my sister who lives on the other side of the river and I told her, "Listen, I went to Buraca, I went to church, and I was so happy because I saw so many Cabo Verdeans there!" My sister, she laughed, [and] she said, "You are just like my son. He also says he doesn't like Portugal; he only wants to be with *negros* [Blacks], only with Cabo Verdeans!" [*laughs*]. But, for example, we have mass on the twenty-ninth of June for the celebration of São Pedro (Saint Peter). It's all community things, all Cabo Verdean. We will all be there, organize a little party, have a day at church. And so the people feel more comfortable and free.

While Nilda's sister jokes that she "just wants to be around Blacks," Nilda recognizes that her attachment to church is not only about an original community. Instead, her gravitation toward Cabo Verdean spaces, such as the church, emerges from her desire to feel "comfortable and free" rather than dislocated as she so often does. Importantly, in religious spaces, she feels the pleasure of joy in a world that consistently tells Black women like her they are out of place, that they don't belong in "antiracial" Portugal.

This is why local church celebrations throughout the year cater to Cabo Verdean and the wider diasporic African community, effectively enabling a dynamic appropriation of cityscapes throughout Europe.[27] The diaspora, similar to any population, holds its tensions and conflicts—between, for example, older and younger generations or newer and more established migrants—but mass, festivals, and other religiously associated events spatially anchor the diasporic identity within Europe through cultural production and practice.

For example, I attended the church celebration that Nilda mentioned on the day of São Pedro (Saint Peter). Long tables featured potluck contributions, including Cabo Verdean *pudim, gufong, catchupa, arroz marisco,* and *jaga-cida* alongside Angolan dishes like *funje* and *mufete.* As I sat with friends in a densely packed room, a youth-led percussion ensemble encouraged the crowd to dance batuque, or *batuku,* enacting an old Cabo Verdean cultural practice that combines poetry, singing, dancing, and drumming and is predominantly prac- ticed by rural women (*batukadeiras*) from the mountainous interior of the island of Santiago, where enslaved Africans once took refuge. The women who practice it often gather in a circle formation, or a *txabeta,* and sing about every- day problems ranging from poverty to colonialism, migration, politics, and gen- der issues.[28] Prohibited by Portugal's colonial authorities and by the Catholic Church, *batuku* survived through the resistance of Cabo Verdean women, and it remains widely popular throughout the diaspora today.[29]

Some critics argue that *batuku* has been co-opted by Lisbon's "diversity" ini- tiatives as it gains wider cultural recognition through the efforts of organized groups of *batukadeiras* who are invited to perform for broader audiences.[30] The fact that Madonna released a 2019 song called "Batuka" reflects the wider rec- ognition of this ancient cultural practice. However, my observations reflect how community-organized church events that occur outside mainstream ven- ues continue to provide pathways toward new understandings of space and belonging through cultural practices, including *batuku.*[31]

Back in the hall, celebrating São Pedro, the youth-led group sat in a circle and began to create a *batuku* beat from balled-up-*pánu di téra*[32]-turned- instruments that they held between their legs and near their knees. A fast cadence reverberated off their fingertips and hands as an older woman sang in *kriolu* about a young mother left behind in Cabo Verde with the forced labor regimes. A group of onlookers clapped to the rhythm of the beat. An elder woman entered the circle, and an onlooker handed over a *pánu,* which the woman tied around her hips before beginning to *da ku torno* by swinging her hips to the sound of the beat. The audience erupted in applause and laughter. Another woman, slightly younger, joined. She, too, placed a *pánu* around her waist, and the women proceeded to dance together, chest against chest. Then a middle- aged woman rose from her chair and joined, hand in hand with a young girl. When this pair returned to their seats, celebrants around them cheered the young girl and softly patted her back in encouragement. One of the girls in the drum procession ran over and pulled a young man onto the stage. When he too placed the *pánu* around his hips and danced, the crowd again erupted in smiles and a mixture of excitement and surprise, and soon another trio of young men were on their feet to *da ku torno*.

Religiously associated community events challenge fixed meanings of racialized otherness, for they provide pathways for cultural practices that inform and inspire diasporic identity.[33] In the colonial era, the Catholic Church repressed *batuku* on account of its "sexually suggestive" behaviors,[34] but it has been sustained through bottom-up creative expressions facilitated by religious gatherings in which African and African-descendant communities draw on Black diasporic histories *and* imbue new localized spaces with new purposes and meanings.[35] Indeed, as argued by Paul Tiyambe Zeleza, diaspora is continuously "made, unmade and remade in the changing conditions in which it lives and expresses itself," and it is an identity that entails a "'here' separate from a 'there,' a 'here' that is often characterized by a regime of marginalization and a 'there' that is invoked as a rhetoric of self-affirmation, of belonging to 'here' differently."[36]

Note, for example, the joy, surprise, and delight of the crowd when young men joined in the *batuku*. *Batuku* is commonly framed as a woman's dance, and gender corporalities emerge from its performances, as Carla Indira Carvalho Semedo's important work has shown.[37] By occupying space via *da ku torno*, performers who were not professional *batukadeiras* could subvert structures of labor, gender, race, and age that aimed to narrowly define them in Portuguese society. Women and girls' performance of a practice deemed savage and sexually suggestive, out of line with the Catholics' civilizing mission, as well as men's participation today constitute an important way Cabo Verdeans "talk back" to stereotyping and victimizing representations of African migrants by white society. Expressing and extending culture, these people of the African diaspora are not, as white Portuguese frame them, perpetually "out of place"[38] but *belong here differently*.

Intriguingly, several study participants who associated religious practice and space with belonging told me that opposing racism was essential to their faith practices. One informant, Helen, had converted, becoming a Jehovah's Witness as a teenager in Cabo Verde because her mother associated the Catholic Church in their city with greed and gossip: "Back then my mom used to say to me, 'Catolica so di boca' [They are Catholics in name only]. My mom spoke about how the Bible taught about co-existing with people, respect, and that we had to respect people out on the streets. If you don't respect people out on the streets, then you can't respect people at home with you either. She gave me that type of education." A fifty-nine-year-old woman who had been in Portugal since the 1980s, Helen still regularly attended services and spoke of the ways her faith and her home church provided her with a strong sense of belonging:

> What I love about my church events and my church is that there we are . . . we are all the same! There's no difference there: we aren't white, we aren't Black. No supervisor, no boss, no manager. No! There we are all the same; we don't have

anything like that. We call everyone sisters and brothers. And we don't care about differences in skin color; we respect people. Respect. Because we all have our defects, nobody is perfect. We all make mistakes. If we see that something happened, we say sorry, we forgive, and then it's over. And it has to be like that. Why? If we want to be loved, we have to love everyone. There's no *negro* [Black], there's no *branco* [white]. We are all the same! We don't make those distinctions there.

Helen relished the feeling of not only ethnic and cultural belonging but *human belonging*. It is through her religious practice and the relationships and values she forges through them that she is able to imagine a different form of belonging, one unencumbered by social categories.

I heard a similar message at a Lisboan mass organized by two local church communities, one with a larger Black and African congregation. Looking out to the multiracial audience, a white priest intoned, "In Lisbon, we have an African community, and we must join the African community, as we are all God's children." But in Helen's version, she evoked the status (supervisor, boss, manager) and racial hierarchies (Black, white) that in other aspects of society so limit Cabo Verdean women's belonging in Portuguese society. For her, her faith provided her with a lens by which to understand the world and her position in it beyond racialized status-based social divisions.

Study respondents' association of belonging with feelings of familial, cultural, *and* human belonging reveals how particular spaces can be both the result of persistent racialized and economic marginalization *and* truly generative spaces through which racially and economically marginalized people build identity, foster creative solidarities, and work toward the futures they dream about. It's within these spaces of Otherness (which Black feminist geographer Katherine McKittrick describes as "demonic grounds") that study participants construct a radical worldview outside the "partial human stories" engendered by the structuring logics of hegemonic whiteness and gendered anti-Blackness.[39] Here, Cabo Verdean women and their kin are anything but invisible.

Centro Comercial Babilónia

Amadora center acts as a sort of transportation hub, with a subway, train, and bus network that connects the neighborhood to the rest of Lisbon proper. Immigrants from Portuguese-speaking African countries make up nearly 75 percent of Amadora's total migrant population[40]; the other residents include Romani, Portuguese (of several racial and ethnic backgrounds), Brazilian, and East and South Asian immigrants, including Pakistani, Chinese, and Indian. A number of my field informants resided in the parishes of Amadora, and the transportation hub was an important place where they came together, especially during their commutes to and from work. These brief, often spontaneous encounters were full of useful information exchanges: local happenings, work

FIG. 6 Amadora Comboio Station. Photo by author.

opportunities, and updates about the goings-on of fellow immigrants. My study participants felt fortunate when they had these serendipitous meetings.

Nearby was another central fixture in several of my informants' lives: the Centro Comercial Babilónia, the first floor of which informants called Babilónia. Babilónia was home to several eateries and an abundance of small rented kiosk spaces selling practically any goods or services familiar and necessary to members of the African diaspora. There were hair salons, barber shops, and hair braiding stations, and shops sold an array of Black American and Brazilian hair care products. Stalls were stuffed with clothing, shoes, handbags, and jewelry nestled up against electronics stores and shops selling African, Asian, and Brazilian pantry staples like an assortment of beans, dried herbs and chilis, cassava flour, and palm oil. And of course, there were counters to book travel and to send money via Western Union.

Two major processes converted Babilónia, founded in 1980, into this diverse marketplace: increased immigration to Portugal at the turn of the twenty-first century and competition from the growth of larger nearby franchises. Shopping centers such as Colombo, Dolce Vita, and Vasco da Gama had already squeezed out many smaller businesses, but the global financial crisis sunk the small businesses that traditionally catered to middle-class (white) Portuguese too. Meanwhile, vendors began taking over the rentals in Babilónia, catering to migrants—which, study informants insisted, marked the space as "dangerous" to others. Yet interviewees resignified urban spaces such as Centro Comercial Babilónia with feelings of community and belonging. In other words, as one informant joked, Babilónia *wasn't for outsiders*. Though she meant that it was too labyrinthine for the uninitiated, her comment held true in a larger sense: most of its patrons were Africans and African descendants, and most of the stores were managed by racial and ethnic minorities. I came to learn that Babilónia was not only a place to access items that helped informants engage in diasporic practices, such as preparing traditional foods, but a place that mediated meaningful connections among members of Lisboan immigrant and minoritized communities as well.

Ana Paula, the twenty-nine-year-old home care worker introduced in chapter 4, frequently visited Babilónia on her way back from work or on her days off. She could pick up a phone card or grocery items the larger supermarkets failed to stock. That was her purpose the day I met her at the entrance—a recipe she wanted to make for out-of-town visitors required *congo*, or pigeon peas. Our first stop was a small ethnic grocery store managed by a friendly South Asian man. As Ana Paula rummaged through the array of colorful peas and grains that lined the shelves and floors, the attendant offered help. With a smile, she replied that she was looking for something from her country (*minha terra*) but would keep trying elsewhere. And so we threaded our way through a cramped hallway lined with electronics stores, greeted by South Asian men at the counters with bright calls of "Bom dia!" "Boa tarde!" and "Olá meninas, estão muitas boas hoje!"[41] Ana Paula sometimes stopped to joke and laugh with them, introducing me as her "American" cousin or commenting that she hadn't seen them in a while. Often, the men directed the conversation toward what was for sale, and at times, Ana Paula promised she would return at the end of the week, when she got paid.

Though the men's commentary was clearly gendered, these exchanges differed from those I observed in the predominantly white areas of Lisbon. In the neighborhoods where my husband and I once lived, such as Benfica or Alameda, we were rarely greeted by passersby, but the more diverse neighborhoods and parishes of Amadora invited interaction. There, we would be greeted in Portuguese or, as when we were in Cabo Verde's city centers, in *kriolu*. The coldness my interviewees complained about with the white Portuguese was in large part assessed in terms of white people's reluctance to greet them in city streets, stores, and hallways. When Ana Paula rented a room with a friend in Benfica, closer to the city center, she remembered,

> I actually rarely saw anyone. But when I saw [white people], it was always that they would pass me in the hallways, and I always would say "boa tarde," because that's how I was raised. And they look at me and say "boa tarde," but they say it in a way like you can tell that they really don't *want* to say "boa tarde." And not just there, but also on the streets, people pass by you while you are walking, and people don't even want to lift their heads and acknowledge you or greet you. They didn't have the *calor humano* [human warmth] that people feel in, for example, places like Babilónia.

FIG. 7 Outside of Centro Comercial Babilónia. Photo by author.

I suggest that it is the "calor humano" that draws people to Babilónia. In spaces like this, race, ethnicity, and nationality coexisted, and Africans and African descendants like Ana Paula could be both Portuguese and Cabo Verdean in ways that they found meaningful. For many informants, Babilónia is a place to congregate and access important items and services, as well as emotive resources such as the feelings of joy, warmth, and family that link their Lisboan neighborhoods to their ancestral homelands and provide them with an ongoing sense of belonging among their multiethnic immigrant communities. Babilónia is a place for "insiders" within a larger societal context that frames people like Ana Paula or the Black, African, Brazilian, and South and East Asian vendors and patrons as "outsiders."

Hair Matters

Specific spaces within and neighboring Babilónia were particularly important for Cabo Verdean women. Tereza worked in an African-owned salon before entering cleaning services. The work was taxing—cleaning the floors and hair styling tools—yet she described that atmosphere in now-familiar terms: "Where I used to work, in the hair salon . . . that was very nice. It's like you feel at home. The people who worked there had children who always came to the salon, they would greet us, ask how we are doing. They would play with us, with the rest of the workers there. And so it's that feeling of being around family. And, for example, when you consider that feeling and compare it to what it was like when

I worked at the other places, I didn't have that feeling there. They weren't warm." Positive associations and depictions of Black femininity and African families were embedded in the culture of Tereza's workspace and its neighborhood.[42] This, of course, largely conflicted with her and other informants' accounts of cleaning and home care work, in which racial tensions with clients, patrons, and colleagues marred on-the-job experiences. In spaces like African-serving salons, however, it was possible to laugh, play, and enjoy gendered solidarity within and across ethnic differences.

I frequently visited one such hair salon with field informants. Forty-nine-year-old Irene resided in a parish further from Amadora's center but often took advantage of a bus transfer to stop by a salon in Amadora over the weekends. On the day I accompanied her, we went to pick up her four-year-old nephew, who was in the care of her sister's friend at a salon where she worked in the area. Irene had agreed to keep him for the night, as she often did when she had a day off from her work in home care.

We found Irene's nephew sitting on the floor with a girl about his age. They had found an unused electrical outlet and were busy watching a YouTube video narrated by a young crafter with a notable Brazilian-Portuguese accent. It was around 2 p.m., and the salon chairs were packed. Brazilian-accented dialogue emanating from a flat-screen TV mixed with conversations among waiting clients and the swirling sounds of hair dryers. A group of Cabo Verdean saleswomen speaking *kriolu* entered carrying large plastic bags filled with clothing. I joined Irene and some other clients in rummaging through the bags of bright, festive dresses as the saleswomen (all of whom appeared to be in their late twenties to midthirties) chatted playfully, mixing Portuguese and *kriolu* as they caught up on work opportunities in the tourist area of Algarve, the price of hair extensions, and the forever backed-up bus schedule. Irene paused, intently examining the belly of one saleswoman who was pregnant; in *kriolu*, Irene declared, "Bô tem mas 3 mês!"—only three more months until her baby would arrive—then turned to an Angolan woman and translated her six-months-pregnant-diagnosis to her in Portuguese. The woman, dark-skinned with puffs of blonde hair peeking out above the cream-colored hair dye packed down onto her roots, nodded in agreement. The pregnant woman, smiling, walked up to the salon mirror, lifting her shirt to show off her round, bronze-colored belly, lovingly caressing it as she proceeded to lift her shirt further to show off her new multicolored bra. A hairdresser sitting in a swivel chair reached over and playfully poked at her breasts, and the room broke into laughter.

For informants like Irene, the salon was a place of connection, pampering, and commerce all at once. Staff and clients had personal connections to various parts of the African diaspora, including Cabo Verde, Angola, Brazil, Senegal, and Guinea-Bissau.[43] And while interactions between African diasporic groups in Portugal may be marked by conflict in some contexts, in this context, respondents like Irene forged many interethnic connections. Irene, for instance, was born in Cabo Verde but had lived in Angola as a child; I would hear her speak with Angolan clients and workers at the salon about her past life as well as how things had changed now that white Portuguese had begun relocating to cities like Luanda and Maputo in Angola and Mozambique. "There are so many Portuguese outside of the country that if someone said to *them* 'Go back to your country,' they wouldn't all fit here," Irene proclaimed in Portuguese after watching a news segment. Murmuring in agreement, the Angolan woman beside her glanced at the television with an eye roll: "Because now they are leaving for Africa, for Angola, because they see that the situation here is very bad! Now there are a lot of Portuguese in Angola, and they are doing well there; they leave for better conditions. The Portuguese read about the good pay, and that's why Angolans are returning home too."

Interested in this exchange, as well as the sardonic lilt of Irene's voice as she extended the category of *immigrant* to the Portuguese, I asked the women if they thought Portuguese immigrants were well received in Africa. The Angolan woman jumped in: "I have family in Angola. And the Angolans say, *e pa*! I sometimes think that they are donkeys themselves because they prefer to give priority to a Portuguese immigrant than to an Angolan that lives there. A person finishes college there, studies there, and they don't have the same opportunities as a Portuguese that goes there in search of work. They treat Portuguese immigrants better than they treat Angolans that live there!" Her words resonated with passionate ones I'd heard from others: the white Portuguese had little appreciation for migrants and racialized communities in Portugal yet migrated to former African colonies when they needed to find their own better economic opportunities. Summing up the absurd contradictions, Irene laughed sarcastically and shouted, "Somos todos imigrantes!" (We are all immigrants!)

Observing Irene's interactions showed me that creating connection, for them, could come from a shared diasporic African identity as well as their shared racialized and gendered social location in Portugal. They did not have equivalent experiences, but they recognized common ground in the shadow of empire. The salon opened space for many possibilities: a gathering place in which racist and sexist imageries of Black womanhood were not activated or employed as they were in the women's workspaces, that fostered the development of political consciousness, and in which women created belonging within and across ethnic difference in Portugal. Irene and her Angolan counterpart's remarks suggest the heterogeneity of those who occupy the subject position of the "migrant," shifting and resignifying the hegemonic discourse of their "otherness." Their shared experiences of being racialized as Black, African-descendant women sustains diasporic connections beyond the borders of nation-states. That is, in knowing what it is like to be "blackened" in a space of nonbelonging, participants like Irene and others are also able to use Blackness—even in the form of something so everyday as hair braiding—as a tool for establishing a collective sense of belonging.

To be sure, the descriptions I've included throughout also give an idea of the embodied resistance strategies that include proudly wearing culturally distinct clothing, jewelry, and hairstyles and frequenting markets that carry imported goods, as well as the ways a more general lack of access to things like culturally appropriate haircare products further marginalizes African and African-descendant women in Portugal. Not only are the bright outfits, matching headscarves, and intricate hairstyles and braids beautiful forms of self-expression and signifiers of Black space; they also push back against dominant narratives that frame Cabo Verdean service and care workers as dirty, unruly, or uncivilized, as my friends and I were called in that busy restaurant.

Hair, in fact, remains a political issue for Black women of the African diaspora. In the fifteenth century, West African hairstyles often expressed a person's identity and social status by age, marital and kinship ties, ethnic identity, religion, and rank. Hair took on a different meaning during the transatlantic slave trade and beyond as white European society made a spectacle of Black women's bodies, demonizing their hair textures and hairstyles as unclean, grotesque, and unsightly and often forcibly shaving the heads of enslaved Africans. It is no wonder, given this tainted history, that Black women have long utilized the aesthetic practice of hairstyling and adornment to resist alienation throughout the diaspora.[44] Enslaved Africans used hairstyling as a survival tactic, often braiding intricate patterns to symbolize ethnic group membership or even to secretly transport survival materials such as rice and seeds across seas. By the 1950s and '60s, Black hair had become central to Black liberation movements across the globe, including the anticolonial movement in Cabo Verde. As scholar Elizabeth Johnson argues, Black hair today is a "physical manifestation of self-identity," a galvanizing symbol of gender, race, and political liberation.[45]

Hair and self-adornment took on particularly complex social and political meanings for several of the Cabo Verdean care workers I met. They often took great care in styling their voluminous tresses, which helped them attenuate their workplace invisibility and the anonymity of their uniforms. In fact, most respondents had dark complexions and very textured hair despite a dominant cultural image of the Cabo Verdean woman as "mixed-race" with brown skin and a looser curl pattern.[46] Their presence as dark-skinned Cabo Verdean women proudly donning Afrocentric hairstyles such as braids, twists, flat tops, and Afros therefore challenged pervasive colorism. Further, their celebration of Black feminine beauty resisted the dehumanizing effects of colonial and postcolonial gendered and racialized labor regimes that attempted to construct Black women as nurturant and nonnurturant care labor units needing no time or energy to spend on their own Black bodies. Their aesthetic practices are a mobilization against the lived experience of nonworth and nonbelonging in a white supremacist, paradoxically "antiracial" context like Portugal.

Recall Tereza, the woman who decried being treated as an outsider when "playing the tourist" with friends. Part of the othering, she explained, related to how whites saw her as an exotic spectacle, a reality that was particularly pronounced with regard to her hair. When we met, she wore long, box spring braids, though she often sported a voluminous Afro that drew attention. Once, she noted, "People were staring like, woooow, 'Is that your hair?'" She grinned when I asked if people really asked that: "Yes! They did! People on the street ask, 'Is that real hair? Is that your hair? How do you wash it?' And I respond, *Just like how you wash your own hair.*' They ask, 'Can I touch it?'" And how did she respond?

> I actually allow some people to touch it because to me they were just curious and it's so different. But with others, you can feel that energy, you feel that there is some maliciousness behind their request, and at other times you can sense it's just curiosity. So sometimes, there are people who want to touch, and I say, "Yes, you can touch. No problem" [*smiles*]. But with others, you get that sense by the manner they speak to you, and I say, "No! you cannot touch!" But I also might say, "My hair is just like yours, it's just that mine is like this!" [*motions around head*] This happens a lot, a lot. I wish I had a photo to show you, but my Afro is seriously e-n-o-r-m-o-u-s.

She smiled proudly as I added, "And beautiful!"

The attention, Tereza said, was both positive and negative—sometimes admiring, sometimes disparaging, sometimes joking. But "I learned how to ignore these ignorant people," she concluded, because "*I love my hair.* And at the end of the day, we are the ones who end up bringing the negative energy home. . . . I used to think . . . 'Uy, why are people like this?' But I know it's because of ignorance. . . . *So in those situations, I just walk on with pride, Afro and all!*"

The range of reactions Tereza experienced is familiar to many women of the African diaspora; their very bodies can be visually "dissected" in public. As argued by scholars like Frantz Fanon and Jin Haritaworn, this is a colonial and voyeuristic event that reinforces difference through the othering of bodies.[47] Indeed, colonial images of Black women's aggressiveness, hypersexuality, unruliness, and being "out of place" render them hypervisible through the construction of their bodies as objects of fascination, scorn, or desire. Yet Tereza manages the emotional vicissitudes of being devalued by "ignorant" people by using sarcasm, choosing when and how to engage, and affirming her pride by intentionally styling her hair in ways that can't be ignored. Thus, while gendered anti-Blackness penalizes and pathologizes Black hair in public spaces, self-presentation and expression constitute Tereza's own form of resistance as she "walk[s] on with pride, Afro and all." Hair and hairstyles are socially and politically powerful.[48]

Kriolu

Today, Portuguese remains the formal language of business, politics, and education, and it is required in many of my informants' workplaces. But *kriolu*, or creole, is the language of everyday life, the language of the diaspora. Its use signifies ethnic difference *and* connects Cabo Verdeans to a broader diasporic identity through a common tongue.[49] Importantly, Cabo Verdean *kriolu* was borne out of colonialism, and it incorporates linguistic features from Portuguese, Spanish, Balante, Mande, Fula, and other languages from the upper Guinea coast.[50] The Portuguese colonial state went so far as to prohibit the speaking of *kriolu* in formal institutions and its publication in literature, a prohibition reflecting fear, domination, and collective control.[51] Today, however, people tell me it is essential to understand *kriolu* to understand Cabo Verde, because *kriolu* also plays into diasporic racial identity construction. As anthropologist Derek Pardue's work on Cabo Verdean male rappers in Lisbon uncovered, using *kriolu* creates a sense of *political* as well as ethnoracial membership.[52] Developed out of colonialist repression, Pardue argues, the language is a "rebellious backtalk against contemporary discourses" that allows for the telling of otherwise untold stories. In anthropological research from Katherine Carter and Judy Aulette, another case study of the continued use of *kriolu*, we also see how Cabo Verdean women from the island of Santiago use it to challenge gendered power relations as they deftly lob cajolery, sarcasm, and hidden meanings.[53]

Most of the foreign-born Cabo Verdean home care and institutional cleaning workers I spoke with had finished at least some high school, which necessarily meant they spoke Portuguese. Yet in Portugal, they were told they didn't speak "real" Portuguese. Bianca, twenty-six, struggled to adjust linguistically when she migrated in her late teens: "Even though people speak Portuguese in Cabo Verde, it's an antique type of Portuguese. So, when we arrived here, I was thinking in *kriolu* and speaking in Portuguese." As she began working, several elders under Bianca's care told her directly that her Portuguese was "bad" or, more commonly, that she spoke "African Portuguese."[54] Comments like these came to study participants from white Portuguese colleagues, too, who subtly commented on the inadequacies of their speech or outright forbade them to speak *kriolu* in front of patrons, care recipients and families, and Portuguese-speaking colleagues. It was within this visible-invisible dyad so poignantly expressed by Bianca that the *kriolu* language emerged in my data as an important vector of belonging:

> The truth is we are not supposed to speak in *kriolu*. Because, according to what our boss tells us, speaking in front of people in a language that they don't understand is something a person does when they lack an education; it's disrespectful. But the truth is we speak our *kriolu* in the workplace and in front of the people we care for. Some of them complain; they suck their teeth and say we are speaking in

a language from our country, a language that they don't understand.... The truth is that we shouldn't speak *kriolu* at work, but that's something I always contest because they tell us not to do it and [*raises voice*] they promise consequences, but it has never happened. It just comes out naturally.

The policing of Bianca's language serves as an ideological border in her workplace, reinforcing notions of belonging and nonbelonging. Her words reflect the pain of hearing her clients remind her that she is not in "her country," that she is a foreigner. Yet her refusal to refrain from speaking in *kriolu* also represents an act of resistance in her workplace. Other respondents similarly reported that they were told by managers to refrain from speaking *kriolu* because others might assume they were talking about them—a gendered, racialized, and xenophobic assumption of deviousness that fit with Portuguese stereotypes of Africans and has been found in other research on service encounters between native-born customers and migrant-origin workers.[55] Like Bianca, they, too, refused to comply. For example, Elisete, a thirty-nine-year-old home care worker of two years at the time of our interview, told me elders and their family members and visiting friends "don't like us to speak *kriolu*" because "they claim they can't understand us, and they don't like it. But I speak to them [elder clients] in Portuguese! But I speak to my colleagues in *kriolu* because we are Cabo Verdean, and it is more natural. But then I receive calls from my boss, and she complains that someone—maybe an old person or maybe their family—called her to tell her that I wasn't speaking in Portuguese to them! Because they tell on us. They get upset!"

Language represents and creates relationships of control and power. This reality is particularly charged in a context where nationality, identity, and language are strongly linked and have, historically, been dispersed throughout the world via colonial domination. However, language also created a space of belonging, even a way to undermine uneven workplace power dynamics, for study participants like Bianca and Elisete. By switching to *kriolu* with ease throughout their workday, respondents defied the organization's requirement that African women be "palatable" to white Portuguese clients and their families. This language fluidity is reminiscent of the literature on "code-switching," which finds that racialized groups must linguistically negotiate two worlds.[56] Here we can understand that this linguistic "double consciousness" is both freeing and challenging for Black women.[57]

Though code-switching is often framed as a matter of surviving in predominantly middle-class white spaces through cultural assimilation, I argue that my respondents' use of *kriolu within* their workspaces actively defies the construction of Black women as Others in need of cultural assimilation. As opposed to changing oneself to optimize the comfort of others, Cabo Verdean care workers instead resort to what Vershawn Young calls "code meshing" by drawing on all their linguistic resources.[58] *Kriolu*, as they put it, came out naturally as they went about their days, and I found that its use (however penalized) resignified their challenging workspaces. *Kriolu* also allowed them to establish cross-ethnic ties with other African or African-descendant colleagues, a reality that, I argue, strengthened their belonging. In this sense, to speak a hybrid language like *kriolu* in Portugal acts as a backtalk to the shadow of empire in which Africans and Portuguese are seen and treated as linguistically and, indeed, racially incompatible.

I noted that study participants commonly switched to *kriolu* when communicating with co-ethnics and their colleagues from Guinea-Bissau, as it seemed to fit with their shared identity.[59] *Kriolu* allowed them to infuse happiness and laughter into their tiring, and at times monotonous, daily routines by connecting to their cultural identity in worksites, hallways, or break rooms. This, in turn, allowed them to collectively cultivate joyful belonging. In one case, a participant had no fellow Cabo Verdeans on her work shift, but Adilson, an employee in the office building she cleaned, was Cabo Verdean and liked to talk with her in *kriolu*. They had a warm relationship that contrasted with the others Myra, thirty-four, had in her workplace:

> We have Angolans, Cabo Verdeans, Portuguese, Brazilian colleagues who work in cleaning services with me. So I can't really speak *kriolu* with anyone there, just with Adilson! I always speak *kriolu* with Adilson.... It's a whole other relationship with him. We are the only *negros* [Blacks] that are there. I mean there are some other *negro* workers there, in cleaning. But not as employees. But with Adilson, you know, we can joke around. We can talk about everything. The other people, the employees, don't really talk to me like that. I don't know if they are scared or what.... There are some that are racist there. Sometimes they look at you and don't even respond, but not Adilson. He always comes by to ask how I am and how my children are, for example.

Being able to communicate with a co-ethnic in her workplace allowed Myra to use words that reflect a colonial history but do not take the perspective of the colonizer, to safeguard her thoughts and feelings and share them selectively, which translated to a feeling of solidarity, belonging, and solace despite the class difference between herself and Adilson. Together, the two conversants resignified the workplace, stripping away a little bit of the power structure that shaped their subordinate social and economic locations.

When activated intentionally, *kriolu* went beyond symbolizing kinship—it became an important tool of resistance. This strategy was especially clear to me during a gathering with a few of my informants from the cleaning services sector. Aline, the forty-eight-year-old host, had that Sunday off from her two jobs. When I shared my interest in *kriolu*, especially that some managers told their workers to speak Portuguese only, one of her guests, Nácia, smiled broadly. "They don't want us to speak *kriolu*, but we do. It comes out!" Nácia worked with a *patroa*, one of the upper-class white Portuguese women who could hire domestic help in the informal market, a few days a week on top of her own job with a cleaning firm. This *patroa* was a lesbian, and her partner made things difficult for Nácia. "She is just like a man," she said. "She wears men's clothing. . . . She, or the *marida*, passes without saying anything to me, if anything is wrong, she gets upset." Here, Nácia plays with Portuguese language conventions, transforming the word for husband, *marido*, to the feminine *marida*, a choice highlighting the misalignment of her employer's intimate relationship with gendered and heteronormative Portuguese language norms while also alluding to the patriarchal distribution of household and social power. Nácia explained to me that she was raised Catholic and was not accustomed to interacting with queer people, but she did not express much of an issue with her employer's lesbian relationship. In fact, she perceived her employer, or *patroa*, as reasonable and fair but identified the problem as "her, my boss's *marida*. She's a disrespectful person. She removes her clothing and throws it on the floor, with the underwear and socks left inside. And sometimes, she leaves her underwear with the dirty pad covered with menstruation! It's a way to humiliate me."

An older woman, Bela, who had labored years as a domestic worker in Portugal, was listening in. She interjected in fervent *kriolu*: "N'ta traba calcinha ku penso na el e n'ta fulhaba dento lixo pan inxinal! Falta respetu! Fulhal dento lixo!"[60] As Bela decried the disrespect and insisted she would throw the woman's underwear in the garbage to teach her a lesson, Nácia frowned and looked away from the group. In Portuguese, she said to me, "I am afraid that my boss would fire me, I'm afraid of losing my job. But Celeste, this is where the *kriolu* comes out! [*smiling*] My boss's *marida*, when she's home, she likes to demand things. And she's like a man! She leaves dishes in the sink, things on the floors. So I have to follow her, picking up all the crap she leaves around the apartment. But what do I do? I speak *kriolu*."

With that, she seamlessly switched back into *kriolu*: "N'flal dento mi, 'ba pa inferno!' Sem medo, n'flal 'ba pa merda.' Or I say things like, 'Oh, dan pa doidu!' when she asks me to do these stupid things."[61]

The guests burst into joyful laughter as Nácia, in the middle of the living room, acted out the scenario, straightening her posture and mumbling curse words and complaints under her breath in *kriolu*: "Ba pa merda! Limpa bu porcaria!" (Go to hell! Clean your own dirty shit!) She added, smiling, "Sometimes, [the *marida*] turns and asks me, 'What did you say?' And I smile and tell her in *Portuguese*-Portuguese, 'Oh, nothing, ma'am. I was just talking to myself and thinking about what I have to do before I leave.'"

In addition to helping form bonds across social divisions, *kriolu* is also an important source of expression, permitting women to stand up for themselves through hidden meanings. While Nácia is clearly in a subordinate position and legitimately afraid to complain outright, she can use *kriolu* to express *and* safeguard her feelings of dissatisfaction and anger over the conditions of her work. Thus, in occupations in which workers are often compelled to perform gendered subservience through silence and labor in solitude as they traverse multiple public, racialized spaces, the *kriolu* language represents an important mechanism for tacit challenges and the application of new meanings to the workplace.

Conclusion

Laboring in the shadow of empire means traversing the several spaces where Cabo Verdean women are marginalized due to their intersecting identities. As this book has shown, Cabo Verdean women in cleaning and home care services are often embedded in spaces of domination, both figuratively and literally. They spend a great deal of time within elders' private homes, traversing racialized and spatialized boundaries between their homes and neighborhood spaces and those located near their workplaces. They may have personal experiences with the everyday gendered racism of being verbally (and, indeed, violently) accosted by white pedestrians and patrons, and they have all witnessed other Black men and women being told to "go back to their countries." Institutional cleaning workers similarly traversed racialized boundaries of space as they traveled to and from work, often associating their invisibility with the spatial and temporal dimensions of their jobs. Both work occupations and the workers' experiences therein represent the dialectic relationship of globalized, gendered, racialized, and capitalist migrations: they are at once hypervisible and invisible as "appropriate" service workers in postindustrial worksites in the shadow of empire.

This is not the only story to be told, however. The challenges of structural racism in "antiracial" Portugal also create spaces for resistance, joy, and subaltern articulation. I argue that it is through reclaimed spaces that Cabo Verdean women creatively *reimagine* a Portugal beyond the shadow of empire. Indeed, Jaqueline Nassy Brown argues, Black Europe and the African diaspora are a "racialized geography of *imagination*" molded by the "*situated encounters*" between members of Black communities.[62] Likewise, situated encounters linking Cabo Verdeans *here* and *there* are negotiated within the localized spaces where African diasporic migrations are culturally specific and similarly racialized. Portugal is not *white* in these spaces, nor are these spaces, literally and singularly, *Black* spaces. In centering *humanness*, *Africanness*, and *Blackness* all at once in their localized and spatialized feelings and practices of joyful belonging, Cabo Verdean care workers resignify spaces otherwise experienced as cold, lacking, or unwelcoming. The imagined places of joyful belonging I describe in this chapter are constructed in tandem with processes of gendered racial formation in Portuguese society. Yet they simultaneously undermine narrow, racist caricatures and stereotypes of Black womanhood assaulting my respondents throughout their travels and toilings. They open room to breathe, share information, celebrate, commiserate, and importantly, feel joy. They represent moments of possibility from within and perhaps beyond the shadow of empire.

7

Laboring beyond the Shadow of Empire

• •

Laboring in the Shadow of Empire demonstrates that Cabo Verdean care service workers are both integral to and marginalized by Portugal's modern urban society. In many ways, the experiences I present in these pages have revealed the contradictions inherent in the holiday with which I opened the manuscript: Portugal's Freedom Day, or Dia da Liberdade. You have read how these African migrant and African-descendant women are "included" in the sense that they have access to legislative status and work in the formal markets, yet their inclusion is conditional, and it is challenged and fragmented in myriad daily interactions. These are the moments that rupture Portugal's claims to antiracialism and bring the racialized and gendered social structure—shaped by legacies of empire and colonialism, patriarchy, white supremacy, and neocapital globalization—to bear at the individual, personal level. The everyday experiences shared by those who labor in eldercare and cleaning services make plain the continuation of the harmful intersectional haunting of colonialist hierarchies well past Cabo Verde's flag independence.

That the struggles encountered by African-descendant women care service workers in the shadow of empire is a global struggle is evident. Throughout Europe, people of African descent experience the varied impacts of systemic racism, including an overrepresentation in segregated schools, police violence, substandard and informal housing, and low-skilled occupations—a fact that holds regardless of their educational qualifications.[1] Antiracist activists and social organizations thus insist that anti-Blackness and its intersectional and colonial underpinnings are widespread throughout Europe. These groups' ongoing critical demands to fight anti-Blackness across Europe draw forth the hypocrisy of racist denial and challenge the global epistemologies that uphold it via white ignorance.

We have also seen a paradox of visibility specific to African-descendant women in Portugal but almost certainly replicated across other racialized and gendered social groups in Europe. The nation's colonial history and unacknowledged racialized and gendered foundations usher in the structural marginalization and ideological invisibility of a large segment of its population, who are nonetheless hypervisible as "citizen outsiders," in the words of sociologist Jean Beaman.[2] They are on streets and on sidewalks; in public transportation, politics, and popular culture; within educational institutions; in national sports; and in workplaces. The presence of a multifaceted African-descendant community in and around Europe, just like the presence of a durable heteropatriarchal white supremacy, *is simply undeniable* in a society where pronouncements of "antiracialism" serve as a tool of coloniality to further obscure the Black presence in Portugal as well as their calls for justice. As Joacine Katar Moreira, one of the first three Black members of the Portuguese parliament, incisively retorts, "Europe is not white. Europe is not a white man. . . . There is no democracy without equity, equality. But also, there is no equality without the voices of ethnic minorities in Europe."[3]

Changing Tides

I began this research in 2014, before the United States had seen the full force of Trumpism and on the cusp of an international surge in the Black Lives Matter (BLM) movement, and my findings remain relevant as European and U.S. voters and legislatures embrace a virulent strain of racial politics. Like Donald Trump in the United States, Geert Wilders in the Netherlands, Marine Le Pen in France, and Jair Bolsonaro in Brazil, André Ventura has learned to use the media to widen his audience and rile his base through divisive racist and xenophobic rhetoric. In 2019, this leader of the Portuguese profascist, far-right Chega Party (in English, "Enough") led an electoral push that gained his party parliamentary seats. Two years later, Ventura stunned the public by securing a third-place finish in Portugal's presidential election. In March 2024, the Chega Party won nearly 19 percent of the votes in a general snap election, putting it on the path to becoming the third largest political force in Portugal.

Even so, Portugal has historically been regarded as a loner in a sea of increasingly rightward-leaning European countries. What can we gather from *this* paradox? As I have argued throughout this book, antiracial ideology represents a collective manifestation of dominant whites' social position in the shadow of empire. Antiracial ideology has historically translated to a national silence about race and racism, institutionalized in Portugal's state bodies and civil society through claims of European exceptionalism. Antiracial ideology also intersects with Portuguese lusotropicalist ideology, which posits that Portugal's colonialism was a kinder, gentler, more "benevolent colonialism" than that imposed by its imperial counterparts. Therefore, the logic goes, the Portuguese were not and are not "racist." Antiracial ideology justifies the racial order via the demobilization of antiracist claims made by antiracist social movements that challenge racial states.

In fact, Ventura's rallying cry, as he led counterprotests in 2020 against those drawing attention to systemic racism in Portugal, was the slogan "Portugal não e racista" (Portugal is not racist). These pernicious words highlight how antiracialism, as a global ideological system of dominance, sustains the inequality that it purports to deny: it aims to naturalize the existence of white supremacy and institutionalized racism evidenced in mechanisms of state control, external ascription, spatial segregation, and of course, everyday racism by rendering them invisible—a fantastical, fictional boogeyman.

As they labor in the shadow of empire, the women I interviewed bear witness to the "fact," to borrow from Frantz Fanon, of systemic gendered anti-Blackness simmering under Portuguese society. These Cabo Verdean women routinely questioned the social impossibility of racism as well as the irony, even absurdity, of the treatment they encountered from white Portuguese people in public spaces and on the job. As postcolonial subjects in a former colonial metropole, they recognized that their social positions were shaped by decades of colonial and anticolonial struggle—in fact, as their migration stories reminded me time and again, they would not be "here" if the Portuguese had never been "there." Today, they recognize that it is also true that if they were not "here," the Portuguese might not be either: their role as laborers in care service occupations is also shaped by a racial and gendered occupational structure within a capitalist system that ultimately needs their stigmatized, low-waged labor to operate, thrive, and manage the challenges of population shifts.

Cabo Verdean women's labor informs their individual and collective feelings of belonging within the shadow of empire. It is primarily through the interactions and interdependencies of *work* that Cabo Verdean women's racial and gender identities are imposed as burdens, limitations, and reasons for exclusion. Still, while seeing themselves racially as Black women, or *mulheres negras*, day to day, many of the women I met also configured their identities in ways that emphasize the specificity of their specific island roots, along with their "Cabo Verdean," "African," and at times "Portuguese" identities. Proud of their multifaceted, diasporic identities, they envision a world beyond hierarchical categories of human difference and challenge the very stage upon which the Portuguese nation and civil society perform white ignorance.

Moving beyond the Shadow of Empire

We are in a moment of change. Activists and communities in Portugal are actively denouncing antiracialism by emphasizing the links between Portugal's colonial past and the pervasive reality of systemic racism in the colonial present. Along with scholars, journalists, everyday people, and international monitoring bodies, these antiracist activists have brought global scrutiny to the Portuguese state, to the widespread systemic racism, racialized surveillance of neighborhoods, and police violence against African, African-descendant, Roma, and other racially minoritized communities inside its borders.

During my fieldwork visits in 2015, a group of eight police officers kidnapped and beat a group of Cabo Verdean men in an ethnic enclave near Lisbon, injuring two Black women bystanders, and protests against racialized police violence unfolded. Soon there were other actions drawing news cameras, and by 2020, when the world woke to the urgent need for a global BLM-led change following the murder of forty-six-year-old George Floyd by Minneapolis Police officers led by Derek Chauvin, my informants would speak of change in the air. In February of that year, antiracist groups marched for Cláudia Simões, an African-descendant woman brutally beaten by Portuguese law enforcement on the streets of Amadora. In May, major cities in Portugal and throughout the world were inundated by protests related to Floyd's death on the pavement of a busy intersection in a midwestern U.S. city. In July, the placards demanded justice for Bruno Candé Marques, a thirty-nine-year-old African-descendant Portuguese man murdered, point blank, on a busy Lisboan street by Evaristo Marinho, a seventy-seven-year-old white Portuguese man who had served as a soldier in the colonial army in Angola. My informants were *always* resolute that *their* lives mattered, but at this moment, they appear even more resolute in demanding that all of Portugal, Europe, and the world accept that fact.

The not-so-surprising irony, however, is that an increase in racist and xenophobic far-right-wing backlash travels alongside these recent developments.[4] It has been clear that the greater visibility of antiracist, intersectional claims *threatens* groups that are positioned as superior within a racialized social system. Thus, at this critical moment, I suggest there is much to gain from the perspectives of Cabo Verdean care service workers facing intersectional social injustice in Portugal. The Cabo Verdean women I spoke to wanted to be treated with dignity and respect, they wanted access to work that provided compensation adequate to sustain their families, and they wanted their families to *belong* in Portuguese society. They understood their centrality to society and the social invisibility of their plight—the unaddressed manifestations of oppressions unique to Black women in Portugal, above and beyond police violence alone.

Possible Ways Forward

The latest resurgence of the long standing Movimento Negro (Black Movement) in Portugal and its continued calls to decolonize Portuguese society are a reminder of how Cabo Verdean transnational care migrants' continued presence in Portugal is directly related to the European imperial and colonial project. As such, Cabo Verdean working women will not experience full equality without the work to decolonize reproductive labor by delivering intersectional, reparatory justice. Here I suggest some possible ways forward.

From the start, care workers must be paid fair and equitable wages. This is paramount. Care work enables people and communities to thrive across generations, yet the level of economic scarcity experienced by this workforce in Portugal and across the globe is unacceptable.

Cabo Verdean care workers' experiences also demonstrate another critical step to undo the harm of systemic racism: the Portuguese state must collect desegregated national census data on race and ethnicity.[5] As many scholars and activists have long argued, this would allow for enhanced intersectional research on and considerations of how racism specifically impacts Africans and African descendants across contexts and social locations (including region, occupational sector, age, gender, education, citizenship, and migration cohort). For example, scholars and reformers would also benefit tremendously from a full accounting of how Cabo Verdean and other African-descendant women's segregation into institutional care service work positions them as appropriate to low-wage, stigmatized "dirty" work, feeding a loop in which labor market sorting is naturalized into an ideological justification for these women's workplace exploitation. In chapters 4 and 5 in particular, I uncovered how this assumption of labor appropriateness has inflected the kinds of work delegated to them and the types and degrees of everyday gendered anti-Black racism they face from clients and their families, employers, and those white Portuguese people who work in the institutional spaces Black women clean (see table 2 in appendix for workplace comparison). Labor appropriateness further intersects with antiracialism through the institutionalized silencing of Black women's claims of discrimination and their overall needs as workers. Together, the "ranking" of these workers on the job via others' assumptions became a steadfast barrier to occupational achievement and dignity.

My findings therefore suggest that the critical work of reducing this inequality will require an overhaul of the norms creating status and power differentials between and among workers. I believe that one way to combat the normativity and privilege of white femininity in these racialized and gendered occupations is for all members of the organizations to recognize the reality of anti-Black gendered racism in Portugal and how it disproportionally impacts Black workers—and that the only way to do that is to attend to, *validate*, and redress the actual experiences of those on the knife's edge of oppression. The emotional harm experienced by care workers when they encounter anti-Black racism from elders and their families, colleagues, and unknown patrons should not be underestimated. A work setting rife with racist microaggressions (if not macroaggressions) generates a profound sense of invalidation among workers. This, in conjunction with low pay and minimal labor protections, feeds into the overall devaluation loop of the work. As I have argued throughout this book, the invisibility of the harm of racism must be made visible if it is to be abolished.

A full recognition of and commitment to fighting gendered anti-Black racism must therefore be institutionalized or Black women will be unable to access formal organizational redress (a lack of access that has been used to dismiss their claims of discrimination as personal/personnel difficulties rather than evidence of a widespread social system). This means listening to the workers' stories of gendered racism and institutionally acknowledging the full range of racism that manifests on the job (including in hiring, firing, promotion, racial harassment, racial microaggressions, the use of racial slurs and colonial rhetoric, and retaliation). This also involves communicating and making accessible state-level antidiscrimination reporting mechanisms around the workplace and developing and communicating comprehensive workplace policies for dealing with all forms of racial discrimination. In turn, managers must communicate what is not acceptable to the full range of organizational actors, including administrators, all staff and personnel, elders *and* their families, building/store employees, and of course, frontline workers.

Of course, eldercare and cleaning work are different forms of work. Given how the nurturant caring labor of home care intersects with a moral ethos to provide care to an aged population, it may be unlikely that elders who suffer from severe diseases will be dismissed altogether from care (recall how Alzheimer's disease, for example, was used to explain away racism in chapter 4). Nonnurturant institutional cleaning labor also poses challenges for redress, as workplace interactions can be infinite for those who labor in large public venues and interact with hundreds of people per day. Still, instead of invalidating workers' experiences by maintaining a culture of silence around everyday racism, efforts could be directed toward taking care of the person and the community that experiences racial harm. At the very minimum, the workplace should be a place of *validation* where workers feel both seen and heard.

Indeed, policies that communicate consequences and avenues for reporting remain critical, but they are not enough. While formal avenues to report racism may exist (for example, the Portuguese Commission for Equality and Against Racial Discrimination) they are underutilized for several reasons, including fear of retaliation or uncertainty that reporting will lead to any meaningful change.[6] Collecting data to understand what challenges racially minoritized employees are facing in order to implement antiracist interventions and policies is also important. Presenting those data in a way that uplifts Black workers' voices and both *problematizes* and *denormalizes* the so-called normal occurrence of gendered racism in caring work is also key.[7]

Additionally, some home care agencies are formalized by the state, others are private organizations, and some are public-private hybrids; the state-run agencies offer union access, but the others lack such avenues for addressing gendered racism. Institutional cleaning firms rely on cheap labor to meet the needs of cash-strapped building owners. While these workers have access to a formal contract, their actual access to unionization is also inconsistent. Expanding union access across both industries *and* prioritizing protections from intersectional discrimination within the hiring organization and union are therefore important additional steps. Indeed, as argued by Joaze Bernardino-Costa, unions provide social spaces that combat the isolation of workspaces and encourage intersectional empowerment versus disempowerment among care workers, where categories such as race, color, class, gender, and citizenship provide critical points of connection to inspire action.[8] However, I must stress that these changes will matter *much* more when Black women are able to access a larger variety of jobs. The abolishment of racial and gender discrimination in the general labor market, along with distributive justice policies in education and employment, will work toward undoing the racializing and gendering of work itself.

The ongoing struggle for fair housing throughout Portugal also constitutes another major part of an antiracist struggle in the shadow of empire. In Lisbon, alongside a global rise in tourism, a tsunami of gentrification has spread across inner-city neighborhoods and beyond, pricing out many residents from long-standing ethnic enclaves. As chapter 6 illustrates, ethnic enclaves offer places of respite in which racialized groups form community and enact critical consciousness. At times, they may become generative spaces for experiencing joy and engaging in political protest and contestation. As several informal housing developments have been destroyed recently and communities are being priced out of their neighborhoods due to the sprawling effects of gentrification in greater metropolitan areas, the state's narrow view of the *bairros* and the struggle for dignified housing in Portugal have become ever clearer.[9]

At an even broader level, the stories I present suggest addressing macrolevel processes from the binds of neoliberal capitalism and the remnants of imperial and colonial power that have upheld institutional cleaning and eldercare work as feminized, racialized, globalized, and postindustrial worksites. For instance, states using neoliberal retrenchment to combat economic uncertainty have relied on the structural disadvantages created by unacknowledged race, gender, class, and national divisions to shunt migrants into high-demand, low-status jobs. At the same time, due to asymmetrical North/South relations, the global economy has generated a parallel demand for feminized immigrant labor through the vast expansion of low-wage service jobs into further devalued sectors. States control the conditions by which migrants can legally enter their borders, creating another way to selectively shape social hierarchies; Portugal, for instance, currently favors family reunification as its major mode of legal entry for African migrants from its former colonies, and so it reinforces the major pathway by which African-descendant women explained they found their way into service and care work. This migration scheme effectively results in a subpopulation of working-class immigrant families, many of whom are concentrated in lower-skilled, often dead-end care service jobs and substandard housing at the city's peripheries.

Thus, increasing access to formalized migration pathways and naturalization for *all migrants* is critically important, but more specific efforts are needed to increase Africans' and African descendants' education and occupational opportunities, allocate state support for their families, and provide access to decent, dignified, and affordable housing, all of which will increase their employment options and understanding of their labor rights. Widespread collective bargaining and unionization efforts will be helpful here too.

On the other end of the migration pathway, in Cabo Verde, more work must be done to undo neoliberal rollbacks of social programs and protections for women and girls. But how? The severe economic consequences of the COVID-19 pandemic have deepened gender poverty gaps while generating the largest decline in economic output in Cabo Verde ever recorded—the second largest in sub-Saharan Africa. The cost of living in Cabo Verde has also soared since the start of the COVID-19 pandemic, which has only been exacerbated by the Russia-Ukraine war. Of course, the decline in tourism during the crisis and the disruption of Ukrainian agriculture explain a large part of this decline. However, *imperial monetary policies* are also implicated in the gendered economic vulnerabilities that have been intensified by the pandemic and the ripple effects of the war. As of 2021, Cabo Verde owes billions of dollars to external creditors, with Portugal being one of the largest bilateral creditors. Cabo Verde currently owes nearly 600 million euros in debt to the government of Portugal and to Caixa Geral de Depósitos, a Portuguese state-owned bank.[10] The solution, according to many advocates, is for debt payments to be channeled into funds earmarked specifically for social programs. A new debt-for-climate deal between Portugal and Cabo Verde that will swap 150 million dollars of "forgiven debt" for investments in a climate fund represents this approach.

To be sure, there is a clear link between climate action and Cabo Verdean women's empowerment, but this debt-for-climate approach, as many climate activists argue, remains insufficient. For one, it requires a nation that contributes very little to global carbon emissions to foot the bill for climate change, and it does not include the much larger share of funds owed to Caixa Geral de Depósitos.[11] But *debt justice*, as convincingly argued by Afro-feminists, recognizes that the chronic debt crises in Africa also stem from a historical legacy of colonial and imperialist power inequalities. Debt-for-climate deals evade economic sovereignty from impacted places, and they implicitly legitimize "West and the Rest" power hierarchies and continued colonial dispossession.[12] One way to dismantle the intersectional haunting of the shadow of empire is for former European empires (and Western disciplinary institutions) to abolish the continuation of imperial monetary policies and to instead pursue true debt cancellation as a central—and necessary—form of reparations.

This brings me to a theoretical process in need of redress: the way gendered anti-Blackness and the devaluation of care service work have intertwined within the contemporary processes of the neocolonial global economy to produce and exacerbate marginalization. For centuries, Western empires advanced their racial capitalist agenda by developing a deeply colonial logic that racialized Black women's ontology as invisible, hypervisible, *and* uniquely appropriate for devalued, so-called dirty work. When it comes to nurturant and nonnurturant caring work today, the tensions and contradictions I describe in this book reflect how coloniality lives on in the enduring societal assumption—on an almost uniformly global scale—that reproductive labor is different from *real* labor. The idea that "dirty work" is motivated by altruism and love or even servility undervalues care work and discredits this work's true economic and social value in our lives. As pointed out by feminist philosopher Joan Tronto, in the absence of a real political imperative to place caring at the center of political life, democracy remains untenable.[13] That is because care workers are excluded from the sphere of care through market imperatives that reframe them not as care *providers* but as care *burdens*. Foremost, without a wide embrace and recognition of the social worth and humanity of the people who carry out the work and a nuanced understanding of care work, whether nurturant or nonnurturant, that bridges the dignity and complexity of this skilled labor, the public may never gain an appropriate awareness of care work, in all its forms, as a *valuable* sociopolitical practice.

We simply need to consider institutional African and African-descendant cleaning workers' and eldercare workers' roles during the COVID-19 pandemic. They were and remain at the front lines—they care for the elders who are immunocompromised and therefore deemed especially vulnerable, and they clean a city's infrastructure in dire need of disinfection during a pandemic. Yet as a reserve labor pool, and despite the contribution they provide to society writ large as nurturant and nonnurturant care laborers, they are often the first to get fired during an economic downturn. By virtue of their work, they are also especially vulnerable to severe illness.

Moreover, the stories I present in this work belong to Cabo Verdean women who work for organizations in which they have no control over the labor process. There is, however, a steady growth of entrepreneurial activity among African descendants in Portugal. Some informants had dreams of renting or owning space to start up their own hair salons or cafés someday; others had relatives and friends who had already done so. It was also not uncommon for informants to send drums and packages to Cabo Verde with goods they had collected over months to be sold at a relative's storefront on the islands. Small numbers of

Cabo Verdean–owned domestic cleaning companies also exist in Portugal. No doubt the employees who labor for these smaller enterprises have distinct experiences working in an environment where staff are co-ethnic at all levels of the organization. The question of Cabo Verdean men's employment is also important, as they have long labored within the agricultural and construction sector, yet growing numbers also fill nonnurturant roles, including food services and institutional cleaning work. A number of Cabo Verdean–owned construction companies also exist throughout Portugal. Even so, I believe the key areas for action that I outline throughout will also improve migrants' and their families' ability to pursue their own personal and collective aspirations, which include entrepreneurial activity.

The final area of improvement identified through my respondents' accounts is perhaps the broadest: Cabo Verdean working women will not have any real equality without high-level recognition and dogged work to eradicate the systemic racism denied by the state, nor without applying the same to gender discrimination. Indeed, intersectional and antiracist scholar-activists and Black feminist organizations based in Portugal are intentional in challenging the effects of the invisibility of Black women's social plight.[14] Recall that gender, unlike race, *is* considered a legitimate social category in Portugal, and addressing it as such will necessarily yield beneficial results for the deconstruction of racism. Cabo Verdean women care service workers' voices thus similarly remind us that the fight against systemic racial inequality must center on the intersections of multiple systems of oppression because listening to and prioritizing their knowledge uncover the fact that gender is bound to race, class, nation, and citizenship so that whiteness and privilege are gendered to the benefit of white men as well as white women. Combating the inequality of the Portuguese labor market requires massive intersectional, decolonial disruption. Intersectionality has always been intended to be a justice-oriented approach, and its emancipatory potential cannot be understated.

Bordering Belonging

Restrictive anti-Black and xenophobic border policies mean that a group like Cabo Verdean women who labor within formal care/service occupations is a great inroad to the lives lived in between and alongside *borders*. To think beyond the border, in other words, we need to look at what happens at the border, at the margins where so many Cabo Verdean women live, raise families, and carve out strategies of resistance (including, in the simplest sense, joy and pride in cultural practices). At the personal level, few of the women I interviewed over the years were personally concerned about issues related to border security and irregular migration, only to the ways these issues impacted their and others' communities. They frequently thought about those who could not migrate legally and found themselves working in precarious, insecure, and dangerous circumstances. Here, where nationality law is considered among Europe's "most generous," the state's continued embrace of *jus soli* in its nationality regime continues to disadvantage postcolonial migrants like those in the Cabo Verdean diaspora. The struggle Black Portuguese are currently leading is a testament to how this diasporic community aims to rewrite the national narrative of belonging and nonbelonging.

Thus, thinking *beyond* the border while also *centering* the border means recognizing the many facets of social belonging. Restrictive policies compel irregular migration throughout Europe in the shadow of empire, but the impact of colonialism extends beyond and seeps through the border, shaping hierarchical ideas of belonging that buttress the nation. It finds its way onto city streets, onto public transportation, and into workplaces. In Europe, where migration is treated like a recent phenomenon, the traumatic impact of centuries of colonialism glides past an intricate system of border security to land on people's doorsteps and temper their opportunities. It finds its way into the intimate spaces of private homes, the corridors and hallways of commercial buildings, and the mouths that hurl insults, mumble recriminations, and boldly ask, "Where are you *from*?"

Places like Portugal purport to embrace liberalism and inclusivity, positioning themselves against the draconian policies of countries like the United States, but challenging white European innocence means recognizing and dismantling the incredible importance of formalized *and* informal borders. It means recognizing how and why a Cabo Verdean woman stands on Portuguese soil on unequal terms. It means laying bare how colonial legacies of impoverishment and the gendered and racial social organization of Europe constitute the long shadow of empire under which women like Maria, Dilza, Jandy, and Mirela labor. It means empathizing deeply with the core frustration facing the Cabo Verdean women whose voices animate this book: their relentless, often unfulfilled desire to belong. Not just as Portuguese workers but perhaps also as Cabo Verdean, or African, or European, or Portuguese individuals, as family members and mothers, sisters and aunts, and cousins and friends with aspirations and rights including dignified treatment in the quotidian politics of urban survival.

Methodological Appendix

Starting in January 2015, I traveled to Portugal and spent nine months in the field informally and formally interviewing eldercare workers and their families and generally observing eldercare workers as they went through their daily routines; more specifically, I rode along with eldercare workers on their travels to work, observing some eldercare home visits, sleeping in my field informants' homes, and helping out with childcare.[1] In addition to these interviews, many of which primarily took place in the private homes of my field informants, I engaged in extended conversations with family members in Cabo Verde during a five-week supplementary field visit to Praia, Cabo Verde, in 2015. I returned to Portugal in the summer of 2016 to conduct additional interviews with care workers and to continue participant observation. In total, I conducted thirty-four formal interviews with Cabo Verdean eldercare workers. In 2019, during a four-month follow-up field visit, I supplemented these data by following up with past informants, informally interviewing some of their family members, and collecting an additional set of twenty-five formal interviews with institutional cleaning workers of Cabo Verdean descent.

These sixteen months of immersive participant observation in the greater metropolitan region of Lisbon, conducted in stages during the years 2015, 2016, and 2019, yielded fifty-nine in-depth and semistructured interviews with Cabo Verdean eldercare and institutional cleaning workers as well as hundreds of informal interviews with informants and their friends and families. My guiding research questions asked how care workers of Cabo Verdean descent experience and make sense of their social inclusion in Portugal and how gender, race, color, occupational status, and nationality are implicated in their everyday experiences. In short, I aimed to document the *process of action* to get a sense of the everyday lives of Cabo Verdean home care and institutional cleaning workers.[2]

All respondents worked in home care or cleaning work for at least one year at the time of the formal interview. Approximately half of the sample consisted of naturalized citizens, five participants were Portuguese-born citizens of Cabo Verdean descent, and the remaining were permanent residents on the pathway to naturalization. Of all fifty-nine respondents, two had a college degree, and five had completed postsecondary training of some kind. Of the remaining forty-five respondents, approximately 75 percent had completed high school. Most eldercare and institutional cleaning respondents had at least one child under their care while residing in Portugal, and nearly half of the respondents engaged in transnational parenting at least once in their lifetimes. All but two of the participants were mothers. Among the foreign born, the women I interviewed had been in the country for an average of twelve years at the time of their interviews. All but three participants cited lineage to the Cabo Verdean archipelago island of Santiago. This is significant, given that Santiago has the strongest historical ties to the transatlantic slave trade, and most Cabo Verdean–origin individuals in Portugal today have ties to Santiago, the majority of whom have darker complexions.[3]

I was able to gain access to a network of Cabo Verdean care workers in Lisbon through existing contacts I made before coming to Portugal, and I developed preliminary research contacts through these relationships. With the use of chain referral sampling techniques, I further recruited study participants by distributing recruitment flyers throughout public spaces in Lisbon, such as bus and metro terminals, commercial centers, and indoor markets, and I began assembling potential research participants through these referrals. These leads then introduced me to friends, family members, and neighbors from other social networks, many of whom connected me with other potential interviewees. To ensure that my recruitment did not target a specific neighborhood, I distributed these fliers both in heavily trafficked spaces located in central Lisbon and in heavily trafficked spaces across the greater Lisbon metropolitan peripheral areas that are home to a larger segment of multigenerational Cabo Verdean and PALOP (Países Africanos de Língua Oficial Portuguesa) families.

Due to the solitary nature of eldercare work, most of my observations of workplace interactions were between workers and the elders they cared for. As my entrance into these settings relied on my participants' own invitation, it is likely that participants invited me to worksites where they had forged a pleasant relationship with an elder. Further, institutional cleaners' early or late-night working schedules also meant that I was unable to observe many interactions between informants and their managers or patrons. It also would have been intrusive to shadow cleaning workers in their public work settings. My analyses of workplace interactions among eldercare workers, therefore, draw primarily from interview data where I asked participants to recall their quotidian experiences at work. Analyses of workplace interactions among cleaning workers also draw heavily on interview data, though I also include participant observation from data collected in public spaces such as large commercial centers. As sociologists Michèle Lamont and Ann Swidler have argued elsewhere, in-depth interviews provide data that may not be gathered through participant observation, especially data concerning identities that are bound to participants' own meaning-making processes.[4] I found that sitting down with participants to discuss and systematically analyze their own experiences related to working and living in Portugal provided insight into how social interactions about race, gender, skin color, and nationality unfold.

I conducted all the semistructured interviews in Portuguese, though I gave participants the option to answer in either Portuguese or Cabo Verdean *kriolu*. When reflecting on their lives in Cabo Verde, respondents often integrated more *kriolu* into their narratives. Interviews lasted anywhere between one to two hours, were generally tape-recorded, and were later transcribed by a native Portuguese-speaking specialist. On the off chance that I was unable to record due to logistical reasons (for example, interviewing in a busy and loud café), I took detailed notes of the conversation during the interview and directly upon completion. Interviews were held in locations chosen by participants. Most respondents preferred being interviewed at their own or a family member's or friend's apartment, though a few respondents selected parks or the quiet corners of local cafés because they sought privacy or felt their homes were too crowded.

My aim was to gather detailed data on quotidian and participant-driven meaning-making among Cabo Verdean care workers who reflect an important segment of the gendered and racially segregated service workforce in Portugal. To do this, I utilized a counternarrative methodology, which builds from the subaltern subject position and explores the stories Black women tell that resist the dominant classificatory order.[5] In the claims they make at a particular moment, speakers employ oppositional knowledge to "expose the construction of the dominant story by suggesting how else it could be told."[6] One way I utilized this methodological approach is by augmenting the interview protocol early on to reflect themes that were gleaned during conversations in the field and emerged from the iterative process of going between memo-ing and collecting data. I asked respondents about their migration stories, what led them to their current employment, how they negotiate their multiple work and family responsibilities, and how they make sense of the work that they do, and I asked them about their feelings of belonging in Portugal. These questions sought perceptions and explanations as well as changes the respondents would make if they had the power to do so. I also asked about or took note of respondents' "talking back" to experiences, situations, stereotypes, and images about Blacks and African descendants that they evoked during our conversations. Interview questions were structured in a way that did not assume that race, nationality, color, or gender were their most salient identity categories but rather allowed participants to reflect on how, if at all, these categories might surface in any way during the politics of everyday life.

The ethnographic data were primarily from participant observation with Cabo Verdean eldercare and institutional cleaning workers and their families in their homes and neighborhood settings in the greater Lisbon metropolitan area. I observed and documented what Cabo Verdean women did in their daily lives, including work but extending beyond it. This research would not have been possible without establishing reciprocity as the cornerstone of my relationship with my field informants. Throughout much of the fieldwork, I spent the night at my informants' homes for five days a week, at minimum, and helped my research participants in any way possible. I provided childcare for many of my informants and participated in the transportation of goods between the United States, Portugal, and Cabo Verde (hair products, food, clothing, etc.). This provided a basis for stronger research relationships. Indeed, "gift-giving" and reciprocity are especially important for establishing rapport with the Cabo Verdean community and follow a cultural and economic tradition of *djunta mon* (hands together), a Cabo Verdean socioeconomy of mutual-support practices that enable survival in Cabo Verde and on Lisbon's economically deprived periphery.[7]

I did not base my participation observation at a particular "bounded" field site, as eldercare and institutional cleaning workers labor long hours with little free time. Thus, I shadowed people as they moved through their various spaces throughout their daily lives.[8] Some of the spaces where I conducted participation observation included two large commercial centers, public parks, African nightclubs, a local indoor market that migrants frequent for specialized goods and services, private workplaces, residential spaces and neighborhoods, bus and train terminals, supermarkets, local churches, immigrant support centers, childcare centers, wedding ceremonies, Cabo Verdean community association events, and town squares. My documentation of detailed field notes while observing private, public, and leisure spaces and events in Portugal and Cabo Verde exposed the difference between what eldercare and cleaning workers report in interviews and what they do in their everyday lives. Thus, more relevant and probing questions emerged from my documentation, coding, and field note analysis that would have been otherwise hidden.

I analyzed the data using a "grounded theory" approach.[9] To do this, I entered all data from interviews into NVivo, a qualitative software program, and coded it line by line, analyzing the transcripts iteratively by switching between coding and writing field memos to allow for the ongoing revision of questions and theoretical claims in light of new data. I then aggregated codes thematically by grouping material around substantive emergent themes, first at broad levels and then into more specific categories within those broad levels. At a later stage of analysis, I further developed concepts by engaging in theoretical dialogue with the existing literature.

Given the sensitive nature of what I observed and heard during field data collection, I am tasked with the challenge of staying true to my informants' words while also guarding participants' confidentiality. Throughout, I use pseudonyms and have altered or omitted identifying demographic characteristics. I also, in some instances, merge people and events in order to ensure confidentiality. This is the case in chapter 3, particularly, where I include portraits of research participants to illustrate the complexity of their stories of migration and finding work in Portugal. Throughout the book I omit the names of work and neighborhood locations and employing organizations to protect the identities of employees.

Researcher Positionality

A body of multiracial feminist and critical race scholarship highlights how co-ethnic researchers often have trouble with the "wisdom" espoused by traditional social science research. That is, typically, researchers have historically been urged to follow an impartial, objective course of observation where their role is to distance themselves to merely observe and document without influencing their study participants.[10] An insider, on the other hand, is assumed to have instant access and almost immediate rapport with study informants due to their shared similarities of race, an assumption that has paradoxically been used to discredit the ability of members of marginalized communities to conduct rigorous, objective research. Yet countless scholars have challenged a one-dimensional insider-outsider dichotomy.[11] The important work of feminist scholar Josephine Beoku-Betts illustrates how an assumed insider status is "based on a process of negotiation rather than granted immediately on the basis of ascribed status."[12] At first, she found that her race, performance of extended kinship networks, and "historical connections as an African" facilitated her access to her research connections as she conducted field research among rural Gullah women in South Carolina.[13] However, she also learned very quickly that the insider status and kin-like relationships she developed with her research participants involved constant negotiation and constant effort to achieve confidence with field informants. To establish trust and rapport, she found herself devoting large blocks of time to some informants; her other identity markers, such as her institutional affiliation, gender, and marital status, mattered in some contexts more than in others, and her shared racial status with her participants gave her special responsibilities to carry out. This reframing of the researcher-subject relationship views positionality as something that fundamentally alters the ethnographic process.

My position in the field was also complex. I was both an outsider and an insider by virtue of my gender, race, class, color, and nationality. Foremost, I am an American researcher—a status that carries enormous responsibility when discussing the lives of any marginalized community of the Global South. I was overwhelmingly privileged when compared to the many Cabo Verdean families I met during my time in Portugal and Cabo Verde. Unlike my informants, I determined my own schedule, and outside of teaching online classes, I did not participate in daily waged work, nor did I have children of my own at the time

I conducted the research for this book. At times introduced as "the American friend" by informants, I realized quickly that my status as "American" signified status to many.

Given that white supremacy is a global structure, race and racism also shaped my everyday experiences as a member of the African diaspora in Portugal. Indeed, informants often expressed solidarity with me by virtue of a shared racial identity despite differences in color, class, and nationality. Race, however, simultaneously served as a marker of both connection and distance within my field sites. This became apparent to me when I traveled through the neighborhood spaces that were not typically frequented by tourists. On some occasions, as I traversed areas where whites predominated, white Portuguese men and women stared, or less frequently, white men called out to me from street corners. While the gaze of white men may be indicative of my gender presentation in the field, their occasional use of the word *pr-ta* when calling me out, a racist term toward Black women, suggests that my experiences were shaped not only by gender but also by race. On one occasion, a white man stared at me as I passed a corner and screamed out "Are you lost, *pr-ta pretinha*!" invoking an incident that occurred in Philadelphia in 2011 when a white man sporting a gray College of Wharton hoodie approached me and a friend of mine as we strolled through the University of Pennsylvania's campus and similarly "asked" us if we were lost in an overtly hostile tone. He then, arms crossed, proceeded to "guard" the entrance to a restaurant to signal that we did not belong.

Further, my status as a light-skinned Black woman of mixed racial background meant that I was privileged by virtue of colorism even while I was able to more readily blend in with others in my main field site who are of a similar phenotype; a long history of racial mixture—both forced and voluntary—in Cabo Verde has influenced the emergence of a creole identity that influenced my experience of often being mistaken for a *certain kind* of Cabo Verdean in Portugal. For example, when I traversed my field site, women or men stopped and asked me for directions, often speaking in Cabo Verdean *kriolu*. While informants generally identified socially as *badia* given their connection to the island of Santiago, I was asked by people I met in passing whether I was from other islands or whether I was *sampajuda*, an identity associated with those Cabo Verdeans who have ties to the islands of Brava and Fogo and the barlavento (windward) islands. The *badia* and *sampajuda* categories represent a regional divide that also assumes a racial context in Cabo Verde, for *badias* from Santiago tend to be darker than mestiço *sampajudas*.[14] Though there are very dark Cabo Verdean residents of all the islands, *badia* has come to represent the Santiaguense from the Cabo Verdean island of Santiago, along with positive rearticulations of Blackness among members of the diaspora.[15] Thus, informants' questioning of whether I was *sampajuda* represents instances in which I was initially read, in passing, as both an insider and an outsider co-ethnic simultaneously.

My personal relationships also impacted the way I was read in the field. My husband, a Cabo Verdean American man born on the Cabo Verdean island of Brava, also resided with me during some field trips, which additionally strengthened my research rapport; older informants seemed especially pleased to know that I was well familiar with Cabo Verdean foods and cultural practices and that I had learned some Cabo Verdean *kriolu* from my partner and his family, particularly his grandmother. I found that informants and their families were often curious about my connections to the Cabo Verdean community in the United States and my frequent past visits to the Cabo Verdean islands. My partner's and my familiarity with the Massachusetts and Rhode Island towns of Dorchester, New Bedford, Brockton, Randolph, and Pawtucket (cities with the largest community of Cabo Verdeans outside of Cabo Verde) also acted as points of connection, as several informants had extended family members living abroad in the United States. I always made sure to discuss some of my own family background with participants who were curious as to why I was interested in their experiences. Upon learning that I had traveled to Cabo Verde extensively, that my husband and my stepfather were immigrants, and that several of my Black American relatives also work in home care agencies in the United States, many of the women I met seemed more at ease and offered details about working and living in Portugal, often without being prompted.

Thus, parts of my identity and personal history provided a sense of trust among participants, but I did not take my ability to connect with my participants for granted or as a given. Instead, my "insider-outsider" positionality was an ongoing, negotiated process, and I had to remain attentive to the very real power dynamics embedded in the research process and my relationships with field informants. To this end, and building from Black and Afro-feminism that prioritizes how cultural experience is essential to a grounded analysis of Black women's lives, relationship-building and reciprocity were cornerstones of my field relationships. I did this by accepting invitations to spend time together and participate in culturally meaningful community events, such as baptisms, religious events, meal preparations, and weekend visits to family and friend's homes. Following the Cabo Verdean cultural tradition of *djunta mon*, I cooked alongside informants, played with their children, and helped around the house with domestic chores. I brought them gifts, such as African American hair products, and I enjoyed my time away from my apartment, making friends and listening to their stories—and sharing some of my own. I also established relationships by carrying gifts from one country to the next. During a field visit to Cabo Verde, for example, I met people who had friends and family in the Lisbon area. As I was traveling back to Portugal, a few people asked me to bring their relatives items such as traditional African cloths, canned Cabo Verdean tuna, or Cabo Verdean treats and homemade specialty foods, such as an array of beans, papaya paste, cookies, butter, and coconut and peanut brittle. I brought several pounds of Portuguese salted codfish with me to the United States and dropped them off at some of my informants' relatives' homes. I was not a distant observer in any sense, for I found it almost impossible to make real connections and collect rich and meaningful stories without reciprocation, by treating others in the same decent, loving, and caring humane ways they were treating me.

My readiness to participate in *djunta mon* mutual-help practices and foster intimate relationships with my informants was, in part, facilitated by racial, ethnic, and cultural connections I shared with informants via my husband's family and my own biological and stepfamilies. Moreover, I believe the fact that I was a participant in gendered reciprocal systems of kinship during my formative years played an especially crucial role in my ability to foster meaningful relationships. This is particularly visible in childcare arrangements, as I often ended up sleeping over at neighbors' and family friends' homes as a kid, many of whom watched over me and later entrusted me to look after their children or grandchildren. These parents, grandparents, and now adult children remain important members of my own chosen family. Though some of these mutual support activities I had grown accustomed to are classed and clearly gendered, I believe they shaped my ability to foster a sense of trust with the several women field informants who played a crucial role in connecting me to other community members. Yet these same informants sometimes brushed over explanations during our conversations, attributing a shared understanding with their curt response. During formal interviews, I sometimes had to encourage them to go past the quick "You know how it is" in order to really collect an explanation of why, for example, some of them believed that "the Portuguese are very racist."

Though I engaged in time-consuming and intimate activities that enriched research relationships, I also had to decline certain requests. While I continuously strove to nurture reciprocal relationships with my informants (after all, they were helping me out tremendously by accepting me into their lives) in a way that was genuine, I also had to constantly consider the ethical dilemmas inherent in our relationships. As highlighted by feminist scholar Miliann Kang, meaningful human exchanges make fieldwork meaningful, "unearth surprising findings," and strengthen research relationships.[16] However, these exchanges also provide researchers with access to highly intimate information about subjects' lives—information that, if not guarded wisely, could easily lead to breaches in confidentiality, causing harm to participants in both their professional and private lives. To produce respectful research that seriously considers my informants' confidentiality along with the important politics of representation, this work represents my attempt to balance the important act of determining which stories to include and which stories to leave out. "Our place in the world," argues Venus Evans-Winters, "shapes how we consume and produce knowledge as well as how we choose to disseminate knowledge."[17] As a sociologist with a profound alliance with migrants and their families, I have done my best to stay as authentic to my participants' stories and voices as possible.

As a final note, sociologist Elizabeth Hordge-Freeman argues that "'bringing your whole self to research' is as much about being reflexive about our bodies and emotions in the field, as it is about embracing the power of our multidimensional identities."[18] Hordge-Freeman's words resonate deeply with me, for I have felt equal parts joy, anger, love, anxiety, and rage throughout the entire research process. I worried that I would not do justice to my informants' stories, but foremost, I feel so much love and respect for the women who opened their world to me. Several have become long-term friends at this point, and the care they took in introducing me to their lives way back then was a treasure. They are—and will always be—the true experts of their own stories. I am humbled by this opportunity to share them.

Table 2
Workplace comparison

Workplace comparison	Cleaning work	Eldercare work
Nurturant versus nonnurturant labor	Primarily nonnurturant	Primarily nurturant
Source of racialized interaction	Frontline colleagues, management, building employees, and (spontaneous) patrons	Frontline colleagues, management, elders, and elders' families
Labor hierarchy	Highly racialized and gendered by task, rank, and promotion	Highly racialized and gendered by task, rank, and promotion
Emotional labor and maintenance	Superficial pleasantries alongside management of emotional response to racism by patrons and colleagues	Personalized, intimate, and engaged care alongside management of emotional response to racism by colleagues and elders and elders' family members
Racialized and gendered colonial ideologies	Black African women associated with criminality (theft), deemed appropriate for "dirty work," and seen as super strong ("work bulls")	Black African women associated with illness and criminality (theft), deemed appropriate for "dirty" work, and seen as superstrong ("work bulls")
Body labor	Sweeping, mopping, scrubbing, and vacuuming; shampooing rugs; cleaning windows, partitions, mirrors, and walls; setting up tables and chairs; cleaning and stocking bathrooms; hauling and emptying rubbish	Checking vital signs; changing diapers and rubbing lotions, medicines, and ointments on the body; dressing and bathing; feeding, moving, carrying, shaving, massaging, and cleaning the body

(continued)

Table 2
Workplace comparison (*continued*)

Workplace comparison	Cleaning work	Eldercare work
Affective dimensions of invisibility and hypervisibility	Performance demands of powerlessness compel workers to create an illusion of invisibility. This invisibility is compounded by the isolated nature of the work itself as well as the overall disregard of their work by patrons. Meanwhile, respondents' *hypervisibility* results from an interplay between structural exclusion and cultural associations of Black women as appropriate targets for control and as appropriate for performing menial labor.	Performance of care labor beyond the purview of the public's eye shapes workers' feeling of invisibility. Meanwhile, respondents' *hypervisibility* results from an interplay between structural exclusion and cultural associations of Black women as appropriate targets for control and as appropriate for performing menial labor. This, along with the intimate nature of the nurturant care labor itself, makes them hypervisible to elders and their families within the confines of isolated private residences.
Antiracialism	Coercive toward silence, compounded by embodied performance demands of invisibility	Coercive toward silence, compounded by workplace professionalism and elder vulnerability/illness discourse
Respondents' conceptualization of work dignity	Respondents resisted characterization of cleaning work as "dirty work" and "slave's work" but viewed racialized and gendered labor hierarchies as assaults on personal dignity	Respondents resisted characterization of eldercare work as "dirty work" and reframed themselves as morally superior for performing socially valuable labor

Suggested Readings

Borges, Sónia Vaz. 2014. *Na pó di spéra: Percursos nos bairros da Estrada Militar, de Santa Filomena e da Encosta Nascente*. Parede, Portugal: Principia.

Cabral, Iva. 2015. *A primeira elite colonial atlántica: Dos "homens honrados brancos" de Santiago à "nobreza da terra."* Praia, Cabo Verde: Livraria Pedro Cardoso.

Dovigo, Maria, Sata Lee Almeida, and Teresa Sales, eds. 2020. *Histórias e Memórias de Mulheres de Cabo Verde em Portugal*. Lisbon: UMAR.

Fikes, Kesha. 2009. *Managing African Portugal: The Citizen-Migrant Distinction*. Durham, N.C.: Duke University Press.

Fortes, Celeste. 2013. "'M t'studa p'mk ter vida k nha mãe tem.' Género e Educação em Cabo Verde." *Ciências sociais unisinos* 49 (1): 80–89.

———. 2015. "As Vendedeiras de Cabo Verde: Circulação de Produtos, Informalidade e Mulheres no Espaço Público de Cabo Verde." In *Visagens de Cabo Verde: Ensaios de antropologia visual e outros ensaios*, edited by José Rogério Lopes, 101–102. Porto Alegre, Brazil: Editora Cirkula.

Henriques, Joana Gorjão. 2016. *Racismo em Português: O lado esquecido do colonialismo*. Lisbon: Tinta da China.

———. 2018. *Racismo no país dos brancos costumes*. Lisbon: Tinta da China.

Lima-Neves, Terza A. Silva, and Aminah N. Fernandes Pilgrim. 2021. *Cabo-Verdean Women Writing, Remembrance, Resistance, and Revolution: Kriolas Poderozas*. London: Lexington Books.

Maeso, Silvia Rodríguez, ed. 2021. *O estado do racismo em Portugal: Racismo antinegro e anticiganismo no direito e nas políticas públicas*. Lisbon: Tinta da China.

Moreira, Patrícia. 2020. *As novas identidades portuguesas*. Lisbon: Chiado.

Tvon. 2020. *Um preto muito português*. Lisbon: Chiado.

Racismo à Portuguesa. n.d. Home page. https://acervo.publico.pt/racismo-a-portuguesa.

Roldão, Cristina. 2019. "Feminismo negro em Portugal: Falta contar-nos." *Público*, January 18. Retrieved February 17, 2021. https://www.publico.pt/2019/01/18/culturaipsilon/noticia/feminismo-negro-portugal-falta-contarnos-1857501.

Roldão, Cristina, Mamadou Ba, and Marta Araújo. 2019. "Recolha de Dados étnico-raciais nos Censos 2021: Um passo à frente no combate ao racismo." *Público*, April 16.

Retrieved July 1, 2021. https://www.publico.pt/2019/04/16/sociedade/opiniao/recolha-dados-etnicoraciais-censos-2021-passo-frente-combate-racismo-1869349.

Semedo, Carla Indira Carvalho. 2020. "A experiência migratória de Cabo-Verdianos para as Roças de São Tomé e Príncipe: Pesquisa de campo." *População e sociedade* 34:87–106.

Glossary

apanha de areia "Sand harvesting." This is a process that involves the extraction of sand and rocks, such as gravel and crushed stone, from the sea for use in construction. Though this process leads to health risks for the harvester as well as land degradation, it remains a viable option for poor rural women.

arroz de marisco A Portuguese and Cabo Verdean dish of seafood rice.

àvontade Portuguese/*kriolu* for "making oneself comfortable."

badia and sampajuda The social categories *badia* and *sampajuda* (or *badjuda*) are culturally positioned in opposition and represent a regional divide that also assumes a racial context in Cabo Verde. Cabo Verdeans often associate *badias* with residents of Santiago, who *tend* to be darker than *sampajudas* from the Barlavento (windward) islands, though there are very dark Cabo Verdean residents of all the islands. Nevertheless, the category *sampajuda* is most associated with residents of the islands of Brava and Fogo, as well as with residents of the *sotavento* islands (southern) such as São Vicente, where "miscegenation" was most prevalent and where a mestiço intermediary elite predominated during Portuguese colonialism. The word *badia* came from the Portuguese word *vadio*, which means lazy and idle. Its derivative, *vadiu*, was used by colonial Portuguese authorities to identify runaway slaves who had settled in self-sustainable maroon communities located in the interior of Santiago. They were, in effect, cast as "lazy" or "aimless" by the authorities because they evaded the colonial hierarchical labor regime, as they were neither enslaved nor free colonial laborers. The Santiaguense from Cabo Verde themselves, however, along with members of the diaspora, have rearticulated the *badia* category to denote resistance and pride in collective identity, Blackness, and Africanity all at once.

bairros de lata "Tin neighborhoods." Bairros de lata are another word used to describe "barracas," or informal or "clandestine" housing developments largely originating in the 1970s. These developments accompanied the migration of African and Portuguese "retornados" (see below) to Portugal during decolonization. Several have since been destroyed by the city's redevelopment initiatives of the twenty-first century.

batuku An old Cabo Verdean cultural practice that combines poetry, singing, dancing, and drumming and is predominantly practiced by rural women (*batukadeiras*) from the mountainous interior of the island of Santiago, where enslaved Africans once took refuge.

boa tarde Good evening.

bom dia Good morning.

branco(a) White (race).

catchupa Cabo Verdean national dish. It is a stew with many variations but often includes hominy, beans, onions, garlic, kale, and pork and/or some other meats.

congo Pigeon peas. Congo also refers to a Cabo Verdean dish often consisting of pigeon peas, beef, and an assortment of vegetables like squash, sweet potatoes, and manioc/yucca.

conta di ojo "Beads of eye." A Cabo Verdean ornament that is worn to protect one from the "evil eye," or evil spirits and negative energy.

da ku torno A dance movement of batuku.

djunta mon *Djunta mon* loosely means "joining hands" in Cabo Verdean *kriolu*. It is a cultural practice of mutual-support that is historically associated with collective rural labor practices in Cabo Verde during drought but has been broadly incorporated into a contemporary socioeconomy of mutual-help practices that enable survival throughout the Cabo Verdean diaspora. See Weeks 2012a, 2012b.

doce di coco A traditional Cabo Verdean treat made of heated coconut and sugar.

fidju Cabo Verdean creole for "daughter/son" that is also used as a term of endearment.

funje Angolan pudding made with cassava flour.

jagacida (or djagacida) A Cabo Verdean dish originating from the island of Fogo and made of corn flour and fried pigeon peas.

lidar Portuguese translation of "to deal with."

Mestiço/mulato Identity category that denotes mixed African and European origins.

mufete Angolan culinary dish often consisting of grilled fish, beans, manioc (cassava), banana bread, sweet potatoes, and musseque flour (farinha musseque).

pánu di téra Traditional Cabo Verdean versatile fabrics made of cotton.

pastel Cabo Verdean deep-fried pastries filled with seasoned tuna fish.

patroa "Mistress." Similar to *senhora* (see below), this term is often used by informants to describe their (woman) employer/manager in domestic work.

peixeira Fishmonger.

pontche A Cabo Verdean drink made of *grogue*, an alcoholic spirit made from sugar cane, mixed with several types of flavoring such as coconut, mint, mango, tamarind, and others.

"pr-ta da merda" Racist gendered expression referring to a woman that translates to "Black piece of shit."

"pr-to(a)" A term that is considered derogatory to denote "Black" but has also been reappropriated by members of the Afro-descendant community.

pudim A Cabo Verdean dessert that is an egg custard.

rabidantes "Informal traders." This is also a Cabo Verdean *kriolu* expression for someone who is good at convincing others.

retornados The Portuguese population that fled the overseas colonies during decolonization. While this term tends to center on the white Portuguese, *retornados* also included some elite Black and mestiço Cabo Verdeans with ties to the colonial administration. Several waves of *badia* Black Africans also migrated to Portugal from Cabo Verde during this time in anticipation of a more exclusionary migration scheme.

senhora Portuguese translation of "ma'am" that is also used by informants to refer to a Portuguese woman employer of a domestic worker. It is a gendered term that denotes a hierarchical work relationship between a *senhora* and the hired domestic whose work she manages and oversees.

sodade A word filled with cultural meaning in Cabo Verde, often referring to the feeling of nostalgia and longing.

trabadju sujo Cabo Verdean *kriolu* for "dirty work." Respondents used this expression to describe the care and service work that many Africans and African descendants carry out in Portugal. Often, they used the term *trabadju sujo* to refer to cleaning and domestic work, eldercare (including home care and work in nursing homes), and restaurant work (especially food services).

toresma A Cabo Verdean snack made of deep-fried pork.

txabeta A formation of *batuku*. The women who practice it often gather in a circle, or *txabeta*, and sing about everyday problems ranging from poverty to colonialism, migration, politics, and gender issues.

"vai para sua terra" Xenophobic insult that translates to "Go back to your country."

Acknowledgments

Writing this book was not easy. My father battled stage 3b colon cancer during the first stages of fieldwork. I began a new job as a professor teaching intersectionality and critical race theory at the beginning of the political takeover by Trumpism. I created a whole human being amid the "dual pandemic," and I struggled with postpartum depression and anxiety following the birth of my little blessed gift of life. But even so, this struggle was accompanied by so much joy and care. I was able to research and write this book because of an army of supporters, some near and others far, that I am forever indebted to. They uplifted me throughout the entire process, reminding me, always, that "yes, I can!"

Foremost, my deepest gratitude goes to the people whose lives animate the pages of this book. So many Cabo Verdean women accepted me into their lives, answered my intrusive questions, and challenged me in the best way possible. I am forever indebted to the care they showed me and the lessons they taught me. Their generosity and intimate knowledge about Portugal and their *terra*, Cabo Verde, allowed my research to take off and thrive. When I felt I was unable to finish, I thought back to the numerous moments of joy and care we experienced as we shared meals, tears, laughs, and stories. Their generosity and trust are truly nourishing, and this book is the product of their willingness to share and be heard. Thank you, all of you.

Without Sidonio and Isabel "Bebe" Ferreira, the book really wouldn't have ever gotten off the ground and into the hands of my editor. I still remember the day I officially met Sidonio in the corner office that would become my place of solace during graduate school. I am honored that he welcomed me into his community and so grateful for the "home schooling" he imparted throughout the years. Sidonio and Bebe helped me recover from the trauma of birthing during one of the most isolating times of my life—a time that I was also supposed to remain productive while caring for a bright-eyed, beautiful baby who was

181

thrust into such a strange, and scary, world. I am also forever indebted to my godmother, Faith Hamilton; mother-in-law Maria Gonsalves and sisters-in-law Carlota Duarte-Carvalho and Judith Grant; aunt-in-laws Ana Lobo and Elisa Goncalves; and dear friends Ximena Maria Abello Hurtado, Karina Arévalo, Julia Arroyo, Celia Almeida, Marvin Bryan, Patricia Cardoso, Mary and Kia Custard, Tamara Dawkins, Salome Duarte, Rina Goncalves, Asiah Lemon, Nilva Massano, Stefanie Robles, Cassaundra Rodriguez, Chaniqua Simpson, Maxine Thompson, Rosy Miranda, Ana Paula Monteiro, Kol Tavares, and Adejah Taylor for their generous support, love, and care during this time. I love y'all so, so much. Thanks for looking out for me.

The brilliant Ximena Maria Abello Hurtado has been my soul sister-scholar for so long, and her academic, emotional, and spiritual support continues to sustain me. Thank you, Xime, for reviewing the manuscript several times, for your pointed and much-needed critiques, and for listening to me ramble on and on (and on) over what must be thousands of calls at this point. I have really grown as a person, mother, and scholar because of you. Thank you for providing me with a home away from home in Massachusetts as you modeled the best kind of feminist solidarity. Your generosity and commitment and love for your work and your community are cherished by so many. Thank you.

I am also indebted to my soul sister-scholar Cassaundra Rodriguez. Your humility, lending ear, and kind soul remain a treasure. Thank you for the peer mentorship during graduate school and beyond, for keeping me grounded, and (most importantly) for getting my jokes! I am also so profoundly blessed for my friendship with the brilliant Johanna Montlouis-Gabriel. Thank you, Johanna, for going above and beyond to provide a welcoming space for me at NC State. I have learned and grown so much from your generous feminist comradery. My brilliant friend Kayla Preito-Hodge, thank you for always looking out for me and showing so much love throughout the years. Thank you for always reminding me that I should never let the academy change me into something I do not want to be. My little one is so blessed to have you all as academic aunties and *ti-tias*. Thank you, all of you, for helping me to the finish line.

I would be remiss if I didn't give a shout-out to the educators that are doing the darn work! I want to thank my high school teacher Mr. Schiffman for teaching my first sociology class ever (and I think it was the first and last sociology class he ever taught). I was hooked immediately! I didn't really understand how radical that was at the time, but I'm certain the thought of a class full of BIPOC high school students learning about social oppression would initiate a tsunami of rage-induced pearl clutching nowadays.

Thank you, Monifa Brison-Mulraine, Fatmir Haskaj, and Riad Nasser for the sociological teachings as an undergrad and for your encouragement to pursue a graduate degree. Professor Monifa Brison-Mulraine was the only African American professor in the Sociology Department, and I am so blessed to have been able to take her college-level Introduction to Sociology class. Her presence and intellect inspired me to become a professor. I am also indebted to Patricia Bazan-Figueras, Delicia Koeneke, and Laureano Corces for their stewardship in the Department of Spanish Language and Literature. Patricia Bazan-Figueras's and Fatmir Haskaj's thesis mentorship and openness to working with an unconventional student like me was life changing. I am grateful to Tukufu Zuberi for taking me on as a naive undergraduate research assistant. I knew very little about a PhD in sociology at the time, but our chats were so generative.

I owe a *huge* debt of gratitude to my stellar advisors, Enobong Hannah Branch and Joya Misra. Thank you, Anna and Joya, for your constant encouragement, your unwavering faith in me and this project, and your continued guidance, friendship, and support throughout the years. Joya's time, wisdom, care, and generosity truly helped me survive graduate school. Thank you for showing so much care and love throughout the years. I am also particularly indebted to Anna for taking me under her wing *way back then*. That first race seminar was so critical to my development as a scholar, and her teaching and mentorship have truly shaped my professional and academic pursuits. Her deep intellectual engagement with race, gender, and labor unearthed so many questions and inspired my work. Importantly, Anna just "gets it," and I love her for that. David Cort's enthusiasm and support motivated me to keep on going during a time of great difficulty. I also cannot thank Jennifer Lundquist enough for offering mentorship and friendship throughout the years. Miliann Kang's early mentorship introduced me to transnational feminism and feminist epistemologies. Her course on Asian and Asian American feminisms was so intellectually generative. I also thank Agustin Laó-Montes for teaching classical sociological theory to PhD students in a way that refused to exalt the work of a small select group of white men from the Global North.

I also want to thank additional professors, friends, and colleagues I met in graduate school who have helped me along the way in numerous ways, including Whitney Battle-Baptiste, Wenona Rymond-Richmond, C. N. Le, Krista Harper, Fareen Parvez, Millie Thayer, Donald and Barbara Tomaskovic-Devey, and Melissa Wooten. I remain in complete awe of the stellar Aurora Vergara-Figueroa. Thank you, Aurora, for looking out for me and for connecting me with Ximena. I will forever cherish our short time together and am so grateful for our continued friendship. Thank you, Ximena Maria Abello Hurtado, Sarita Orellana, Ester Orellana, Nini Hayes, Castriela Hernandez, Leta Hooper, Dario Vasquez Padilla, Stefanie Robles, Mahala Stewart, and Lydia Washington for creating community with me. Finally, I want to especially thank the administrative and professional staff at the University of Massachusetts–Amherst, North Carolina State University, and Boston University who made every angle of my research possible. Beth Berry, Juliet Carvajal, Micheal Chapman, Joyce Christian, Matthew Dineen, Elise Esprit, Garret Hobbs, Heather Ockington, Linda Orlandi, Cindy Patten, Erin Seiling, Marcus Shaw, Carletta Smith, Maureen

Warner, and Wendy Wilde: Your kind words, excellent humor, and warm hearts forever uplifted/uplift me, and I appreciate everything that you do.

I have to say that one of the true joys of being a professor is the great privilege of connecting with brilliant undergraduate students throughout my time at the University of Massachusetts–Amherst, North Carolina State University, and Boston University. These include Monique Smith, Sarah Andrade, Chantal Barbosa, Jaz Bertrand, Brianna Brooks, Ciara Crosby, Jody Delano, Jeffrey Dinger, Amy Lam, Kelem Makonnen, Jennifer Martins, Jaz Bertrand, Lajeanesse Harris, Kayla Palazzo, Lauren Deseré Sellars, Wei Wang, and many others. Many have since graduated and have gone on to pursue their passions (for example, as public servants, doulas, nurses, and musicians). I also truly cherish the time spent with the graduate students at NC State, particularly those who enrolled in my seminar on intersectionality. You have all pushed me in the best way possible, and I have learned so much from teaching you. Thank you so much for those treasured memories. I finished this book while teaching my first-ever class at Boston University. Thank you to the entire spring 2023 class of Sociology of Family for such a great and invigorating introduction to Boston University.

I was able to research and write this book thanks to financial support from several sources, including the National Science Foundation, the American Sociological Association, North Carolina State University and Boston University Sociology Departments, and the UMass graduate school. I am especially appreciative of Krista Harper's instrumental guidance in the Culture and Heritage in European Societies & Spaces (CHESS) program. My wonderful CHESS cohort—Berra Topcu, Dana Conzo, Cary Speck, and Eleanor Finely—was a blessing as I jumped into fieldwork. I am also indebted to the American Sociological Association's Minority Fellowship Program for believing in me. Finally, I completed this book thanks to a much-needed full semester of paid parental leave provided by Boston University. I am happy to say that I most definitely *did not* write much during this time, and there's no doubt that I wouldn't have been able to return to a life in academia in one piece without this generous leave (that did not include unnecessary employment stipulations). This needs to be universal for *all parents*.

Portions of chapter 4 were published in an abbreviated form as "Reproducing the Privilege of White Femininity: An Intersectional Analysis of Home Care" in the journal *Sociology of Race and Ethnicity*. I am thankful to David Brunsma, David Embrick, the anonymous reviewers, and Kevin Zevallos for their support in shaping this work. I also have had the great fortune to present portions of *Laboring in the Shadow of Empire* across the country. I thank the American Sociological Association, the Eastern Sociological Association, and the Association of Black Sociologists, along with the University of Wisconsin's Center for European Studies, Sociology of Gender (Fem Sem) of the Department of Sociology and African Studies for the opportunity to present my work. I also thank Melissa Wooten for inviting me to present at the Race and Organizations mini-conference at the Eastern Sociological Association and Jean Beaman for the great opportunity to present at the American Sociological Association's Special Session on Colorblind Racism in the U.S. and Globally.

My editor, Peter Mickalus, believed in my project since the outset, and I am so honored to have developed this book with series editors Enobong Branch and Adia Harvey Wingfield at Rutgers University Press. I am also so appreciative of the initial editorial support offered by Kristy Johnson on the book proposal, and I am incredibly lucky to have worked with the fabulous, funny, fellow plant lover, and all together brilliant Letta Page on the full manuscript. Letta, your jargon slaying saved my book! Also, thanks to the wonderful Elena Shih's fortuitous recommendation, Sanya Hyland's copyediting magic helped me across the finish line. I also owe a gigantic debt of gratitude to Jean Beaman and Erynn Masi de Casanova, who, as reviewers, pushed me in the best ways possible. Jean Beaman's continued mentorship has been a true treasure. Herbert Rodrigues's translation support was a godsend, and I am so thankful for the hours and hours of Portuguese and Cabo Verdean language tutoring offered by Adelaide Monteiro and Susana Perry.

Maxine Thompson deserves the biggest appreciation for the dogged work she carried out to make sure that I was protected at North Carolina State University. As my faculty mentor, Maxine went toe-to-toe to keep me from unnecessary committee work, for she knew I needed the space and time to get the book off the ground. Maxine made it clear since the first day I interviewed that my voice mattered, and I benefited immeasurably from our self-care excursions, our surreptitious office meetings, and our good laughs. I wouldn't have survived the first few years on the tenure track without Maxine's care.

I am so thankful for the hard work Elan Hope carried out to make sure that there was a generative space outside of our departments for Black women junior scholars. Several early parts of my book were written in the good company of Ronisha Browdy, Qiana R. Cryer-Coupet, Elan Hope, Ebony Jones, Johanna Montlouis-Gabriel, and Brean'a Parker. Thanks to Johanna's hard work to sustain an intellectual community during the pandemic, I was so fortunate to join a virtual writing group with an amazing group of academic women scholars. Thank you, Julia Arroyo, Abigail E. Celis, Susan Leonard, Brean'a Parker, Elizabeth Saylor, and Cara Snyder for all the love, jokes, and motivation to get the darn thing done. I am also grateful for the additional mentorship provided by Sarah Bowen, Kim Ebert, and Melvin Thomas. Finally, I am immeasurably grateful for the friendship, love, and support I continue to receive from April Fernandes and Wenjie Liao, my two badass academic sisters. I forever miss our little "hot water" hideaways, but I am so grateful to remain comrades regardless of where academic life takes us.

Since my arrival at Boston University, the care shown by my colleagues has been a true gift, and I have benefited immeasurably from their goodwill. I truly remain in awe that I get to work with such a group of brilliant, fierce, and funny scholars (humor is, in fact, my life source). I am especially thankful to Japonica Brown-Saracino, Heba Gowayed, Saida Grundy, Nazli Kibria, Ashley Mears, Sarah Miller, and Ana Villarreal. A heartfelt thanks goes to Jessica Simes, who has accompanied me on this hectic "mamademic" ride. Thank you, Jess, for making me feel like I truly belong.

The writing process has been so, so long and would not have been possible without the encouragement of my family. My "little big sister" has been the best sibling anyone could ask for, graciously dealing with my crowding of her living space with books, bags, and papers during family visits. My little brother also endured years of me taking over his bedroom. *Super Mario* video games, graphic novels like *Diary of a Wimpy Kid*, Legos, snap circuits, and board games entertained the energetic kid while I was up to my ears in books, but I do feel that I missed out on savoring some of those precious moments. Never again. I remain in awe of the young teenager that he has become and am blessed to share this accomplishment with him.

A special note of profound gratitude goes to my aunt, Janice Curington. I am a sociologist today because of my "Auntie-mama." She has *always* been there to encourage me to keep on and keep going during the hard days, and she taught me what unconditional love looks like. She attended all my milestones and had zero problem telling my committee members that they were blocking her view. She was never too tired to listen to me wrangle over the politics of academia, and she always made me feel heard and seen. She remains a fierce and staunch advocate for justice, and I must thank my late grandparents, Janie and George Curington, for raising such a stellar daughter. We did it, Mama J!

My little one, your arrival into this world was the most frightening of times, but it also marks the beginning of the best of times. Believe it or not, I finished chapter 6 in North Carolina while bouncing on a yoga ball as you nestled on my chest (whatever gets them to sleep, they say). Having you join in on the fun has been a complete blessing, and I have learned so much from you. Your kisses, cries, giggles, and smiles help me remember what's important. My hope is that you one day recognize your own history from within these pages. This book is dedicated to your grandma "Ma" Maria and your vovó—two fierce Cabo Verdean migrant women whose embeddedness in caring labor has paved the way for you.

Finally, my biggest and most heartfelt thanks go to my husband, my love, my rock, my champion, our foundation. Thank you for the relentless labor of love you have carried out across cities, states, and continents. Thank you for the big and little things, your sense of humor, and your commitment to our family. You are the main reason I maintained equanimity while writing this book. Thank you for making this book possible. I love you. Onward!

Notes

Introduction

1 A racist and derogatory term for a Black woman.
2 Cabo Verdean kriolu translation: "Daughter."
3 Popular cotton cloths, originating in Cabo Verde during the fifteenth century and based on Upper Guinean production methods. These fabrics have been worn by Cabo Verdean women into the 1800s and are still widely popular today as a cultural artifact.
4 Coconut brittle.
5 Tuna pastries.
6 Fried pork skins.
7 Cabo Verdean kriolu translation: "Hey, great life.... What's up?"
8 Migration Integration Policy Index 2015.
9 Lugones 2007; Oyěwùmí 1997; Tamale 2020; Quijano 2000.
10 Lugones 2007, 2010.
11 Folbre 1994; Glenn 2010; Hochschild 1997; Molinier 2013; Tronto 2013; Wall and Guerreiro 2005.
12 Du Bois 1999; Rollins 1985; Saunders 1982.
13 de Casanova 2013; Duffy 2011; Gutiérrez-Rodríguez 2010; Pereira 2010.
14 Saunders 1982.
15 Tinhorão 1988.
16 Pereira 2010; T. Santos 2014.
17 Fikes 2009; Pereira 2013.
18 See, for example, Hondagneu-Sotelo (2001) 2007; Lan 2006; Lutz 2011; Parreñas (2001) 2015; Rosenbaum 2017; Romero 2002; Triandafyllidou 2010; Triandafyllidou and Maroukis 2012.
19 Sassen 1988, 2000.
20 Sahraoui 2019, 5.
21 Ally 2009, 2010; Gaitskell et al. 1983; Thobejane and Khosa 2019. Also see SADSAWU 2024.
22 See, for example, Alves and Vergara-Figueroa 2019; Carneiro 2011; Falcón 2008; Figueiredo 2011; Harth-Terré 1973; Hurtado and Mornan 2015; Mera 2014; Organización Internacional para las Migraciones (OIPM) n.d.; Posso 2008.

23 Andall 2000; Branch 2011; Brown 2011; Condon et al. 2013; Fikes 2009; Gutiérrez-Rodríguez 2010; Jones 2009; Marchetti 2014; Rollins 1985; Sahraoui 2019.

24 Smith 2016.

25 McKittrick 2006; Spillers 1987.

26 Gordon 2008.

27 Boulila 2019b, 25.

28 A. Cabral 1979b.

29 Emejulu and Sobande 2019.

30 Small 2018.

31 Boris and Parreñas 2010.

32 Collins (2000) 2014; Emejulu and Sobande 2019; Essed 1991; hooks 1989; Kilomba 2008; Tamale 2020.

33 McKittrick 2006, 121.

34 Andall 2000; Crenshaw 1989; Emejulu and Sobande 2019; Romero 2002; Rollins 1985.

35 Andall 2000; Avril and Cartier 2014; Batalha and Carling 2008; Bettio, Simonazzi, and Villa 2006; Degiuli 2016; Fikes 2009; Roig 2015; Marchetti 2014.

36 Góis 2008.

37 For a discussion of Ukrainian migration to Portugal, see Fonseca, Esteves, and McGarrigle 2016; and Fonseca, Pereira, and Esteves 2014.

38 Ambrosini 2015; Lan 2006; Liebelt 2011; Triandafyllidou 2010; Lutz 2011; Parreñas 2022.

39 In Rhacel Parreñas's latest work, she identifies how the legal framework of states binds domestic workers to their employers in several Middle Eastern contexts, resulting in the severing of workers' rights via turning migrant workers into "unfree labor." For example, domestic workers may not be able to change employers or terminate their employment, and they have no power in deciding where they will work or who they work for. See Parreñas 2022.

40 Pereira 2013.

41 Glenn 1992.

42 Parreñas (2001) 2015.

43 For a discussion of care work and care worker informality and illegality in Europe, see Triandafyllidou 2010.

44 M. Abrantes 2014.

45 My approach, which seeks to go beyond an illegality-formality nexus by foregrounding gendered racism and coloniality, connects with the important work on global care chains. Nicola Yeates, for example, argues that the research on care transnationalization may inadvertently "renaturalize the nation-state" by focusing only on care chains that "transcend international state borders" (see Yeates 2012, 136). Likewise, though informants may have followed the classic path of transnational mothering upon their initial departure from Cabo Verde to Portugal, what is particularly common among the well-established migrants I interviewed is the experience of a care deficit *within Portugal*. In some cases, the international direction of the transfer may be distinct from what is generally reported in the literature (mothers migrating abroad and leaving children behind with paid or unpaid caregivers), with Cabo Verdean care workers sending their Portuguese-born children *back* to Cabo Verde to be cared for by relatives left behind. This is a topic I am pursuing in additional research.

46 See, for example, Andall 2000; Anderson 2000; Bernardino-Costa 2014; de Casanova 2019; Gutiérrez-Rodríguez 2010; Hondagneu-Sotelo (2001) 2007; Lutz 2011; Rollins 1985; and Romero 2002.

47 Glenn 1992.

48 Duffy 2007.

49 See Boris and Parreñas 2010.

50 See Stacey 2011. According to Stacey, the emotive nature of home care work provides workers with an identity she refers to as a "caring self," in which workers construct paid caregiving as a dignified, altruistic, and specialized service that only a select few can deliver.

51 Anderson 2000.

52 For a discussion of antiracialism in Portugal, see Araújo and Maeso 2016; Maeso and Araújo 2017; and Maeso 2021.

53 Boulila 2019a, 2019b; Essed 1991; Gilroy 1992; Goldberg 2002; Hawthorne 2022; Roig 2017; Wekker 2016.

54 Mills 1997.

55 Bonilla-Silva 1997.

56 Goldberg 2015.

57 Keaton 2023, 8.

58 For color-blind ideology, see Bonilla-Silva ([2003] 2021). For mestizaje, see Sawyer (2005). For a discussion of how these ideologies strategically employ race to disavow the state's complicity in perpetuating racism, see Goldberg (2002) and Keaton (2023).

59 Hall 2019.

60 Lentin 2004.

61 Vale de Almeida 2022; Givens and Case 2014.

62 Goldberg 2015.

63 Araújo 2013.

64 Portugal's revised antidiscrimination law, Law No. 93/2017, establishes a legal framework for combating discrimination based on racial and ethnic origin, color, nationality, descent, and territory of origin. The law also broadened to encompass different forms of discrimination (direct, indirect, multiple forms of discrimination) and includes harassment as a form of discrimination. While these changes are critical, scholars have remained skeptical of the legislation's ability to acknowledge and combat institutional racism as well as the everyday forms of quotidian racism experienced by minoritized communities. See Maeso et al. 2020; and Maeso 2021.

65 Fleming 2017.

66 Araújo 2013; Dias and Dias 2012; Maeso and Araújo 2017; Small 2017.

67 Freyre (1933) 1944; Freyre 1953.

68 Vale de Almeida 2006.

69 Araújo and Maeso 2016.

70 Batalha 2004; Borges 2014; Dias and Dias 2012; Fikes 2009; J. Henriques 2018; J. Henriques 2016b; Maeso 2021; Pereira 2010; T. Santos 2014.

71 P. Abrantes and Roldão 2019; Roldão 2016; Seabra et al. 2011, 2016.

72 Alves and Ba 2015; Raposo et al. 2019; Raposo and Varela 2017.

73 Bonilla-Silva (2003) 2021.

74 For examples, see Beaman 2017; Brown 2005, 2009; Emejulu and Sobande 2019; El-Tayeb 2011; Essed 1991; Fikes 2009; Hawthorne 2022; Keaton 2006; Kilomba 2008; Moreira 2020; Small 2017; Tvon 2020; and Wekker 2016.

75 Bonilla-Silva 1997; Du Bois (1903) 2009; Omi and Winant (1986) 2015.

76 Beaman 2022; Collins 2019; Collins and Bilge 2016; Crenshaw 1989, 1991; Davis 1981; Essed 1991; Hull, Bell-Scott, and Smith 1982; D. King 1988; Motsi-Khatai 2020; Tamale 2020.

77 Crenshaw 1989.

78 Essed 1991.
79 Casaca 2010; Lyonette, Crompton, and Wall 2007; Matias, Andrade, and Fontaine 2012; A. Santos 2016; Tavora 2012.
80 IPUMS International. n.d.; González 2014; European Institute for Gender Equality n.d.
81 Cantante 2014; V. Ferreira 2010.
82 Reskin 1993.
83 See Fikes 2009; Pereira 2010.
84 Fikes 2009.
85 Batalha 2004.
86 Collins (2000) 2014.
87 For examples, see Carla Fernandes 2015; FEMAFRO n.d.; Kilomba 2020; and Roldão 2019.
88 For some excellent examples that focus on hybridity, see Andrade-Watkins 2006; Halter 1993; Sánchez Gibau 2005; Okpalaoka 2008. See Saucier 2015 for an example that gives greater primacy to race and Liu 2021 for an example that centers the intersection of race and ethnicity.
89 Capitalization conventions for romance languages differ from those of the English language in that adjectives are generally not capitalized. However, as others have long argued, I believe capitalizing *Black* is important, for it underscores self-determination of Blackness as a political identity versus a simple descriptor. Yet I also recognize that using a capitalized *B* may impose a U.S.-centric frame upon the lived experiences of my research participants. Still, Black radical traditions and global antiracist movements throughout Europe have, at times, drawn on capitalization to reclaim imposed (yet denied) racial identities.

Of note, several scholars have rightly argued that leaving *white* in lowercase is important in the U.S. context, for the force of racialization has not denied whites ethnic identity choices. I likewise have decided to keep *white* in lowercase when referring to white Portuguese throughout the book because whites in Portugal have long been treated as unquestionably Portuguese, whereas Blacks of various ethnic backgrounds have long been denied full national belonging. Though I have decided to keep *Black* capitalized in line with English language conventions of capitalizing pronouns (Irish American, Asian, etc.) and important arguments made regarding the importance of accounting for the structurally and historically rooted dimensions of Black identities, I do recognize there are limitations. Self-identification from the paradoxical space of being both "blackened" and made invisible is a powerful act of resistance, and I do not wish to erase that in my retelling of my informants' narratives. Thus, throughout the book I use lowercase when racial and ethnic identity categories are in their original Portuguese language.

Chapter 1   The Making of a Gendered and Racialized Care Sector in Portugal

1 Braudel 1980.
2 For a discussion, see Nimako and Small 2009; and Mayblin and Turner 2021.
3 OECD 2008a, 2008b; Oliveira and Pires 2010; Peixoto and Sabino 2009.
4 Machado and Abranches 2005.
5 Lobban 1995; Saunders 1982; Tinhorão 1988.
6 de Sousa Santos 2011, 399; de Sousa Santos 2016.
7 Tinhorão 1988.

8 Tinhorão 1988. Also see I. Henriques 2021 for a historical discussion of the African presence in Lisbon.

9 I. Henriques 2013. Though Catholicism was a central pillar of colonialism via the Portuguese civilizing mission, Black Catholic brotherhoods offered spaces and places of resistance and respite. Nossa Senhora do Rosário dos Homens Pretos was the first Black fraternity of Lisbon, established in the sixteenth century. For a historical discussion, see J. Fonseca, *Religião e liberdade* (2016). Sociologist Cristina Roldão notes that many Black women were involved in these spaces despite not being able to be formal members in many cases. See Roldão 2019.

10 I. Henriques 2019; Tinhorão 1988.

11 Tinhorão 1988.

12 For a history of the slave trade in Cabo Verde, see Carreira 1972 and Carreira 1982.

13 Patterson 1988.

14 As Walter Rodney's work shows, any difference between bartering and threatening was dubious. See Rodney (1972) 2018.

15 Carreira 1982.

16 Carreira 1982; Fortes and Challinor 2020.

17 Batalha 2004; Carreira 1982; Meintel 1984.

18 Jerónimo 2015.

19 Ishemo 1995.

20 Carreira 1982.

21 Glenn 2002.

22 Hartman 1997; Kilomba 2008.

23 Yuval-Davis 1997.

24 Carreira 1982, 107.

25 Carter and Aulette 2009.

26 Spillers 1987.

27 Åkesson 2004; Carreira 1982; Fikes 2009; Patterson 1988.

28 Brooks 2010.

29 Bigman 1993. This colonial project arguably reflects modern forms of resource extraction. For example, Cabo Verde allows European vessels to fish in its exclusive economic zone. This, in turn, restricts local African fishers from benefiting from local resources, whether through catching (larger numbers of men) or sales/fishmongering (larger numbers of women).

30 Brooks 2010, 107.

31 Carter and Aulette 2009; Carreira 1982.

32 Patterson 1988.

33 Carter and Aulette 2009.

34 Carreira 1982, 155.

35 Fortes 2015; Grassi 2003.

36 Martins 1891.

37 Carreira 1982; Meintel 1984.

38 Wooten and Branch 2012.

39 Fortes and Challinor 2020.

40 I. Cabral 2015.

41 Tamale 2020.

42 G. Fernandes, 2000; Saucier 2015.

43 Lobban 1995, 58.

44 I. Henriques 2013, 87.

45 I. Henriques 2013, 87.

46 Ferreira 1946, 255.

47 This ideology of assimilation was taken up by numerous European empires and is perhaps most strongly exemplified in the African French Empire, where the French used a "civilizing mission" as justification to require that colonized Africans shed themselves of their culture, religions, and languages via "Frenchification." However, this assimilation never translated to full inclusion. See Daughton 2006.

48 Semedo 2020.

49 Costa (1975) 2011. Historical accounts suggest that the initial arrival of Cabo Verdean voluntary migrants predated the whaling boom of the nineteenth century. See Carreira 1982.

50 Batalha 2004.

51 The social categories of *badia* and *sampajuda* (or *badjuda*) are culturally positioned in opposition and represent a regional divide that also assumes a racial context in Cabo Verde. Cabo Verdeans often associate *badias* with residents of Santiago, who tend to be darker than *sampajudas* from the *barlavento* (windward) islands, though there are very dark Cabo Verdean residents of all the islands. Nevertheless, Cabo Verdeans often associate the category with residents of the islands of Brava and Fogo, as well as with residents of the sotavento (southern) islands such as São Vicente, where "miscegenation" was most prevalent and where a *mestiço* intermediary elite predominated during Portuguese colonialism. See the glossary for an expanded discussion of etymology.

52 Fikes 2009.

53 Baganha 1998.

54 Lobo 2011; Cruz 2016.

55 Fikes 2009.

56 Batalha 2004. See Salgueiro, "Bairros clandestinos na periferia de Lisboa" (1977), for a historical examination of the early emergence of these communities.

57 During the twentieth century, long-standing colonial images that depicted Africans as "savage" and animalistic intersected with Portuguese scientific racism, which relentlessly sought to prove the genetic and biological inferiority of Blacks. See Matos 2013; and I. Henriques 2013.

58 Batalha 2004; Fikes 2009.

59 See Borges 2014.

60 Borges 2014; Cammett 2015; Dias and Dias 2012; Fassin 2013; Fredette 2014; Keaton 2006; Raposo et al. 2019; Wacquant 2008.

61 Davidson (1969) 2017.

62 A. Cabral 1979a.

63 Araújo 2013.

64 Freyre 1953.

65 The PAIGC was founded in Bissau in 1956 by Júlio Almeida, Amílcar and Luís Cabral (Amílcar Cabral was assassinated on the eve of decolonization, in 1973, by a PAIGC guerrilla fighter who is believed to have been working with Portuguese agents), Fernando Fortes, Aristides Pereira, and Elisée Turpin—some of whom were associated with the Casa dos Estudantes do Império and several of its members, including Lilica Boal and Agostinho Neto. The stories of the colonial struggle, however, often uplift men's leadership and centrality, whereas the incredible contributions made by women toward liberation remain hidden. Some of these freedom fighters that were key in the movement toward freedom were Brinsam, Ana Maria Cabral, Coba Sambu, Dori Silveira, Elizabeth Reis, Eva Gomes, Fatoumata Diallo, Fatu Turé, Francisca Pereira, Joana Gomes, Zau eh D' Pove, Zezinha Chantre, Tutu Evora, Ernestina "Titina" Silá, and many others. See Lima-Neves 2009 and Ly 2014. Also, the ongoing U.S.-based

"PAIGC/PAICV Women Warriors Project" aims to honor the many "hidden figures" of the struggle for independence. See Cabo Verde & Guinea-Bissau Women Warrior Project 2023.

66 Andrade 2002.
67 Lobban 1995.
68 Batalha 2004.
69 An estimated five hundred thousand to eight hundred thousand colonial settlers and their ancestors fled back to Portugal (primarily from Mozambique and Angola) between 1974 and 1979. See Arenas 2015. Also see the glossary for more detail.
70 Ascensão 2015.
71 Goldberg 2006.
72 de Sousa 2017; J. Henriques 2018, 2016c.
73 Guerreiro 2014.
74 Horta and White 2008; Wall and Nunes 2010.
75 Parents are entitled to 120 or 150 consecutive days of parental leave, which can be shared by fathers and mothers after the birth. Parents may also take an extended parental leave after the initial parental leave for 30 days. See Guerreiro 2014.
76 Lyonette, Crompton, and Wall 2007.
77 World Bank 2022; Varela 2020.
78 Coelho 2010; Joël, Dufour-Kippelen, and Samitca 2010; Torres 2008.
79 For example, "Program 1992–1993" was open to workers and nonworkers who had been in the country prior to April 15, 1992, and regularized 38,364 individuals. "Program 1996" required proof of involvement in a professional activity, a basic ability to speak Portuguese, a clean criminal history, and authorized housing, and it regularized 35,000 people (67 percent of them from the PALOP nations). Decree-Law No. 244/98 reduced the required period of residence from twenty to ten years for a permanent resident visa. Family reunification was also included as a right. Law-Decree No. 4/2001 offered regularization to individuals residing in Portugal who had secured a valid work permit and regularized 170,000 people. The creation of the one-year "stay permit" accompanied this regularization program, which was in practice a temporary work stay visa granted based on the possession of a work contract and could be renewed for a maximum of five years. This permit made it possible for immigrants to sponsor relatives, and immigrants could apply for a resident permit at the end of five years. See Piçarra and Gil 2012. In 2004, Regulatory-Decree No. 6/2004 of April 26, article 71, permitted the regularization of immigrants who could provide proof that they paid into social security and tax administration for a minimum period of ninety days prior to the law. See Peixoto and Sabino 2009.
80 R. King 2000.
81 SOS Racismo 2002. Decree-Law No. 4/2001 requires employers to guarantee at least a year of employment; thus, labor visas are now required to be updated yearly, and the employer controls migrant residency. Decree-Law No. 29/2012 implements minimum financial and criminal penalties for companies or individuals that employ undocumented immigrants and imposes more stringent eligibility requirements on foreign local hires.
82 Decree-Law No. 253/94 was amended to allow migrants from Portuguese-speaking countries to apply for long-term residence status after a period of five years, though non-EU migrants from non-Portuguese-speaking countries were eligible only after a period of eight years. See Horta and White 2008.
83 Walia 2021.

84 The Portuguese language requirement persisted in the new law and is more demanding, as candidates are required to pass Portuguese language tests administered by the Ministry of Education and to possess a language degree from an official Portuguese school. See Peixoto and Sabino 2009.

85 A child born in Portugal to foreign parents acquires Portuguese nationality, provided that at least one of their parents has "de facto" resided in Portugal for one year, irrespective of legal status.

86 Migration Integration Policy Index 2015.

87 Lan 2018; Portes and Rumbaut 2001.

88 Fikes 2009; Peixoto 2009.

89 Wall and Nunes 2010. Also see Carling 2002 and 2008 for a discussion of the impact of policy on Cabo Verdean migrant flows in the twentieth century.

90 Tamale 2020.

91 Carter and Aulette 2009.

92 While MPD tends to dominate throughout much of the twenty-first century, on November 9, 2021, José Maria Neves of PAICV (the offshoot of PAICG) was sworn in as the new President of Cabo Verde.

93 Tamale 2020; Carter and Aulette 2009.

94 Many of these loans have been made via state-run banks. Interest rates tend to be high, with reports of some ranging from 7 to 9 percent. See Mata 2020, 164.

95 Rodney (1972) 2018.

96 See Quadri 2018 for a discussion of the serious drawbacks of SAPs.

97 These economic processes, ushered in by the global neoliberalization of a world economy, are also entangled with an intricate system of border security that underpins the Fortress of Europe. That is, in the push to harmonize border controls in the Schengen Zone, the externalization of border security has become a major feature of EU policy. While international aid has been linked to deregulation via international lenders, the European Commission also increasingly requires aid and trade agreements with African countries to preemptively control migration. During the early 2000s, European efforts at outsourcing migration controls were directed to Cabo Verde, along with Senegal, Mauritania, and Morocco, allowing EU ships to access waters close to African countries in order to prevent African migration to Spain via the Canary Islands. As argued by Harsha Walia, these processes of "imperial containment" convey the project of Europe, where the circuits of gendered labor migration emerge as a result of the entanglement of neoliberalism, border securitization, and structural adjustment policies—all extensions of colonial legacies of impoverishment. See Bourdet 2000; Walia 2021.

98 Esquivel 2016.

99 Furtado 2021.

100 Sparr 1994.

101 Instituto Nacional de Estatística 2015; World Bank 2018.

102 Tamale 2020.

103 Åkesson, Carling, and Drotbohm 2012.

104 Bettio, Simonazzi, and Villa 2006.

105 I do not intend to suggest that white Portuguese women are no longer employed in caring professions. On the contrary, white Portuguese rural and poor women often do not have any other option but to seek work in *care work*, usually at similar wage rates as African immigrants or African-descendant nationals. It is significant, then, to consider African and African-descendant institutional workers' micro workplace interactions with white Portuguese women who are members of the dominant group yet share an equal work status with Black women. As chapters 4 and 5 illustrate, study

respondents find that these women use race to exert their dominance in an otherwise stigmatized profession. Also see Fikes 2009.

106 Farris 2015.
107 For example, in April 2011, Portugal received a financial bailout from EU-ECB-IMF "troika" lenders. See Peixoto (2011) for a discussion of how immigrant labor was impacted by austerity.
108 Farris 2015.
109 As the data for this book were collected in stages from 2015 to 2019, it is important to note, however, that some care sectors that employ substantial African and African-descendant workers have been especially hit by the COVID-19 global pandemic, such as cleaning work. Nurturant care workers have also faced increased vulnerability during this time.
110 For an example of how similar processes limited the opportunities of Black domestic workers in the United States during the twentieth century, see Enobong Branch's *Opportunity Denied: Limiting Black Women to Devalued Work* (2011).
111 See Joël, Dufour-Kippelen, and Samitca 2010; and Pedroso 2014.
112 Guerreiro 2014; Lopes 2016; Mestheneos 2011.
113 Stacey 2011; Soares 2019.
114 Duffy 2011.
115 Batalha 2004.
116 M. Abrantes 2014; Catarino and Oso 2000; Fikes 2009; Pereira 2010; Santos, Romão, and Cerqueira 2023.
117 Pereira 2010.

Chapter 2 Converging Differences

1 Fortes 2013.
2 This is not to suggest that gendered surveillance does not occur in Portugal. Given the use of social media (Facebook) as well as the embeddedness of the Cabo Verdean migrant community in Lisbon, many informants did face surveillance. However, several informants indicated that they were glad to separate from some of the "gossip" among family systems in Cabo Verde, and they associated migration with greater feelings of personal autonomy in accomplishing daily activities independent of relationships with men and older women.
3 Andall 2000; Lutz 2011; Parreñas (2001) 2015.
4 Parreñas (2001) 2015.
5 Small 2018.
6 Grassi 2003.
7 Theodore, Gutelius, and Burnham 2019; Triandafyllidou 2010.
8 Glenn 1992; Palmer 1989.
9 Constable 2014.

Chapter 3 Confronting Everyday Gendered Racism in Portugal

1 Essed 1991.
2 Kilomba 2008, 11.
3 Wekker 2016.
4 Lentin 2020.
5 Lentin 2020, 48. Also see Lentin 2018.
6 Essed and Muhr 2018.

7 Essed 1991, 52.
8 Keaton 2023.
9 Matos 2013.
10 Perry 2013; Ducre 2018.
11 Hall (2003) 2021.
12 "Daughter" (Cabo Verdean *kriolu*)
13 Note that *pr-ta* has been written out in full in certain quotes in this chapter where the term is being reclaimed and affirmed by the speaker.
14 Keaton 2023.
15 See, for example, Adamkiewicz and Graz 2016.
16 "Pr-ta da merda" translates roughly to "Black piece of shit," and it is gendered in that it refers specifically to a Black woman.
17 "Go back to your country."
18 McKittrick 2011, 948.
19 Arendt 1970.
20 hooks 1989.
21 Emejulu and Sobande 2019.
22 J. Henriques 2022.

Chapter 4   Negotiating and Challenging Gendered Racism in Home Care

1 Lan 2006, 11.
2 Degiuli 2016; Olasunkanmi-Alimi, Natalier, and Mulholland 2022.
3 Kang 2010.
4 Avril and Cartier 2014.
5 Glenn 1992; Marchetti 2014; Romero 2002; Sahraoui 2019.
6 Ray 2019, 46. Also see Acker 1990 and 2006.
7 Gutiérrez-Rodríguez 2010.
8 Gutiérrez-Rodríguez 2010, 5.
9 Evetts 2003; Ruchti 2012.
10 Matos 2013.
11 Bell and Nkomo 2003; Durr and Wingfield 2011; Evans 2013; Kennelly 1999.
12 Wingfield and Alston 2014.
13 Weber 1958.
14 Lorde (1984) 2007.
15 Du Bois (1935) 2007.
16 Branch 2011.
17 Wooten and Branch 2012.
18 Brandão 2016; also see Cole 2015; Fekete 2009.
19 J. Henriques 2018.
20 Collins (2000) 2014.
21 See, for example, Neely 2002.
22 Folbre 2012.
23 Borelli et al. 2017.
24 Collins (2000) 2014.
25 Awumbila et al. 2019; Brites 2014; Pande 2012; Rollins 1985.
26 While the literature on domestic workers finds that accusations of stealing are common and reflect power differentials between employer and employee, it is important to note that theft may also constitute an act of resistance to that power and a response to poverty. See, for example, Francis 2020.

27 Hondagneu-Sotelo (2001) 2007. For some additional examples, see Ozyegin and Hondagneu-Sotelo 2008; Salzinger 1997; and Tuominen 2008.

28 Brown 2011.

29 Glenn 2010; Parreñas (2001) 2015.

30 Calavita 2005; Yukich 2013.

31 Dodson and Zincavage 2007; Doyle and Timonen 2009; Olasunkanmi-Alimi, Natalier, and Mulholland 2022; Stevens, Hussein, and Manthorpe 2012; Uttal and Tuominen 1999.

32 Dodson and Zincavage 2007; Gutiérrez-Rodríguez 2010; Marchetti 2014; Rollins 1985; Sahraoui 2019; Uttal and Tuominen 1999; Wingfield 2010, 2019.

33 Wingfield 2010, 2013.

34 Ruchti 2012.

35 Rodriquez 2014.

36 Araújo and Maeso 2016; Maeso and Araújo 2017.

37 Acker 2006; Acker 1990.

38 Adia Harvey Wingfield's excellent work illustrates the embeddedness of racial ideology within workplaces. For examples, see Wingfield 2019, 2013, 2010; and Wingfield and Alston 2014. Other examples include Ray 2019; and Wooten 2019.

39 Said in *kriolu*.

Chapter 5 Negotiating and Challenging Gendered Racism in Cleaning Work

1 "F-ck."

2 "Good morning."

3 Emejulu and Sobande 2019; Frisina and Hawthorne 2018.

4 "Good morning, good afternoon."

5 Ehrenreich and Hochschild 2003.

6 Collins (2000) 2014; Morgan 2021; Saunders 1982; Tinhorão 1988.

7 Guibentif, 2011.

8 França and de Oliveira 2021; Torresan 2021.

9 de Casanova 2013.

10 Fikes 2009.

11 Essed 1991.

12 Durr and Wingfield 2011; Hochschild (1983) 2012.

13 Rollins 1985; Wingfield and Alston 2014.

14 Araújo and Maeso 2016; Boulila 2019a; Goldberg 2015.

15 Portuguese revised antidiscrimination Law No. 93/2017 establishes a legal framework for combating discrimination based on racial and ethnic origin, color, nationality, descent, and territory of origin. The law was also broadened to encompass different forms of discrimination (direct, indirect, multiple forms of discrimination) and includes harassment as a form of discrimination. Still, scholars and activist groups argue that this altered policy remains inadequate for combating structural racism. See, for example, Ba 2021; and Maeso, Alves, and Fernandes 2021.

16 In the end, the officers were charged with crimes ranging from bodily harm to kidnapping. However, to the disappointment of the victims and supporters, accusations of racial hatred and torture were dropped by the public ministry.

17 "Days off."

Chapter 6 Spaces and Places of Joyful Belonging

1 An alcoholic beverage made of sugar cane.
2 A snack made of fried pork.
3 A dish made with pigeon peas, beef or pork, and vegetables such as collard greens, carrots, sweet potatoes, and butternut squash.
4 A stew with many variations that typically includes dried collard greens, hominy, beans, onions, garlic, and pork.
5 Deep-fried pastries filled with seasoned tuna fish.
6 "Today is a day to celebrate. It's a day to be proud. We are a beautiful people. . . . But most of all, we are strong!"
7 Reproduced by permission from Africa Nostra.
8 Gilroy 1992, 158.
9 Fikes 2008, 57.
10 McKittrick 2006.
11 Ducre 2018.
12 Eduardo Ascensão refers to these developments as "post-colonial slums," given their link to twentieth-century postcolonial out-migrations, and they have many similarities to informal settlements in the Global South (derelict buildings, lack of ownership, lack of infrastructure, and stigmatization by the wider society). For more information on the genesis of these areas in Portugal, see Ascensão 2015.
13 "Daughter."
14 Social housing in Portugal is public property owned by municipalities, while a smaller share of this housing is owned by the Institute of Housing and Urban Renewal (IHRU), which is a government-run institute.
15 Ascensão 2015; J. Henriques 2016a; Varela 2020; Wacquant 2007.
16 Borges 2014; Brown 2005; Gilroy 1993.
17 For examples, see Barwick and Beaman 2019; Garrido Castellano and Raposo 2020; McGarrigle 2016; Tester and Wingfield 2013; and Walton 2016.
18 Borges 2014.
19 "Hands together."
20 Portuguese/*kriolu* for "making oneself comfortable." *Àvontade* denotes more than physical comfort, encompassing feelings of being able to relax and be oneself. Informants typically used this word when discussing their feelings navigating racially segregated neighborhood settings where Africans predominate, though it's used in other contexts as well. I recall that I was once invited to an informant's friend's home for lunch. I brought a bag of fish to fry as a gift, and my informant brought some wine. The friend's husband asked if I needed utensils, and I indicated that I had difficulty eating fish with a fork and knife (a European custom), and the friend smiled and said, "Àvontade." I understood this to mean that I could use my hands. Though I am an outsider, I believe my willingness (and indeed happiness) to eat the fish just as everyone else was illustrated that we could all be at ease, or *àvontade*, as we sat around the small balcony table. The friend ended up Facebook messaging me a few days later and told me that she found someone I could potentially interview.
21 "Poor thing."
22 "Do you need a ride?" It's significant that Layla uses the word *nho*, which denotes respect.
23 "My mother is from Fogo and my dad is from Praia."
24 "But *I am* from Praia." See the glossary for an expanded discussion of *badia*.
25 "My people."
26 See Barwick and Beaman 2019; and Tester and Wingfield 2013.

27 M. Johnson 2020; McGarrigle 2016; Saraiva 2008.
28 Nogueira 2011; Semedo 2009.
29 Carter and Aulette 2009.
30 Stepanik 2019.
31 Hawthorne 2019.
32 Traditional Cabo Verdean versatile fabrics made of cotton.
33 Hall 1990; Gilroy 1993.
34 Fikes 1998.
35 Florvil 2020.
36 Zeleza 2005, 41.
37 Semedo 2009.
38 Hawthorne 2019.
39 McKittrick 2006, 135.
40 The aforementioned PALOP countries include Angola, Cabo Verde, Guinea-Bissau, São Tomé and Príncipe, and Mozambique.
41 "Hi, girls, you are very pretty today."
42 A major issue that drives consumers to participate in this racial enclave economy includes the use of beauty and fashion to empower Black women in spaces that cater to Afrocentric hair and features. U.S.-based research finds that the salon offers a lucrative enterprise for Black owners. Several participants of mine had dreams of opening their own salons in the future. One participant's cousin who also worked in home care had opened a small salon in a rented space by the time I finished fieldwork. See Wingfield 2008.
43 During some visits, a few phenotypically white women with Lisboan accents entered the space, usually friends accompanying teenaged or young adult Black women.
44 See Banks 2000; Craig 2002; Ford 2015; Greensword 2022; E. Johnson 2016; and Majali, Coetzee, and Rau 2017.
45 E. Johnson 2016.
46 For a discussion of colorism among diasporic Cabo Verdeans, see Sánchez Gibau 2005; and Sánchez 1999.
47 Several scholars of race and gender have noted the centrality of the body in the racialization process of Black people in general. For example, to Du Bois ([1903] 2009), the veil symbolizes the intersubjective process by which racial difference is constructed through the body; the racialized see themselves through the eyes of those who racialize their body as Black and therefore Other. In Frantz Fanon's classic essay on the "fact of Blackness," Fanon (2016) argues that Blackness is not an essential identity but rather thrust upon individuals through a racialization process that visually dissects them as racial Others in relation to whites. Patricia Hill Collins's ([2000] 2014) work on controlling images illustrates how gender and sexual ideologies are also implicated in the racialization of bodies; men and women of color are often stereotypically represented in popular culture as having excessive, unruly, and hypersexual bodies. Sabrina Strings's important work in *Fearing the Black Body* (2019) highlights the centrality of the body in constructing and validating contemporary racial, gender, and class inequality and difference.
48 This aspect of my research is part of an ongoing research inquiry. I am interested in respondents' utilization of hair styling and self-adornment to challenge the invisibility they experience while at work. While conducting interviews and field observations, I took note of how respondents often wore visible cultural artifacts while at work, including the Portuguese *figa* (closed fist) and the popular Cabo Verdean *conta di ojo* (evil eye). Curiously, this was most pronounced among institutional cleaning workers who largely associated their work with feelings of invisibility.

49 Semedo 2009. Cape Verdean creole, or *kriolu*, has island-specific variants throughout the archipelago, however.
50 Pardue 2012, 2015.
51 Fanon (1952) 1967.
52 Pardue 2015.
53 Carter and Aulette 2009, 24.
54 The reference "African Portuguese" likely does, in part, refer to objective national variations in Portuguese language. However, there is also a long history of racist stereotypes of Black people's supposed speech deficiencies throughout the Iberian Peninsula. Throughout sixteenth- and eighteenth-century Portugal, for example, "Língua de Preto" (Black language) appeared in Vilancicos de Negro, a popular minstrel performance that mimicked Black African people's speech, music, and mannerisms in a caricatured manner. See Tinhorão 1988.
55 Kang 2010.
56 Meghji 2019; Du Bois (1903) 2009; Pattillo-McCoy (1999) 2003.
57 I use the term *double consciousness* here to emphasize that code-switching is more than just a survival strategy. Similar to Stuart Hall's insistence that Black Europe is "in but not of Europe," the double consciousness of code-switching is a result of being racialized in a world where Black people reside within yet outside of a white mainstream. See Du Bois (1903) 2009; and Hall (2003) 2021.
58 Code meshing is described as "combining two or more dialects, language systems, and/or communication modes to effectively write and speak within the multiple domains of society." The point of departure from code-switching is that it does not actively reinforce racism. See Young et al. 2018, 87.
59 Guinea-Bissauan colleagues did speak *Guinea-Bissauan* kriolu, and both groups could understand one another.
60 "I would take the underwear with the pad and throw it in the garbage to teach her a lesson! Disrespect! Throw it in the garbage!"
61 "I said to her under my breath, 'Go to hell!' Without fear, I tell her to 'eat shit.' Or I say things like 'Oh! You take me for a fool.'"
62 Brown 2009 (emphasis mine).

Chapter 7 Laboring beyond the Shadow of Empire

1 Council of Europe Commissioner for Human Rights 2020.
2 Beaman 2017.
3 Moreira 2020.
4 Casquilho-Martins, Belchior-Rocha, and Alves 2022.
5 Though attempts to add the race and ethnicity question to the official census have been consistently denied, in early 2023 Portugal began collecting the ethnic-racial origins of people who have lived in Portugal for at least twelve months via the small-scale Pilot Survey on Living Conditions, Origins, and Trajectories of the Resident Population. However, data from a large-scale, nationally representative source remain critical. To be sure, several activists, organizations, and scholars in Portugal continue to stress the critical importance of the collection of racial data by the state. For details, see Roldão, Ba, and Araújo 2019; and Ba et al. 2017.
6 Alves and Maeso 2021; Ba 2021.
7 Their stories could be shared during employee meetings or in other venues, which would call out the problematic behavior patterns. One way to do this could be through providing workers with an easy-to-use platform for anonymously

documenting experiences and observations of racism. To take it a step further, workers' anonymized stories could also be distributed among elders and their family members and building employees. Partnerships with local feminist and antiracist organizations would prove especially beneficial. See Penn Medicine 2024.

8 Bernardino-Costa 2014.

9 Ascensão 2015; J. Henriques and Moutinho 2016.

10 Cabo Verde owes 150 million euros in debt to the government of Portugal and an additional 430 million to Caixa Geral de Depósitos. The World Bank and African Development Bank are also major creditors, with Cabo Verde owing $523 million and $263 million, respectively. See Appel 2023 for a discussion of how the partial replacement of European banks with Pan-African banks may further extend racial and imperial power.

11 PORTUGAL.GOV.PT 2023.

12 For an example, see NAWI Afrifem Macroeconomics Collective 2023.

13 Tronto 2013.

14 Ramalho da Silva 2020; European Network Against Racism 2020; Roldão 2019.

Methodological Appendix

1 Though I was unable to frequently visit workspaces, I implemented a "follow the people" strategy whenever possible. This led me to observe the importance of space (public/private) in experiences of and responses to intersectional oppression in Lisbon. See Marcus 1998.

2 Becker 1996, 1998.

3 Batalha 2004; Fikes 2009.

4 Lamont and Swidler 2014.

5 Solórzano and Yosso 2002.

6 Harris, Carney, and Fine 2000, 13.

7 Gallardo 2014; Weeks 2012a, 2012b.

8 Marcus 1998.

9 Strauss and Corbin 1997.

10 See Evans-Winters 2019; Twine and Warren 2000; and Young 2008.

11 For examples, see Collins 1986; Grundy 2022; Hordge-Freeman 2018; Mayorga-Gallo and Hordge-Freeman 2017; and Reyes 2020.

12 Beoku-Betts 1994, 417.

13 Beoku-Betts 1994, 417.

14 For a discussion of the etymology of these words, see Batalha 2004; and Fikes 2009.

15 These categories are not mutually exclusive, however. Given the reality of interisland migration, several informants I met who identified as *badia* nevertheless explained that one of their parents or grandparents was *sampajuda*.

16 Kang 2000, 45.

17 Evans-Winters 2019, 3.

18 Hordge-Freeman 2018.

References

Abrantes, Miguel. 2014. "'I Know It Sounds Nasty and Stereotyped:' Searching for the Competent Domestic Worker." *Gender, Work & Organization* 21 (5): 427–442.

Abrantes, Pedro, and Cristina Roldão. 2019. "The (Mis)Education of African Descendants in Portugal: Towards Vocational Traps?" *Portuguese Journal of Social Science* 18 (1): 27–55.

Acker, Joan. 1990. "Hierarchies, Jobs, Bodies: A Theory of Gendered Organizations." *Gender & Society* 4 (2): 139–158.

———. 2006. "Inequality Regimes: Gender, Class, and Race in Organizations." *Gender & Society* 20 (4): 441–464.

Adamkiewicz, Ewa A., and Austria Graz. 2016. "White Nostalgia: The Absence of Slavery and the Commodification of White Plantation Nostalgia." *Aspeers* 9:13–31.

Åkesson, Lisa. 2004. "Making a Life: Meanings of Migration in Cape Verde." PhD diss., Department of Social Anthropology, University of Gothenburg. Retrieved May 25, 2023. https://gupea.ub.gu.se/handle/2077/16304.

Åkesson, Lisa, Jørgen Carling, and Heiki Drotbohm. 2012. "Mobility, Moralities and Motherhood: Navigating the Contingencies of Cape Verdean Lives." *Journal of Ethnic and Migration Studies* 38 (2): 237–260.

Ally, Shireen. 2009. *From Servants to Workers: South African Domestic Workers and the Democratic State*. Ithaca, N.Y.: Cornell University Press.

———. 2010. "Domestics, 'Dirty Work' and the Affects of Domination." *South African Review of Sociology* 42 (2): 1–7.

Alves, Ana Rita, and Mamadou Ba. 2015. "Da violência policial nos bairros ao racismo institucional do Estado." *Le Monde Diplomatique—Edição Portuguesa*, 2015, pp. 16–17.

Alves, Ana Rita, and Silvia Rodríguez Maeso. 2021. "A racialização do espaço pela mão da política local: Anticiganismo, habitação e segregação territorial." In *O estado do racismo em Portugal: Racismo antinegro e anticiganismo no direito e nas políticas públicas*, edited by Silvia Rodríguez Maeso, 157–180. Lisbon: Tinta da China.

Alves, Jaime, and Aurora Vergara-Figueroa. 2019. "The Branch of Paradise: Geographies of Privilege, Multiculturalism and Black Social Suffering in Cali, Colombia." In *Comparative Racial Politics in Latin America*, edited by Kwame Dixon and Ollie A. Johnson III, 183–2010. New York: Taylor & Francis.

Ambrosini, Maurizio. 2015. "Irregular but Tolerated: Unauthorized Immigration, Elderly Care Recipients, and Invisible Welfare." *Migration Studies* 3 (2): 199–216.

Andall, Jacqueline. 2000. *Gender, Migration and Domestic Service: The Politics of Black Women in Italy*. New York: Ashgate.

Anderson, Bridget. 2000. *Doing the Dirty Work? The Global Politics of Domestic Labour*. New York: Zed Books.

Andrade, Elisa Silva. 2002. "Cape Verde." In *A History of Postcolonial Lusophone Africa*, edited by Chabal, Patrick, 264–290. Bloomington: Indiana University Press.

Andrade-Watkins, Claire. 2006. *Some Kind of Funny Porto Rican? A Cape Verdean American Story*. Providence, R.I.: SPIA Media Productions.

Appel, Hannah. 2023. "Pan African Capital? Banks, Currencies, and Imperial Power." *Journal of Cultural Economy* 16 (3): 392–408. https://doi.org/10.1080/17530350.2023.2177322.

Araújo, Marta. 2013. "Challenging Narratives on Diversity and Immigration in Portugal: The (De)Politicization of Colonialism and Racism." In *Migrant Marginality: A Transnational Perspective*, edited by Philip Kretsedemas, Jorge Capetillo-Ponce, and Glenn Jacobs, 27–46. New York: Routledge.

Araújo, Marta, and Silvia Rodríguez Maeso. 2016. *The Contours of Eurocentrism: Race, History, and Political Texts*. Lanham, Md.: Rowman & Littlefield.

Arenas, Fernando. 2015. "Migrations and the Rise of African Lisbon: Time-Space of Portuguese (Post)Coloniality." *Postcolonial Studies* 18 (4): 353–366.

Arendt, Hannah. 1970. *On Violence*. New York: Harcourt.

Ascensão, Eduardo. 2015. "Slum Gentrification in Lisbon, Portugal: Displacement and the Imagined Futures of an Informal Settlement." In *Global Gentrifications: Uneven Development and Displacement*, edited by Loreta Lees, Hyun Bang Shin, and Ernesto López-Morales, 37–58. Bristol, U.K.: Policy Press.

Avril, Christelle, and Marie Cartier. 2014. "Subordination in Home Service Jobs: Comparing Providers of Home-Based Child Care, Elder Care, and Cleaning in France." *Gender & Society* 28 (4): 609–630.

Awumbila, Mariama, Priya Deshingkar, Leander Kandilige, Joseph Kofi Teye, and Mary Setrana. 2019. "Please, Thank You and Sorry—Brokering Migration and Constructing Identities for Domestic Work in Ghana." *Journal of Ethnic and Migration Studies* 45 (14): 2655–2671.

Ba, Mamadou. 2021. "A legislação antirracista: Uma manta de retalhos entre a negação e a ineficácia." In *O estado do racismo em Portugal: Racismo antinegro e anticiganismo no direito e nas políticas públicas*, edited by Silvia Rodríguez Maeso., 307–321. Lisbon: Tinta da China.

Ba, Mamadou, Ana Fernandes, Carla Fernandes, José Pereira, Anabela Rodrigues, and Cristina Roldão. 2017. "A urgência de um combate real às desigualdades étnico-raciais e ao racismo." *Le Monde Diplomatique*, February.

Baganha, Maria. 1998. "Immigrant Involvement in the Informal Economy: The Portuguese Case." *Journal of Ethnic and Migration Studies* 24 (2): 367–385.

Banks, Ingrid. 2000. *Hair Matters: Beauty, Power, and Black Women's Consciousness*. New York: New York University Press.

Barwick, Christine, and Jean Beaman. 2019. "Living for the Neighbourhood: Marginalization and Belonging for the Second-Generation in Berlin and Paris." *Comparative Migration Studies* 7 (1): 1–17.

Batalha, Luís. 2004. *The Cape Verdean Diaspora in Portugal: Colonial Subjects in a Postcolonial World*. Lanham, Md.: Rowman & Littlefield.

Batalha, Luís, and Jørgen Carling, eds. 2008. *Transnational Archipelago: Perspectives on Cape Verdean Migration and Diaspora*. Amsterdam: Amsterdam University Press.

Beaman, Jean. 2017. *Citizen Outsider: Children of North African Immigrants in France*. Oakland: University of California Press.

———. 2022. "Black Feminism and Transnational Solidarity: Mobilization against Police Violence in France." *Esclavages & Post-esclavages: Slaveries & Post-Slaveries* 6. https://doi.org/10.4000/slaveries.6563.

Becker, Howard S. 1996. "The Epistemology of Qualitative Research." In *Ethnography and Human Development: Context and Meaning in Social Inquiry*, edited by Richard Jessor, Anne Colby, Richard A. Shweder, 53–71. Chicago: University of Chicago Press.

———. 1998. *Tricks of the Trade: How to Think about Your Research While You're Doing It*. Chicago: University of Chicago Press.

Bell, Ella L. J. Edmondson, and Stella Nkomo. 2003. *Our Separate Ways: Black and White Women and the Struggle for Professional Identity*. Brighton, Mass.: Harvard Business Press.

Beoku-Betts, Josephine. 1994. "When Black Is Not Enough: Doing Field Research among Gullah Women." *NWSA Journal* 6 (3): 413–433.

Bernardino-Costa, Joaze. 2014. "Intersectionality and Female Domestic Workers' Unions in Brazil." *Women's Studies International Forum* 46:72–80.

Bettio, Francesca, Annamaria Simonazzi, and Paola Villa. 2006. "Change in Care Regimes and Female Migration: The 'Caredrain' in the Mediterranean." *Journal of European Social Policy* 16 (3): 271–285.

Bigman, Laura. 1993. *History and Hunger in West Africa: Food Production and Entitlement in Guinea-Bissau and Cape Verde*. Westport, Conn.: Greenwood Press.

Bonilla-Silva, Eduardo. 1997. "Rethinking Racism: Toward a Structural Interpretation." *American Sociological Review* 62 (3): 465–480.

———. (2003) 2021. *Racism without Racists: Color-Blind Racism and the Persistence of Racial Inequality in the United States*. Lanham, Md.: Rowman & Littlefield.

Borelli, Jessica L., Katherine S. Nelson, Laura M. River, Sara A. Birken, and Corrine Moss-Racusin. 2017. "Gender Differences in Work-Family Guilt in Parents of Young Children." *Sex Roles* 76 (5–6): 356–368.

Borges, Sónia Vaz. 2014. *Na pó di spéra: Percursos nos bairros da Estrada Militar, de Santa Filomena e da Encosta Nascente*. Parede, Portugal: Principia.

Boris, Eileen, and Rhacel Salazar Parreñas. 2010. *Intimate Labors: Cultures, Technologies, and the Politics of Care*. Palo Alto, Calif.: Stanford University Press.

Boulila, Stefanie Claudine. 2019a. "Race and Racial Denial in Switzerland." *Ethnic and Racial Studies* 42 (9): 1401–1418.

———. 2019b. *Race in Post-racial Europe: An Intersectional Analysis*. Lanham, Md.: Rowman & Littlefield International.

Bourdet, Yves. 2000. "Reforming the Cape Verdean Economy. The Economics of Mudança." *Afrika Spectrum* 35 (2): 121–163.

Branch, Enobong. 2011. *Opportunity Denied: Limiting Black Women to Devalued Work*. New Brunswick, N.J.: Rutgers University Press.

Brandão, Inês Maria Calvo. 2016. "Deuses em movimento: O caso dos Muçulmanos Guineenses em Lisboa." Master's thesis, Department of Sociology—FCSH, Universidade Nova de Lisboa. Retrieved August 4, 2020. https://run.unl.pt/handle/10362/19613.

Braudel, Fernand. 1980. "History and the Social Sciences: The Longue Durée." In *On History*, 25–54. Chicago: University of Chicago Press.

Brites, Jurema. 2014. "Domestic Service, Affection and Inequality: Elements of Subalternity." *Women's Studies International Forum* 46:63–71. https://doi.org/10.1016/j.wsif.2014.03.009.

Brooks, George E. 2010. *Western Africa and Cabo Verde, 1790s–1830s: Symbiosis of Slave and Legitimate Trades*. Bloomington, Ind.: Author House.

Brown, Jacqueline Nassy. 2005. *Dropping Anchor, Setting Sail: Geographies of Race in Black Liverpool*. Princeton, N.J.: Princeton University Press.

———. 2009. "Black Europe and the African Diaspora: A Discourse on Location." In *Black Europe and the African Diaspora*, edited by Darlene Clark Hine, Trica Danielle Keaton, and Stephen Small, 201–211. Champaign: University of Illinois Press.

Brown, Tamara M. 2011. *Raising Brooklyn: Nannies, Childcare, and Caribbeans Creating Community*. New York: New York University Press.

Cabo Verde & Guinea-Bissau Women Warrior Project. 2023. Facebook. Retrieved February 27, 2024. https://www.facebook.com/groups/636727608335089.

Cabral, Amílcar. 1979a. "The Facts about Portuguese Colonialism." In *Unity and Struggle: Speeches and Writings of Amilcar Cabral*, 17–27. New York: Monthly Review Press.

———. 1979b. *Unity and Struggle: Speeches and Writings of Amilcar Cabral*. New York: Monthly Review Press.

Cabral, Iva. 2015. *A primeira elite colonial atlántica: Dos "homens honrados brancos" de Santiago à "nobreza da terra."* Praia, Cabo Verde: Livraria Pedro Cardoso.

Calavita, Kitty. 2005. *Immigrants at the Margins: Law, Race, and Exclusion in Southern Europe*. Cambridge: Cambridge University Press.

Cammett, Ann. 2015. "Confronting Race and Collateral Consequences in Public Housing." *Seattle University Law Review* 39 (4): 1123–1155.

Cantante, Frederico. 2014. "Desigualdades de género no topo dos ganhos salariais em Portugal." *Observatório das Desigualdades e-Working Papers*, Working Paper No. 1/2014. Retrieved July 1, 2021. https://observatoriodasdesigualdade.files.wordpress.com/2014/11/desigualdades-de-gc3a9nero-no-topo-dos-ganhos_frederico-cantante_od-e-working-paper-n-c2ba-1_2014.pdf.

Carling, Jørgen. 2002. "Cape Verde: Towards the End of Emigration." Migration Policy Institute. Retrieved July 1, 2021. http://www.migrationpolicy.org/article/cape-verde-towards-end-emigration.

———. 2008. "Policy Challenges Facing Cape Verde in the Areas of Migration and Diaspora Contributions to Development." *Oslo: PRIO*. Retrieved July 1, 2021. https://www.prio.org/Publications/Publication/?x=7298.

Carneiro, Sueli. 2011. *Racismo, sexismo e desigualdade no Brasil*. São Paulo: Selo Negro.

Carreira, António. 1972. *Cabo Verde: Formação e extinção de uma sociedade escravocrata (1460–1878)*. Bissau, Guiné-Bissau: Centro de Estudos da Guiné Portuguesa.

———. 1982. *The People of the Cape Verde Islands: Exploitation and Emigration*. Hamden, Conn.: Archon Books.

Carter, Katherine, and Judy Aulette. 2009. *Cape Verdean Women and Globalization: The Politics of Gender, Culture, and Resistance*. New York: Palgrave Macmillan.

Casaca, Sara Falcão. 2010. "A (des)igualdade de género e a precarização do emprego." In *A igualdade de mulheres e homens no trabalho e no emprego em Portugal: Políticas e circunstâncias*, edited by Virgínia Ferreira, 261–291. Lisbon: Comissão para a Igualdade no Trabalho e no Emprego / Ministério do Trabalho e da Solidariedade Social.

Casquilho-Martins, Inês, Helena Belchior-Rocha, and David Ramalho Alves. 2022. "Racial and Ethnic Discrimination in Portugal in Times of Pandemic Crisis." *Social Sciences* 184 (11): 1–19.

Catarino, Christine, and Laura Oso. 2000. "La inmigración femenina en Madrid y Lisbon: Hacia una etnización del servicio doméstico y de las empresas de limpieza." *Papers: Revista de sociología* 60:183–207.

Coelho, Lina. 2010. "Mulheres, família e desigualdade em Portugal." PhD diss., Department of Economics, Universidad de Coimbra. Retrieved May 25, 2023. https://www.academia.edu/82165737/Mulheres_fam%C3%ADlia_e_desigualdade_em_Portugal.

Cole, Mike. 2015. *Racism: A Critical Analysis*. London: Pluto Press.

Collins, Patricia Hill. 1986. "Learning from the Outsider Within: The Sociological Significance of Black Feminist Thought." *Social Problems* 33 (6): S14–S32.

———. (2000) 2014. *Black Feminist Thought: Knowledge, Consciousness, and the Politics of Empowerment*. New York: Routledge.

———. 2019. *Intersectionality as Critical Social Theory*. Durham, N.C.: Duke University Press.

Collins, Patricia Hill, and Sirma Bilge. 2016. *Intersectionality*. Hoboken, N.J.: John Wiley & Sons.

Condon, Stephanie, Emmanuelle Lada, Amélie Charrualt, and Agnès Romanini. 2013. "Promoting Integration for Migrant Domestic Workers in France." *International Migration Papers* no. 117. Retrieved July 1, 2021. https://www.ilo.org/wcmsp5/groups/public/---ed _protect/---protrav/---migrant/documents/publication/wcms_222299.pdf.

Constable, Nicole. 2014. *Born out of Place: Migrant Mothers and the Politics of International Labor*. Berkeley: University of California Press.

Costa, Manuel E., Sr. (1975) 2011. *The Making of the Cape Verdean*. Bloomington, Ind.: Author House.

Council of Europe Commissioner for Human Rights. 2020. *Combating Racism and Racial Discrimination against People of African Descent in Europe*. Retrieved February 27, 2024. https://rm.coe.int/combating-racism-and-racial-discrimination-against-people-of-african -d/1680a1c0b6.

Craig, Maxine Leeds. 2002. *Ain't I a Beauty Queen? Black Women, Beauty, and the Politics of Race*. New York: Oxford University Press.

Crenshaw, Kimberlé. 1989. "Demarginalizing the Intersection of Race and Sex: A Black Feminist Critique of Antidiscrimination Doctrine, Feminist Theory and Antiracist Politics." *University of Chicago Legal Forum* 8 (1): 139–167.

———. 1991. "Mapping the Margins: Intersectionality, Identity Politics, and Violence against Women of Color." *Stanford Law Review Review* 43 (6): 1241–1299.

Cruz, Carmen Helena. 2016. "Maternidades e paternidades no interior de Santiago: Ribeira da Barca." In *Estudos sociais cabo-verdianos*. Vol. 4, *Género e sociabilidades no interior de Santiago*, edited by Carmelita de Afonseca Silva and Miriam Steffen Vieira, 19–40. Praia: Universidade de Cabo Verde.

Daughton, James Patrick. 2006. *An Empire Divided: Religion, Republicanism, and the Making of French Colonialism, 1880–1914*. New York: Oxford University Press.

Davidson, Basil. (1969) 2017. *No Fist Is Big Enough to Hide the Sky: The Liberation of Guinea-Bissau and Cape Verde, 1963–74*. London: Zed Books.

Davis, Angela Y. 1981. *Women, Race, & Class*. New York: Vintage.

de Casanova, Erynn Masi. 2013. "Embodied Inequality: The Experience of Domestic Work in Urban Ecuador." *Gender & Society* 27 (4): 561–585.

———. 2019. *Dust and Dignity: Domestic Employment in Contemporary Ecuador*. Ithaca, N.Y.: Cornell University Press.

Degiuli, Francesca. 2016. *Caring for a Living: Migrant Women, Aging Citizens, and Italian Families*. New York: Oxford University Press.

de Sousa, Anna Naomi. 2017. "The Portuguese Denied Citizenship in Their Own Country: Members of Afro-descendant Communities, Rendered 'Foreigners' Due to a Discriminatory Nationality Law, Are Speaking Up." *Al Jazeera*, March 23. Retrieved July 1, 2021. https://www.aljazeera.com/indepth/features/2017/03/portuguese-denied-citizenship -country-170302084810644.html.

de Sousa Santos, Boaventura. 2011. "Portugal: Tales of Being and Not Being." *Portuguese Literary and Cultural Studies* 19 (20): 399–443.

———. 2016. "A New Vision of Europe: Learning from the South." In *Demodiversity: Toward Post-abyssal Democracies*, edited by Boaventura de Sousa Santos, 31–53. New York: Routledge.

Dias, Beatriz. 2021. "O combate ae o racismo não pode esperar." In *O estado do racismo em Portugal: Racismo antinegro e anticiganismo no direito e nas políticas públicas*, edited by Silvia Rodríguez Maeso, 301. Lisbon: Tinta da China.

Dias, Bruno Peixe, and Nuno Dias. 2012. *Imigração e racismo em Portugal: O lugar do outro.* Lisbon: Edições 70/Le Monde diplomatique.

Dodson, Lisa, and Rebekah N. Zincavage. 2007. "'It's like a Family' Caring Labor, Exploitation, and Race in Nursing Homes." *Gender & Society* 21 (6): 905–928.

Doyle, Martha, and Virpi Timonen. 2009. "The Different Faces of Care Work: Understanding the Experiences of the Multi-cultural Care Workforce." *Ageing & Society* 29 (3): 337–350.

Du Bois, W. E. B. (1903) 2009. *The Souls of Black Folk.* New York: Oxford University Press.

———. (1935) 2007. *Black Reconstruction in America: Toward a History of the Part Which Black Folk Played in the Attempt to Reconstruct Democracy in America, 1860–1880.* Oxford: Oxford University Press.

———. 1999. "The Servant in the House." In *Darkwater: Voices from within the Veil*, 63–69. New York: Dover.

Ducre, Kishi Animashaun. 2018. "The Black Feminist Spatial Imagination and an Intersectional Environmental Justice." *Environmental Sociology* 4 (1): 22–35.

Duffy, Mignon. 2007. "Doing the Dirty Work: Gender, Race, and Reproductive Labor in Historical Perspective." *Gender & Society* 21 (3): 313–336.

———. 2011. *Making Care Count: A Century of Gender, Race, and Paid Care Work.* New Brunswick, N.J.: Rutgers University Press.

Durr, Marlese, and Adia M. Harvey Wingfield. 2011. "Keep Your 'N' in Check: African American Women and the Interactive Effects of Etiquette and Emotional Labor." *Critical Sociology* 37 (5): 557–571.

Ehrenreich, Barbara, and Arlie Russell Hochschild, eds. 2003. *Global Woman: Nannies, Maids, and Sex Workers in the New Economy.* New York: Henry Holt and Company.

El-Tayeb, Fatima. 2011. *European Others: Queering Ethnicity in Postnational Europe.* Minneapolis: University of Minnesota Press.

Emejulu, Akwugo, and Francesca Sobande, eds. 2019. *To Exist Is to Resist: Black Feminism in Europe.* London: Pluto Press.

Esquivel, Valeria. 2016. "Power and the Sustainable Development Goals: A Feminist Analysis." *Gender & Development* 24 (1): 9–23.

Essed, Philomena. 1991. *Understanding Everyday Racism: An Interdisciplinary Theory.* Thousand Oaks, Calif.: Sage.

Essed, Philomena, and Sara Louise Muhr. 2018. "Entitlement Racism and Its Intersections: An Interview with Philomena Essed, Social Justice Scholar." *Ephemera* 18 (1): 183–201.

European Institute for Gender Equality. n.d. "Gender Equality Index 2019: Portugal." Retrieved July 1, 2021. https://eige.europa.eu/publications/gender-equality-index-2019 -portugal.

European Network Against Racism. 2020. "Urgent Solidarity Call to Support Portuguese Anti-racist Activists." Retrieved July 1, 2021. https://www.enar-eu.org/Urgent-solidarity -call-to-support-Portuguese-anti-racist-activists.

Evans, Louwanda. 2013. *Cabin Pressure: African American Pilots, Flight Attendants, and Emotional Labor.* Lanham, Md.: Rowman & Littlefield.

Evans-Winters, Venus E. 2019. *Black Feminism in Qualitative Inquiry: A Mosaic for Writing Our Daughter's Body.* New York: Routledge.

Evetts, Julia. 2003. "The Sociological Analysis of Professionalism: Occupational Change in the Modern World." *International Sociology* 18 (2): 395–415.

Falcón, Sylvanna M. 2008. "Mestiza Double Consciousness: The Voices of Afro-Peruvian Women on Gendered Racism." *Gender & Society* 22 (5): 660–680.

Fanon, Frantz. (1952) 1967. *Black Skin, White Masks*. New York: Grove Press.

———. 2016. "The Fact of Blackness." In *Postcolonial Studies: An Anthology*, edited by Pramond K. Nayar, 15–31. Malden, Mass.: John Wiley & Sons.

Farris, Sara R. 2015. "Migrants' Regular Army of Labour: Gender Dimensions of the Impact of the Global Economic Crisis on Migrant Labor in Western Europe." *Sociological Review* 63 (1): 121–143.

Fassin, Didier. 2013. *Enforcing Order: An Ethnography of Urban Policing*. Cambridge: Polity Press.

Fekete, Liz. 2009. *A Suitable Enemy: Racism, Migration and Islamophobia in Europe*. London: Pluto Press.

FEMAFRO. n.d. Home page. Retrieved February 1, 2023. https://femafro.pt.

Fernandes, Carla Marisa. 2015. "Media étnicos, novas tecnologias e visibilidade dos afrodescendentes em Portugal: O caso do audioblogue Rádio AfroLis." Master's thesis, Comunicação, Cultura e Tecnologias da Informação, University Institute of Lisboa, ISCTE. Retrieved October 1, 2021. https://repositorio.iscte-iul.pt/handle/10071/10378.

Fernandes, Gabriel Antônio Monteiro. 2000. "Entre a Europeidade e a Africanidade: Os marcos da colonização/descolonização no processo de funcionalização identitária em Cabo Verde." Repositório Institucional da UFSC. Retrieved July 1, 2021. https://repositorio.ufsc .br/xmlui/bitstream/handle/123456789/79058/231358.pdf.

Ferreira, Vicente. 1946. "Alguns aspectos da política indígena de Angola." In *Antologia colonial portuguesa I*, 220. Lisbon: Agência Geral das Colónias.

Ferreira, Virgínia. 2010. "A evolução das desigualdades entre salários masculinos e femininos: Um percurso irregular." In *A igualdade de mulheres e homens no trabalho e no emprego em Portugal: Políticas e circunstâncias*, edited by Virgínia Ferreira, 139–190. Lisbon: Comissão para a Igualdade no Trabalho e no Emprego / Ministério do Trabalho e da Solidariedade Social. Retrieved July 1, 2021. https://estudogeral.sib.uc.pt/handle/10316/44009.

Figueiredo, Angela. 2011. "Condições e contradições do trabalho doméstico em Salvador." In *Tensões e experiências: Um retrato das trabalhadoras domésticas de Brasília e Salvador*, edited by Natalia Mori, Soraya Fleischer, Angela Figueiredo, Joaze Bernardino-Costa, and Tânia Cruz, 89–131. Brasília: Centro Feminista de Estudos e Assessoria.

Fikes, Kesha. 1998. "Domesticity in Black and White: Assessing Badia Cape Verdean Challenges to Portuguese Ideals of Black Womanhood." *Transforming Anthropology* 7 (2): 5–19.

———. 2008. "Diasporic Governmentality: On the Gendered Limits of Migrant Wage-Labour in Portugal." *Feminist Review* 90 (1): 48–67.

———. 2009. *Managing African Portugal: The Citizen-Migrant Distinction*. Durham, N.C.: Duke University Press.

Fleming, Crystal Marie. 2017. *Resurrecting Slavery: Racial Legacies and White Supremacy in France*. Philadelphia: Temple University Press.

Florvil, Tiffany N. 2020. *Mobilizing Black Germany: Afro-German Women and the Making of a Transnational Movement*. Champaign: University of Illinois Press.

Folbre, Nancy. 1994. *Who Pays for the Kids? Gender and the Structures of Constraint*. New York: Taylor & Francis.

———. 2012. *For Love and Money: Care Provision in the United States*. New York: Russell Sage Foundation.

Fonseca, Jorge. 2016. *Religião e liberdade: Os negros nas irmandades e confrarias portuguesas (séculos XV a XIX)*. Retrieved April 17, 2023. https://research.unl.pt/ws/portalfiles/portal/ 3334367/Religiao_e_Liberdade_WEB_1_.pdf.

Fonseca, Maria Lucinda, Alina Esteves, and Jennifer McGarrigle. 2016. "The Economic Crisis as a Feedback-Generating Mechanism? Brazilian and Ukrainian Migration to Portugal." In

Beyond Networks, edited by Oliver Bakewell, Godfried Engbersen, Maria Lucinda Fonseca, and Cindy Hors, 113–133. London: Palgrave Macmillan.

Fonseca, Maria Lucinda, Sónia Pereira, and Alina Esteves. 2014. "Migration of Ukrainian Nationals to Portugal: Changing Flows and the Critical Role of Social Networks." *Central and Eastern European Migration Review* 3 (1): 115–130.

Ford, Tanisha C. 2015. *Liberated Threads: Black Women, Style, and the Global Politics of Soul.* Chapel Hill: University of North Carolina Press.

Fortes, Celeste. 2013. "'M t'studa p'mk ter vida k nha mãe tem.' Género e educação em Cabo Verde." *Ciências sociais unisinos* 49 (1): 80–89.

———. 2015. "As vendedeiras de Cabo Verde: Circulação de produtos, informalidade e mulheres no espaço público de Cabo Verde." In *Visagens de Cabo Verde: Ensaios de antropologia visual e outros ensaios*, edited by José Rogério Lopes, 101–102. Porto Alegre, Brazil: Editora Cirkula.

Fortes, Celeste, and Elizabeth Challinor. 2020. "Women in Cape Verde." *Oxford Research Encyclopedia of African History.* Retrieved July 1, 2021. https://doi.org/10.1093/acrefore/9780190277734.013.575.

França, Thais, and Stefanie Prange de Oliveira. 2021. "Brazilian Migrant Women as Killjoys: Disclosing Racism in 'Friendly' Portugal." *Cadernos Pagu* 63.

Francis, Leigh-Anne. 2020. "'Steal or Starve:' Black Women's Criminal Work in New York City, 1893 to 1914." *Journal of Women's History* 32 (4): 13–37.

Fredette, Jennifer. 2014. *Constructing Muslims in France: Discourse, Public Identity, and the Politics of Citizenship.* Philadelphia: Temple University Press.

Freyre, Gilberto. (1933) 1944. *The Masters and the Slaves: A Study in the Development of Brazilian Civilization.* New York: Alfred E. Knopf.

———. 1953. *Um Brasileiro em terras portuguêsas: Introdução a uma possível luso-tropicologia, acompanhada de conferências e discursos proferidos em Portugal e em terras lusitanas e ex-lusitanas da Ásia, da África e do Atlântico.* Rio de Janeiro: J. Olympio.

Frisina, Annalisa, and Camilla Hawthorne. 2018. "Italians with Veils and Afros: Gender, Beauty, and the Everyday Anti-racism of the Daughters of Immigrants in Italy." *Journal of Ethnic and Migration Studies* 44 (5): 718–735.

Furtado, Clementina Baptista de Jesus. 2021. "Public Policies and Gender Equality in Cabo Verde from the Study on the Use of Time to the National Care System." In *Cabo-Verdean Women Writing, Remembrance, Resistance, and Revolution: Kriolas Poderozas*, edited by Terza A. Silva Lima-Neves, and Aminah N. Fernandes Pilgrim, 105–119. London: Lexington Books.

Gaitskell, Deborah, Judy Kimble, Moira Maconachie, and Elaine Unterhalter. 1983. "Class, Race and Gender: Domestic Workers in South Africa." *Review of African Political Economy* 10 (27/28): 86–108.

Gallardo, Francisco José Cuberos. 2014. "Djunta-mon: Migración Caboverdiana y prácticas de ayuda mutua en la periferia de Lisboa." *Perifèria: Revista d'investigació i ormació en antropologia* 19 (2): 4–28.

Garrido Castellano, Carlos, and Otávio Raposo. 2020. "Bottom-up Creativity and Insurgent Citizenship in 'Afro Lisboa': Racial Difference and Cultural Commodification in Portugal." *Cultural Dynamics* 32 (4): 328–351.

Gilroy, Paul. 1992. *There Ain't No Black in the Union Jack.* New York: Routledge.

———. 1993. *The Black Atlantic: Modernity and Double Consciousness.* London: Verso.

Givens, Terri E., and Rhonda Evans Case. 2014. *Legislating Equality: The Politics of Anti-discrimination Policy in Europe.* New York: Oxford University Press.

Glenn, Evelyn Nakano. 1992. "From Servitude to Service Work: Historical Continuities in the Racial Division of Paid Reproductive Labor." *Signs: Journal of Women in Culture and Society* 18 (1): 1–43.

———. 2002. *Unequal Freedom*. Cambridge, Mass.: Harvard University Press.

———. 2010. *Forced to Care: Coercion and Caregiving in America*. Cambridge, Mass.: Harvard University Press.

Góis, Pedro. 2008. *Comunidade(s) Cabo-Verdiana(s): As múltiplas faces da imigração Cabo-Verdiana*. ACIDI, IP. Retrieved July 1, 2021. https://core.ac.uk/download/pdf/144048705.pdf.

Goldberg, David Theo. 2002. *The Racial State*. Malden, Mass.: Blackwell.

———. 2006. "Racial Europeanization." *Ethnic and Racial Studies* 29 (2): 331–364.

———. 2015. *Are We All Post-racial Yet?* Cambridge: Polity Press.

González, Pilar. 2014. "Gender Issues of the Recent Crisis in Portugal." *Dans Revue de l'OFCE* 2 (133): 241–275. https://www.cairn.info/revue-de-l-ofce-2014-2-page-241.htm.

Gordon, Avery F. 2008. *Ghostly Matters: Haunting and the Sociological Imagination*. Minneapolis: University of Minnesota Press.

Grassi, Marzia. 2003. *Rabidantes: Comércio espontâneo transnacional em Cabo Verde*. Praia, Cabo Verde: Imprensa de Ciências Sociais.

Greensword, Sylvane Ngandu-Kalenga. 2022. "Historicizing Black Hair Politics: A Framework for Contextualizing Race Politics." *Sociology Compass* 16 (8): e13015.

Grundy, Saida. 2022. *Respectable: Politics and Paradox in Making the Morehouse Man*. Oakland: University of California Press.

Guerreiro, Maria das Dores. 2014. "Family Policies in Portugal." In *Handbook of Family Policies across the Globe*, edited by Mihaela Robila, 195–201. New York: Springer.

Guibentif, Pierre. 2011. "Rights Perceived and Practiced: Results of a Survey Carried Out in Portugal as Part of the Project 'Domestic Work and Domestic Workers: Interdisciplinary and Comparative Perspectives.'" Centro de Estudos sobre a Mudança Socioeconómica e o Território (Dinâmia-CET) (Centre for Socioeconomic Change and Territorial Studies), Instituto Universitário de Lisboa, ISCTE-IUL. Unpublished manuscript. Retrieved May 11, 2023. https://citeseerx.ist.psu.edu/document?repid=rep1&type=pdf&doi=1f4d79ea914ca1b2062490e009ed5ccb13fd094f.

Gutiérrez-Rodríguez, Encarnación. 2010. *Migration, Domestic Work and Affect: A Decolonial Approach on Value and the Feminization of Labor*. New York: Routledge.

Hall, Stuart. 1990. "Cultural Identity and Diaspora." In *Identity: Community, Culture, Difference*, edited by Jonathon Rutherford, 222–237. London: Lawrence & Wishart.

———. (2003) 2021. "'In but Not of Europe:' Europe and Its Myths." In *Selected Writings on Race and Difference*, edited by Paul Gilroy and Ruth Wilson Gilmore, 374–385. Durham, N.C.: Duke University Press.

———. 2019. "The West and the Rest: Discourse and Power." In *Essential Essays*. Vol. 2, *Identity and Diaspora*, edited by David Morely, 141–184. Durham, N.C.: Duke University Press.

Halter, Marilyn. 1993. *Between Race and Ethnicity: Cape Verdean American Immigrants, 1860–1965*. Urbana: University of Illinois Press.

Harris, Anita, Sarah Carney, and Michelle Fine. 2000. "Counter Work: Theorising the Politics of Counter Stories." *International Journal of Critical Psychology* 4 (2): 6–18.

Harth-Terré, Emilio. 1973. *Negros e Indios: Un estamento social ignorado del Perú colonial*. Lima: Librería-Editorial Juan Mejía Baca.

Hartman, Saidiya V. 1997. *Scenes of Subjection: Terror, Slavery, and Self-Making in Nineteenth-Century America*. New York: Oxford University Press.

Hawthorne, Camilla. 2019. "Black Matters Are Spatial Matters: Black Geographies for the Twenty-First Century." *Geography Compass* 13 (11): 1–13.

———. 2022. *Contesting Race and Citizenship: Youth Politics in the Black Mediterranean*. Ithaca: Cornell University Press.

Henriques, Isabel Castro. 2013. "Africans in Portuguese Society: Classification Ambiguities and Colonial Realities." In *Imperial Migrations*, edited by Eric Morier-Genoud and Michel Cahen, 72–103. London: Palgrave Macmillan.

———. 2019. *Mulheres Africanas em Portugal: O discurso das imagens (séculos XV–XXI)*. Lisbon: Secretária de Estado para a Cidadania e a Igualdade ACM. https://www.acm.gov.pt/documents/10181/27754/Mulheres_africanas_pt.pdf.

———. 2021. *Roteiro histórico de uma Lisboa Africana séculos XV–XXI*. Lisbon: Edições Colibri.

Henriques, Joana Gorjão. 2016a. "Este é o apocalipse dos 'sem direito' a casa." *Público*, December 11. Retrieved February 22, 2023. https://www.publico.pt/2016/12/11/sociedade/reportagem/este-e-o-apocalipse-dos-sem-direito-a-casa-1754071.

———. 2016b. *Racismo em Português: O lado esquecido do colonialismo*. Lisbon: Tinta da China.

———. 2016c. "Retrato da desigualdade racial em Portugal: Associações elaboraram retrato das desigualdades raciais em Portugal com dados que vão da educação à habitação." *Público*, December 6. Retrieved July 1, 2021. https://www.publico.pt/2016/12/05/sociedade/noticia/-os-numeros-da-desigualdade-racial-em-portugal-1753490.

———. 2018. *Racismo no país dos brancos costumes*. Lisbon: Tinta da China.

———. 2022. "Três polícias vão a julgamento no caso de agressão a Cláudia Simões." *Público*, June 20. https://www.publico.pt/2022/06/20/sociedade/noticia/tres-policias-vao-julgamento-caso-agresssao-claudia-simoes-2010648.

Henriques, Joana Gorjão, and Vera Moutinho. 2016. "Entrevista: Quando saímos de casa dos pais, também não batemos à porta da câmara." *Público*, December 11. Retrieved July 1, 2021. https://www.publico.pt/2016/12/11/sociedade/noticia/quando-saimos-de-casa-dos-pais-tambemnao-batemos-a-porta-da-camara-1754075.

Hochschild, Arlie Russell. (1983) 2012. *The Managed Heart*. Berkeley: University of California Press.

———. 1997. *The Time Bind: When Work Becomes Home and Home Becomes Work*. Berkeley: University of California Press.

Hondagneu-Sotelo, Pierette. (2001) 2007. *Domestica: Immigrant Workers Cleaning and Caring in the Shadows of Affluence*. Berkeley: University of California Press.

hooks, bell. 1989. *Talking Back: Thinking Feminist, Thinking Black*. Boston: South End Press.

Hordge-Freeman, Elizabeth. 2018. "'Bringing Your Whole Self to Research': The Power of the Researcher's Body, Emotions, and Identities in Ethnography." *International Journal of Qualitative Methods* 17 (1): 1–9.

Horta, Ana Paula Beja, and Paul White. 2008. "Post-colonial Migration and Citizenship Regimes: A Comparison of Portugal and the United Kingdom." *Revista migrações* 4:33–57.

Hull, Akasha Gloria T., Patricia Bell-Scott, and Barbara Smith, eds. 1982. *All the Women Are White, All the Blacks Are Men, but Some of Us Are Brave: Black Women's Studies*. New York: Feminist Press.

Hurtado, Vicenta Moreno, and Debaye Mornan. 2015. "¿Y el derecho à la ciudad? Aproximaciones sobre el racismo, la dominación patriarcal y estrategias feministas de resistencia en Cali, Colombia." *Revista CS* 16:89–110.

Instituto Nacional de Estatística. 2015. "Anuário estatístico." Retrieved December 10, 2021. https://ine.cv/wp-content/plugins/ine-download-attachments-by-zing-developers/includes/download.php?id=6739.

IPUMS International. n.d. "Return to Work: Occupation Variables List." Retrieved March 20, 2024. https://international.ipums.org/international-action/variables/PT1991A_0437#integrated_variables_section.

Ishemo, Shubi L. 1995. "Forced Labour and Migration in Portugal's African Colonies." In *The Cambridge Survey of World Migration*, edited by Robin Cohen, 162–165. Cambridge: Cambridge University Press.

Jerónimo, Miguel Bandeira. 2015. *The "Civilising Mission" of Portuguese Colonialism, 1870–1930*. New York: Palgrave Macmillan.

Joël, Marie-Eve, Sandrine Dufour-Kippelen, and Sanda Samitca. 2010. "Long-Term Care in Portugal: Some Elements of Context." *ENEPRI Research Report*, no. 84. Retrieved May 15, 2023. http://aei.pitt.edu/14607/1/Portugal.pdf.

Johnson, Elizabeth. 2016. *Resistance and Empowerment in Black Women's Hair Styling*. New York: Routledge.

Johnson, Michelle. 2020. *Remaking Islam in African Portugal: Lisbon–Mecca–Bissau*. Bloomington: Indiana University Press.

Jones, Jacqueline. 2009. *Labor of Love, Labor of Sorrow: Black Women, Work, and the Family, from Slavery to the Present*. New York: Basic Books.

Kang, Miliann. 2000. "Researching One's Own: Negotiating Co-ethnicity in the Field." In *Cultural Compass: Ethnographic Explorations of Asian America*, edited by Martin F. Manalansan, 38–48. Philadelphia: Temple University Press.

———. 2010. *The Managed Hand: Race, Gender and the Body in Beauty Service Work*. Berkeley: University of California Press.

Keaton, Trica Danielle. 2006. *Muslim Girls and the Other France: Race, Identity Politics, & Social Exclusion*. Bloomington: Indiana University Press.

———. 2023. *#You Know You're Black in France When: The Fact of Everyday Antiblackness*. Boston: MIT Press.

Kennelly, Ivy. 1999. "'That Single-Mother Element': How White Employers Typify Black Women." *Gender & Society* 13 (2): 168–192.

Kilomba, Grada. 2008. *Plantation Memories: Episodes of Everyday Racism*. Münster, Germany: Unrast Verlag.

———. 2020. *Memórias da plantação: Episódios de racismo cotidiano*. Rio de Janeiro: Editora Cobogó.

King, Deborah K. 1988. "Multiple Jeopardy, Multiple Consciousness: The Context of a Black Feminist Ideology." *Signs: Journal of Women in Culture and Society* 14 (1): 42–72.

King, Russell. 2000. "Southern Europe in the Changing Global Map of Migration." In *Eldorado or Fortress? Migration in Southern Europe*, edited by Russell King, Gabriella Lazaridis, and Charalambos Tsardanidis, 3–26. London: Palgrave Macmillan.

Lamont, Michèle, and Ann Swidler. 2014. "Methodological Pluralism and the Possibilities and Limits of Interviewing." *Qualitative Sociology* 37 (2): 153–171.

Lan, Pei-Chia. 2006. *Global Cinderellas: Migrant Domestics and Newly Rich Employers in Taiwan*. Durham, N.C.: Duke University Press.

———. 2018. *Raising Global Families: Parenting, Immigration, and Class in Taiwan and the US*. Palo Alto, Calif.: Stanford University Press.

Lentin, Alana. 2004. *Racism and Anti-racism in Europe*. London: Pluto Press.

———. 2018. "Beyond Denial: 'Not Racism' as Racist Violence." *Continuum* 32 (4): 400–414.

———. 2020. *Why Race Still Matters*. Hoboken, N.J.: John Wiley & Sons.

Liebelt, Claudia. 2011. *Caring for the "Holy Land": Filipina Domestic Workers in Israel*. New York: Berghahn Books.

Lima-Neves, Terza A. Silva. 2009. "Heroinas d'nos terra: Cabo Verdean Women, 34 Years after Independence." Terza Silva Lima-Neves, PhD. June 2009. Retrieved June 22, 2023. https://www.terzalimaneves.com/the-tea-with-dr-t/heroinas-dnos-terra-cabo-verdean-women-34-years-after-independence.

Liu, Callie Watkins. 2021. "Where Blackness and Cape Verdeanness Intersect: Reflections of Monoracial and Multiethnic Reality in the United States." In *Cabo-Verdean Women Writing, Remembrance, Resistance, and Revolution: Kriolas Poderozas*, edited by Terza A. Silva Lima-Neves and Aminah N. Fernandes Pilgrim, 151–165. London: Lexington Books.

Lobban, Richard A. 1995. *Cape Verde: Crioulo Colony to Independent Nation*. Boulder, Colo.: Westview Press.

Lobo, Andréa. 2011. "'Making Families' Child Mobility and Familiar Organization in Cape Verde." *Vibrant: Virtual Brazilian Anthropology* 8 (2): 197–219.

Lopes, Alexandra. 2016. "Portugal: Quasi-privatization of a Dual System of Care." In *Long-Term Care for the Elderly in Europe: Development and Prospects*, edited by Bent Greve, 59–74. London: Routledge.

Lorde, Audre. (1984) 2007. "Age, Race, Class, and Sex: Women Redefining Difference." In *Sister Outsider* by Audre Lorde, 104–114. New York: Penguin Books.

Lugones, María. 2007. "Heterosexualism and the Colonial/Modern Gender System." *Hypatia* 22 (1): 186–219.

———. 2010. "Toward a Decolonial Feminism." *Hypatia* 25 (4): 742–759.

Lutz, Helma. 2011. *The New Maids: Transnational Women and the Care Economy*. New York: Zed Books.

Ly, Aliou. 2014. "Promise and Betrayal: Women Fighters and National Liberation in Guinea-Bissau." *Feminist Africa* 19:24–42.

Lyonette, Clare, Rosemary Crompton, and Karin Wall. 2007. "Gender, Occupational Class and Work–Life Conflict: A Comparison of Britain and Portugal." *Community, Work and Family* 10 (3): 283–308.

Machado, Fernando Luís, and Maria Abranches. 2005. "Caminhos limitados de integração social: Trajectórias socioprofissionais de Cabo-Verdianos e hindus em Portugal." *Sociologia, problemas, e prácticas* no. 48 (May–August 2005): 67–89. http://hdl.handle.net/10071/194.

Maeso, Silvia Rodríguez, ed. 2021. *O estado do racismo em Portugal: Racismo antinegro e anticiganismo no direito e nas políticas públicas*. Lisbon: Tinta da China.

Maeso, Silvia Rodríguez, Ana Rita Alves, and Sara Fernandes. 2021. "A implementação da legislação de combate a discriminação racial em Portugal: uma abordagem sociolegal." In *O estado do racismo em Portugal: Racismo antinegro e anticiganismo no direito e nas políticas públicas*, edited by Silvia Rodríguez Maeso, 33–57. Lisbon: Tinta da China.

Maeso, Silvia Rodríguez (coord.), Ana Rita Alves, Sara Fernandes, and Inês Oliveira. 2020. "Direito, estado e sociedade: Uma análise da legislação de combate ao racismo em Portugal." *Caderno de apresentação de resultados do projeto COMBAT*. Retrieved January 1, 2022. https://www.ces.uc.pt/ficheiros2/files/Combat_Booklet_Caderno_junho_2020.pdf.

Maeso, Silvia Rodríguez, and Marta Araújo. 2017. "The (Im)plausibility of Racism in Europe: Policy Frameworks on Discrimination and Integration." *Patterns of Prejudice* 51 (1): 26–50.

Majali, Zukiswa, Jan K. Coetzee, and Asta Rau. 2017. "Everyday Hair Discourses of African Black Women." *Qualitative Sociology Review* 13 (1): 158–172.

Marchetti, Sabrina. 2014. *Black Girls: Migrant Domestic Workers and Colonial Legacies*. Leiden, Netherlands: Brill.

Marcus, George E. 1998. *Ethnography through Thick and Thin*. Princeton, N.J.: Princeton University Press.

Martins, Joao Augusto. 1891. *Cape Verde, Madeira e Guiné*. Lisbon: Livraria de Antonio M. Pereira.

Mata, Maria Eugénia. 2020. *The Portuguese Escudo Monetary Zone: Its Impact in Colonial and Post-colonial Africa*. London: Palgrave.

Matias, Marisa, Cláudia Andrade, and Anne Marie Fontaine. 2012. "The Interplay of Gender, Work and Family in Portuguese Families." *Work Organisation, Labour and Globalisation* 6 (1): 11–26.

Matos, Patrícia Ferraz de. 2013. *The Colours of the Empire: Racialized Representations during Portuguese Colonialism*. New York: Berghahn Books.

Mayblin, Lucy, and Joe Turner. 2021. *Migration Studies and Colonialism*. Cambridge: Polity Press.

Mayorga-Gallo, Sarah, and Elizabeth Hordge-Freeman. 2017. "Between Marginality and Privilege: Gaining Access and Navigating the Field in Multiethnic Settings." *Qualitative Research* 17 (4): 377–394.

McGarrigle, Jennifer. 2016. "Islam in Urban Spaces: The Residential Incorporation and Choices of Muslims in Lisbon." *Journal of Ethnic and Migration Studies* 42 (3): 437–457.

McKittrick, Katherine. 2006. *Demonic Grounds: Black Women and the Cartographies of Struggle*. Minneapolis: University of Minnesota Press.

———. 2011. "On Plantations, Prisons, and a Black Sense of Place." *Social & Cultural Geography* 12 (8): 947–963.

Meghji, Ali. 2019. *Black Middle-Class Britannia: Identities, Repertoires, Cultural Consumption*. Manchester, U.K.: Manchester University Press.

Meintel, Deirdre. 1984. *Race, Culture, and Portuguese Colonialism in Cabo Verde*. Syracuse, N.Y.: Syracuse University Press.

Mera, Alda. 2014. "Conseguir trabajo siendo indígena o afro es un verdadero 'camello.'" *El País*, April 30. Retrieved July 1, 2021. https://www.elpais.com.co/cali/conseguir-trabajo -siendo-indigena-o-afro-es-un-verdadero-camello.html.

Mestheneos, Elizabeth. 2011. "Ageing in Place in the European Union." *Global Ageing* 7 (2): 17–24.

Migration Integration Policy Index. 2015. "Portugal." Retrieved June 12, 2023. http://mipex .eu/Portugal.

Mills, Charles W. 1997. *The Racial Contract*. Ithaca, N.Y.: Cornell University Press.

Molinier, Pascale. 2013. *Le travail du care*. Paris: La Dispute.

Moreira, Joacine Katar. 2020. "Precisamos da justiça social na Europa." YouTube. Retrived February 27, 2024. https://www.youtube.com/watch?v=d8jdxUI_Yo8.

Moreira, Patrícia. 2020. *As novas identidades portuguesas*. Lisbon: Chiado.

Morgan, Jennifer L. 2021. *Reckoning with Slavery: Gender, Kinship, and Capitalism in the Early Black Atlantic*. Durham, N.C.: Duke University Press.

Motsi-Khatai, Wadzanai. 2020. "Intersectional Discrimination in Europe: Relevance, Challenges and Ways Forward." European Network Against Racism and Center for Intersectional Justice, September 14. Retrieved July 1, 2021. https://www.intersectionaljustice.org/ publication/2020-09-14-intersectional-discrimination-in-europe-relevance-challenges-and -ways-forward.

NAWI Afrifem Macroeconomics Collective. 2023. Our Knowledge Portal. Retrieved May 1, 2023. https://www.nawi.africa/portal/page/2/?thematic_area=debt&country#038 ;country.

Neely, Megan Tobias. 2002. *Hedged Out: Inequality and Insecurity on Wall Street*. Oakland: University of California Press.

Nimako, Kwame, and Stephen Small. 2009. "Theorizing Black Europe and African Diaspora: Implications for Citizenship, Nativism, and Xenophobia." In *Black Europe and the African Diaspora*, edited by Darlene Clark Hine, Trica Danielle Keaton, and Stephen Small, 212–237. Chicago: University of Illinois Press.

Nogueira, Gláucia Aparecida. 2011. "Batuko, património imaterial de Cabo Verde. Percurso histórico-musical." Master's thesis, Department of Social Sciences and Humanities, Universidade de Cabo Verde. Retrieved July 1, 2021. https://core.ac.uk/download/pdf/38680099 .pdf.

OECD (Organisation for Economic Co-operation and Development). 2008a. *Jobs for Immigrants: Labour Market Integration in Belgium, France, the Netherlands, Portugal; Summary and Recommendations Portugal*. Paris: OECD. Retrieved July 1, 2021. http://www.oecd .org/portugal/41708423.pdf.

———. 2008b. "The Labour Market Integration of Immigrants and Their Children in Portugal." In *Jobs for Immigrants: Labour Market Integration in Belgium, France, the Netherlands, Portugal*, 269–331. Paris: OECD. Retrieved July 1, 2021. https://doi.org/10.1787/9789264055605-en.

Okpalaoka, Chinwe L. 2008. "'You Don't Look like One, So How Are You African?': How West African Immigrant Girls in the US Learn to (Re)negotiate Ethnic Identities in Home and School Contexts." PhD diss., ED Policy and Leadership, Ohio State University. Retrieved May 25, 2023. http://rave.ohiolink.edu/etdc/view?acc_num=osu1230605597.

Olasunkanmi-Alimi, Temitope, Kristin Natalier, and Monique Mulholland. 2022. "Everyday Racism and the Denial of Migrant African Women's Good Caring in Aged Care Work." *Gender, Work & Organization* 29 (4): 1082–1094.

Oliveira, Catarina Reis, and Cláudia Pires. 2010. "Imigração e sinistralidade laboral." *Observatório da imigração*, vol. 41. Lisbon: Alto Comissariado para a Imigração e Diálogo Intercultural (ACIDI). Retrieved July 1, 2021. https://www.om.acm.gov.pt/documents/58428/177157/OI_41.pdf.

Omi, Michael, and Howard Winant. (1986) 2015. *Racial Formation in the United States*. New York: Routledge.

Organización Internacional para las Migraciones (OIPM). n.d. "UTRASD, red de mujeres Afrocolombianas que transforman el servicio doméstico en Colombia." Retrieved July 1, 2021. https://colombia.iom.int/es/stories/utrasd-red-de-mujeres-afrocolombianas-que-transforman-el-servicio-domestico-en-colombia.

Oyěwùmí, Oyèrónkẹ́. 1997. *The Invention of Women: Making an African Sense of Western Gender Discourses*. Minneapolis: University of Minnesota Press.

Ozyegin, Gul, and Pierette Hondagneu-Sotelo. 2008. "Conclusion: Domestic Work, Migration and the New Gender Order in Contemporary Europe." In *Migration and Domestic Work: A European Perspective on a Global Theme*, edited by Helma Lutz, 207–220. New York: Routledge.

Palmer, Phyllis. 1989. *Domesticity and Dirt: Housewives and Domestic Servants in the United States, 1920–1945*. Philadelphia: Temple University Press.

Pande, Amrita. 2012. "From 'Balcony Talk' and 'Practical Prayers' to Illegal Collectives: Migrant Domestic Workers and Meso-level Resistances in Lebanon." *Gender & Society* 26 (3): 382–405. https://doi.org/10.1177/0891243212439247.

Pardue, Derek. 2012. "Cape Verdean Kriolu as an Epistemology of Contact." *Cadernos de estudos africanos* 24:73–94.

———. 2015. *Cape Verde, Let's Go: Creole Rappers and Citizenship in Portugal*. Champaign: University of Illinois Press.

Parreñas, Rhacel Salazar. (2001) 2015. *Servants of Globalization: Women, Migration and Domestic Work*. Stanford, Calif.: Stanford University Press.

———. 2022. *Unfree: Migrant Domestic Work in Arab States*. Stanford, Calif.: Stanford University Press.

Patterson, David K. 1988. "Epidemics, Famines, and Population in the Cape Verde Islands, 1580–1900." *International Journal of African Historical Studies* 21 (2): 291–313.

Pattillo-McCoy, Mary. (1999) 2003. *Black Picket Fences: Privilege and Peril among the Black Middle Class*. Chicago: University of Chicago Press.

Pedroso, Paulo. 2014. "Portugal and the Global Crisis: The Impact of Austerity on the Economy, the Social Model and the Performance of the State." Friedrich Ebert Stiftung. Retrieved July 1, 2021. https://library.fes.de/pdf-files/id/10722-20220207.pdf.

Peixoto, João. 2009. "New Migrations in Portugal: Labour Markets, Smuggling and Gender Segmentation." *International Migration* 47 (3): 185–210.

———. 2011. "How the Global Recession Has Impacted Immigrant Employment: The

Portuguese Case." In *Migration and the Great Recession: The Transatlantic Experience*, edited by Demetrios G. Papademetriou, Madeleine Sumption, and Aaron Terrazas, 106–125. Washington, D.C.: Migration Policy Institute. Retrieved June 8, 2023. https://www.migrationpolicy.org/sites/default/files/publications/mpi-migrationgreatrecession-2011-final-webversion.pdf.

Peixoto, João, and Catarina Sabino. 2009. "Immigration, Emigration and Policy Developments in Portugal (ARI)." *Real Instituto Elcano (RIE)*. Retrieved May 18, 2023. https://media.realinstitutoelcano.org/wp-content/uploads/2009/07/ari117-2009-peixotosabino-immigration-emigration-policy-portugal.pdf.

Penn Medicine. 2024. *Lift Every Voice: Capturing and Intervening on Experiences of Racism in Health Care*. Center for Health Care Transformation & Innovation. Retrieved February 27, 2024. https://chti.upenn.edu/lift-every-voice.

Pereira, Sónia. 2010. *Trabalhadores de origem africana em Portugal: Impacto das novas vagas de imigração*. Lisbon: Edições Colibri.

———. 2013. "Replacement Migration and Changing Preferences: Immigrant Workers in Cleaning and Domestic Service in Portugal." *Journal of Ethnic and Migration Studies* 39 (7): 1141–1158.

Perry, Keisha-Khan Y. 2013. *Black Women against the Land Grab: The Fight for Racial Justice in Brazil*. Minneapolis: University of Minnesota Press.

Piçarra, Nuno, and Ana Rita Gil. 2012. "Country Report: Portugal." *EUDO Citizenship Observatory, Robert Schuman Centre for Advanced Studies, European University Institute, Florence*. Retrieved May 18, 2023. https://cadmus.eui.eu/bitstream/handle/1814/19632/RSCAS_EUDO_CIT_2012_8.pdf.

Portes, Alejandro, and Rubén G. Rumbaut. 2001. *Legacies: The Story of the Immigrant Second Generation*. Berkeley: University of California Press.

PORTUGAL.GOV.PT. 2023. "Portugal Supports Cape Verde's Green and Energy Transition." Portugal.gov.pt. Retrieved June 20, 2023. https://www.portugal.gov.pt/en/gc23/communication/news-item?i=portugal-supports-cape-verdes-green-and-energy-transition.

Posso, Jeanny. 2008. "Mecanismos de discriminación étnico-racial, clase social y género: La inserción laboral de mujeres negras en el servicio doméstico de Cali." In *Pobreza, exclusión social y discriminación étnico-racial en América Latina y el Caribe*, edited by María del Carmen Zabala Argüelles, 215–240. Bogotá: Siglo del Hombre Editores; CLACSO.

Quadri, Maryam Omolara. 2018. "Neoliberalism and the Paradox of Poverty Reduction: A Synthesis of the Poverty Reduction Strategy Paper Experience in Benin and Nigeria." *Africology: Journal of Pan African Studies* 11 (7): 186–203.

Quijano, Aníbal. 2000. "Coloniality of Power and Eurocentrism in Latin America." *International Sociology* 15 (2): 215–232.

Ramalho da Silva, Beatriz. 2020. "Portugal: Deadly Racism, Far-Right Growth Draw Global Concern." *Al Jazeera*, September 14. Retrieved January 22, 2021. https://www.aljazeera.com/features/2020/9/14/portugal-deadly-racism-far-right-growth-draw-global-concern.

Raposo, Otávio, Ana Rita Alves, Pedro Varela, and Cristina Roldão. 2019. "Negro drama: Racismo, segregação e violência policial nas periferias de Lisboa." *Revista crítica de ciências sociais* 119:5–28.

Raposo, Otávio, and Pedro Varela. 2017. "Faces do racismo nas periferias de Lisboa. Uma reflexão sobre a segregação e a violência policial na Cova da Moura." Paper presented at the IX Congresso Português de Sociologia: *Portugal, Território de Territórios*. Lisbon: Associação Portuguesa de Sociologia. Retrieved July 1, 2021. https://estudogeral.sib.uc.pt/handle/10316/87147.

Ray, Victor. 2019. "A Theory of Racialized Organizations." *American Sociological Review* 84 (1): 26–53.

Reskin, Barbara. 1993. "Sex Segregation in the Workplace." *Annual Review of Sociology* 19 (1): 241–270.

Reyes, Victoria. 2020. "Ethnographic Toolkit: Strategic Positionality and Researchers' Visible and Invisible Tools in Field Research." *Ethnography* 21 (2): 220–240.

Rodney, Walter. (1972) 2018. *How Europe Underdeveloped Africa*. Brooklyn, N.Y.: Verso Trade.

Rodriquez, Jason. 2014. *Labors of Love: Nursing Homes and the Structures of Care Work*. New York: New York University Press.

Roig, Émilia. 2015. "Gender Equality for Some at the Cost of Others: Deciphering the Intersectional Discrimination of Racialized Care Workers in France and Germany." PhD diss., Department of Political Science, École Doctorale—Université de Lyon. Retrieved May 25, 2023. https://www.theses.fr/2015LYO20018.

———. 2017. "Uttering 'Race' in Colorblind France and Post-racial Germany." In *Rassismuskritik und Widerstandsformen*, edited by Karim Fereidooni and Meral El, 613–627. Wiesbaden, Germany: Springer.

Roldão, Cristina. 2016. "Os afrodescendentes no sistema educativo português: Racismo institucional e continuidades coloniais." In *Tecendo redes antirracistas: Africas, Brasis, Portugal*, edited by Anderson Ribeiro Oliva, Majorie Nogueira Chaves, Renisia Cristina Gracia Filice, and wanderson flor do nascimento. São Paulo: Autêntica Editora.

———. 2019. "Feminismo negro em Portugal: Falta contar-nos." *Público*, January 18. Retrieved February 17, 2021. https://www.publico.pt/2019/01/18/culturaipsilon/noticia/feminismo -negro-portugal-falta-contarnos-1857501.

Roldão, Cristina, Mamadou Ba, and Marta Araújo. 2019. "Recolha de Dados étnico-raciais nos Censos 2021: Um passo à frente no combate ao racismo." *Público*, April 16. Retrieved July 1, 2021. https://www.publico.pt/2019/04/16/sociedade/opiniao/recolha-dados-etnicoraciais -censos-2021-passo-frente-combate-racismo-1869349.

Rollins, Judith. 1985. *Between Women: Domestics and Their Employers*. Philadelphia: Temple University Press.

Romero, Mary. 2002. *Maid in the USA*. New York: Routledge.

Rosenbaum, Susanna. 2017. *Domestic Economies: Women, Work, and the American Dream in Los Angeles*. Durham, N.C.: Duke University Press.

Ruchti, Lisa C. 2012. *Catheters, Slurs, and Pickup Lines: Professional Intimacy in Hospital Nursing*. Philadelphia: Temple University Press.

Sahraoui, Nina. 2019. *Racialised Workers and European Older-Age Care*. Cham, Switzerland: Springer International.

Salgueiro, Teresa Barata. 1977. "Bairros clandestinos na periferia de Lisboa." *Finisterra* 12(23). Retrieved May 24, 2023. https://doi.org/10.18055/Finis2281.

Salzinger, Leslie. 1997. "A Maid by Any Other Name: The Transformation of 'Dirty Work' by Central American Immigrants." In *Situated Lives: Gender and Culture in Everyday Life*, edited by Louise Lamphere, Helena Ragoné, and Patricia Zavella, 271–292. New York: Routledge.

Sánchez, Gina Elizabeth. 1999. "Diasporic Transformations: Race, Culture and the Politics of Cape Verdean Identity." PhD diss., Department of Anthropology, University of Texas at Austin.

Sánchez Gibau, Gina. 2005. "Contested Identities: Narratives of Race and Ethnicity in the Cape Verdean Diaspora." *Identities: Global Studies in Culture and Power* 12 (3): 405–438.

Santos, Ana Luísa Sousa. 2016. "Discriminação laboral sobre as mulheres no mercado de trabalho micaelense." Master's thesis, Department of History, Philosophy and the Arts, Universidade dos Açores. Retrieved July 1, 2021. https://repositorio.uac.pt/handle/10400 .3/3789.

Santos, Maria Helena, Núria Romão, and Carla Cerqueira. 2023. "Gender, Class, and

Ethnicity: Perspectives of White Portuguese and Black African Women on Labor Dynamics in the Cleaning Sector." *Social Sciences* 12 (20): 1–19.

Santos, Tiago. 2014. "ENAR Shadow Report 2012–13 on Racism and Related Discriminatory Practices in Employment in Portugal." *European Network against Racism*. Retrieved July 1, 2021. https://www.academia.edu/6586092/ENAR_Shadow_Report_2012_13_on_Racism _and_related_discriminatory_practices_in_employment_in_Portugal.

Saraiva, Clara. 2008. "Transnational Migrants and Transnational Spirits: An African Religion in Lisbon." *Journal of Ethnic and Migration Studies* 34 (2): 253–269.

Sassen, Saskia. 1988. *The Mobility of Labor and Capital: A Study in International Investment and Labor Flow*. New York: Cambridge University Press.

———. 2000. "Women's Burden: Counter-geographies of Globalization and the Feminization of Survival." *Journal of International Affairs* 53 (2): 503–524.

Saucier, P. Khalil. 2015. *Necessarily Black: Cape Verdean Youth, Hip-Hop Culture, and a Critique of Identity*. East Lansing: Michigan State University Press.

Saunders, A. C. De C. M. 1982. *A Social History of Black Slaves and Freedmen in Portugal, 1441–1555*. Cambridge: Cambridge University Press.

Sawyer, Mark Q. 2005. *Racial Politics in Post-revolutionary Cuba*. Cambridge: Cambridge University Press.

Seabra, Teresa, Sandra Mateus, Elisabete Rodrigues, and Magda Nico. 2011. "Trajetos e projetos de jovens descendentes de imigrantes à saída da escolaridade básica." *Observatório da imigração*, vol. 47. Lisbon: Alto Comissariado para a Imigração e Diálogo Intercultural (ACIDI). Retrieved July 1, 2021. https://ec.europa.eu/migrant-integration/sites/default/ files/2012-05/docl_27413_612833835.pdf.

Seabra, Teresa, Cristina Roldão, Sandra Mateus, and Adriana Albuquerque. 2016. "Caminhos escolares de jovens Africanos (PALOP) que acedem ao ensino superior." *Observatório das migrações*, vol. 57. Lisbon: Alto-Comissariado para as Migrações I.P. (ACM, I.P.). Retrieved July 1, 2021. https://www.om.acm.gov.pt/documents/58428/177157/ESTUDO+57_web .pdf.

Semedo, Carla Indira Carvalho. 2009. "*Mara sulada e dã ku torno*: Performance, gênero e corporeidades no grupo de Batukadeiras de São Martinho Grande (Ilha de Santiago, Cabo Verde)." Master's thesis, Department of Social Anthropology, Universidade Federal do Rio Grande do Sul. Retrieved May 25, 2023. https://lume.ufrgs.br/bitstream/handle/10183/ 16227/000695072.pdf.

———. 2020. "A experiência migratória de Cabo-Verdianos para as roças de São Tomé e Príncipe: Pesquisa de campo." *População e sociedade* 34:87–106.

Small, Stephen. 2017. *20 Questions and Answers on Black Europe*. The Hague: Amrit.

———. 2018. "Theorizing Visibility and Vulnerability in Black Europe and the African Diaspora." *Ethnic and Racial Studies* 41 (6): 1182–1197.

Smith, Christen A. 2016. *Afro-paradise: Blackness, Violence, and Performance in Brazil*. Champaign: University of Illinois Press.

Soares, Miguel Gomes. 2019. "Serviço de apoio domiciliário na saúde em Portugal." Master's thesis, Department of Economics—Service Management, University of Porto. Retrieved June 12, 2023. https://repositorio-aberto.up.pt/bitstream/10216/123693/2/364430.pdf.

Solórzano, Daniel G., and Tara J. Yosso. 2002. "Critical Race Methodology: Counter-storytelling as an Analytical Framework for Education Research." *Qualitative Inquiry* 8 (1): 23–44.

SOS Racismo. 2002. *A imigração em Portugal: Os movimentos humanos e culturais em Portugal*. Lisbon: SOS Racismo.

South African Domestic Service and Allied Workers Union (SADSAWU). 2024. "About Us." Retrieved February 27, 2024. http://www.sadsawu.com/about-us.html.

Sparr, Pamela, ed. 1994. *Mortgaging Women's Lives: Feminist Critiques of Structural Adjustment*. London: Zed Books.

Spillers, Hortense J. 1987. "Mama's Baby, Papa's Maybe: An American Grammar Book." *Diacritics* 17 (2): 65–81.

Stacey, Clare L. 2011. *The Caring Self: The Work Experiences of Home Care Aides*. Ithaca, N.Y.: Cornell University Press.

Stepanik, Hanna. 2019. "On Notions of (In)visibility and Diaspora Space: The Case of *Batuku* as a Popular Cultural Practice in Lisbon." *Vienna Journal of African Studies* 36 (19): 75–100.

Stevens, Martin, Shereen Hussein, and Jill Manthorpe. 2012. "Experiences of Racism and Discrimination among Migrant Care Workers in England: Findings from a Mixed-Methods Research Project." *Ethnic and Racial Studies* 35 (2): 259–280.

Strauss, Anselm, and Juliet M. Corbin, eds. 1997. *Grounded Theory in Practice*. Thousand Oaks, Calif.: Sage.

Strings, Sabrina. 2019. *Fearing the Black Body: The Racial Origins of Fat Phobia*. New York: New York University Press.

Tamale, Sylvia. 2020. *Decolonization and Afro-Feminism*. Ottawa: Daraja Press.

Tavora, Isabel. 2012. "The Southern European Social Model: Familialism and the High Rates of Female Employment in Portugal." *Journal of European Social Policy* 22 (1): 63–76.

Tester, Griff, and Adia M. Harvey Wingfield. 2013. "Moving Past Picket Fences: The Meaning of 'Home' for Public Housing Residents." *Sociological Forum* 28 (1): 70–84.

Theodore, Nik, Beth Gutelius, and Linda Burnham. 2019. "Workplace Health and Safety Hazards Faced by Informally Employed Domestic Workers in the United States." *Workplace Health & Safety* 67 (1): 9–17.

Thobejane, Tsoaledi Daniel, and Sibongile Khosa. 2019. "On Becoming a Domestic Worker: The Case of Mpumalanga Province, South Africa." *OIDA International Journal of Sustainable Development* 12 (3): 27–38. Retrieved June 12, 2023. https://ssrn.com/abstract=3438994.

Tinhorão, José Ramos. 1988. *Os negros em Portugal: Uma presença silenciosa*. Lisbon: Caminho.

Torres, Anália. 2008. "Women, Gender, and Work: The Portuguese Case in the Context of the European Union." *International Journal of Sociology* 38 (4): 36–56.

Torresan, Angela. 2021. "Postcolonial Social Drama: The Case of Brazilian Dentists in Portugal." *Critique of Anthropology* 41 (2): 165–186.

Triandafyllidou, Anna, ed. 2010. *Irregular Migration in Europe: Myths and Realities*. London: Routledge.

Triandafyllidou, Anna, and Thanos Maroukis. 2012. *Migrant Smuggling*. New York: Palgrave Macmillan.

Tronto, Joan C. 2013. *Caring Democracy: Markets, Equality, and Justice*. New York: New York University Press.

Tuominen, Mary C. 2008. "The Right and Responsibility to Care: Oppositional Consciousness among Family Child Care Providers of Color." *Journal of Women, Politics & Policy* 29 (2): 147–179.

Tvon, Telma. 2020. *Um preto muito português*. Lisbon: Chiado.

Twine, France Winddance, and Jonathan W. Warren. 2000. *Racing Research, Researching Race: Methodological Dilemmas in Critical Race Studies*. New York: New York University Press.

Uttal, Lynette, and Mary Tuominen. 1999. "Tenuous Relationships: Exploitation, Emotion, and Racial Ethnic Significance in Paid Child Care Work." *Gender & Society* 13 (6): 758–780.

Vale de Almeida, Miguel. 2006. "On the Lusophone Postcolony: 'Culture,' 'Race,' 'Language.'" Rutgers University, Department of Spanish and Portuguese Studies. Retrieved July 1, 2021.

https://www.yumpu.com/en/document/read/12907707/on-the-lusophone-postcolony
-miguel-vale-de-almeida.

———. 2022. "Ninguém imagina de verdade um Português negro." In *Portuguese Literary and Cultural Studies*. Vol. 34/35, *The Open Veins of the Postcolonial: Afrodescendants and Racisms*, edited by Inocência Mata and Iolanda Évora, 32–41. Dartmouth, Mass.: Tagus Press, Center for Portuguese Studies and Culture, University of Massachusetts Dartmouth. Retrieved May 5, 2023. https://ojs.lib.umassd.edu/index.php/plcs/article/view/PLCS34 _35_Almedia_page32/1329.

Varela, Pedro. 2020. "Hortas urbanas de Cabo-Verdianos: Sociabilidades e resistência quotidiana nas margens de Lisboa." *Análise social* 3 (236): 534–559.

Wacquant, Loïc. 2007. "Territorial Stigmatization in the Age of Advanced Marginality." *Thesis Eleven* 91 (1): 66–77.

———. 2008. *Urban Outcasts: A Comparative Sociology of Advanced Marginality*. Cambridge: Polity Press.

Walia, Harsha. 2021. *Border and Rule: Global Migration, Capitalism, and the Rise of Racist Nationalism*. Chicago: Haymarket Books.

Wall, Karin, and Maria das Dores Guerreiro. 2005. "A divisão familiar do trabalho." In *Famílias em Portugal: Percursos, interacções, redes sociais*, edited by Karin Wall, 303–362. Lisbon: Imprensa de Ciências Sociais.

Wall, Karin, and Catia Nunes. 2010. "Immigration, Welfare and Care in Portugal: Mapping the New Plurality of Female Migration Trajectories." *Social Policy and Society* 9 (3): 397–408.

Walton, Emily. 2016. "'It's Not Just a Bunch of Buildings': Social Psychological Investment, Sense of Community, and Collective Efficacy in a Multiethnic Low-Income Neighborhood." *City & Community* 15 (3): 231–263.

Weber, Max. 1958. "The Three Types of Legitimate Rule." *Berkeley Publications in Society and Institutions* 4 (1): 1–11.

Weeks, Samuel. 2012a. "'As You Receive with One Hand, So Should You Give with the Other': The Mutual-Help Practices of Cape Verdeans on the Lisbon Periphery." Master's thesis, Department of Social and Cultural Anthropology, Instituto de Ciências Sociais, Universidade de Lisboa. Retrieved July 1, 2021. http://hdl.handle.net/10451/6773.

———. 2012b. "Marxian Crisis, Maussian Gift: The Mutual-Help Practices of Lisbon's Cape Verdean Labor Immigrants in an Age of Austerity." *Cadernos de estudos africanos* 24:27–43.

Wekker, Gloria. 2016. *White Innocence: Paradoxes of Colonialism and Race*. Durham, N.C.: Duke University Press.

Wingfield, Adia Harvey. 2008. *Doing Business with Beauty: Black Women, Hair Salons, and the Racial Enclave Economy*. Lanham, Md.: Rowman & Littlefield.

———. 2010. "Are Some Emotions Marked 'Whites Only'? Racialized Feeling Rules in Professional Workplaces." *Social Problems* 57 (2): 251–268.

———. 2013. *No More Invisible Man: Race and Gender in Men's Work*. Philadelphia: Temple University Press.

———. 2019. *Flatlining: Race, Work, and Health Care in the New Economy*. Oakland: University of California Press.

Wingfield, Adia Harvey, and Renée Skeete Alston. 2014. "Maintaining Hierarchies in Predominantly White Organizations: A Theory of Racial Tasks." *American Behavioral Scientist* 58 (2): 274–287.

Wooten, Melissa E. 2019. "Race, Organizations, and the Organizing Process." In *Race, Organizations, and the Organizing Process*, edited by Melissa Wooten, 1–14. Bingley, U.K.: Emerald.

Wooten, Melissa E., and Enobong Hannah Branch. 2012. "Defining Appropriate Labor: Race,

Gender, and Idealization of Black Women in Domestic Service." *Race, Gender & Class* 19 (3/4): 292–308.

World Bank. 2018. "International Development Association Project Appraisal Document on a Proposed Credit in the Amount of SDR 7.3 Million to the Republic of Cabo Verde for a Social Inclusion Project." Retrieved July 1, 2021. http://documents .worldbank.org/curated/en/102181545015798577/pdf/CABO-VERDE-PAD-11262018 -636805945700219570.pdf.

———. 2022. "Labor Force, Female (% of Total Labor Force)—Portugal." Retrieved March 20, 2024. https://data.worldbank.org/indicator/SL.TLF.TOTL.FE.ZS?locations=PT.

Yeates, Nicola. 2009. *Globalizing Care Economies and Migrant Workers: Explorations in Global Care Chains*. London: Palgrave Macmillan.

Young, Alford A., Jr. 2008. "White Ethnographers on the Experiences of African American Men: Then and Now." In *White Logic, White Methods: Racism and Methodology*, edited by Tukufu Zuberi and Eduardo Bonilla-Silva, 179–200. Lanham, Md.: Rowman & Littlefield.

Young, Vershawn Ashanti, Rusty Barrett, Y'shanda Young-Rivera, and Kim Brian Lovejoy. 2018. *Other People's English: Code-Meshing, Code-Switching, and African American Literacy*. Anderson, S.C.: Parlor Press.

Yukich, Grace. 2013. "Constructing the Model Immigrant: Movement Strategy and Immigrant Deservingness in the New Sanctuary Movement." *Social Problems* 60 (3): 302–320.

Yuval-Davis, Nira. 1997. "Women, Citizenship and Difference." *Feminist Review* 57 (1): 4–27.

Zeleza, Paul Tiyambe. 2005. "Rewriting the African Diaspora: Beyond the Black Atlantic." *African Affairs* 104 (414): 35–68.

Index

Note: Figures and tables are indicated by page numbers in *italics*.

About the Author

CELESTE VAUGHAN CURINGTON is an intersectional sociologist and assistant professor of sociology and women's and gender studies at Boston University. Her published work has appeared in *Sociology of Race and Ethnicity*, *Du Bois Review*, *Race and Social Problems*, and *American Sociological Review*. She completed her PhD in sociology from the University of Massachusetts–Amherst.